T0278506

Praise for the Foundations for Spirit-Filled Christianity Series

"I am amazed at how North American and European Christians continue to ignore the dramatic changes in global Christianity. These changes are not insignificant. They call for serious revisions in the Christian mission, ecumenism, and theological training. One of the most dramatic shifts has been the rapid rise of Pentecostal/Charismatic spirituality. It is safe to say that in all forms of the global church—Protestant, Roman Catholic, and Orthodox—people are increasingly seeing themselves as Spirit-filled believers. Unfortunately, colleges and seminaries often lack textbooks that address these changes. This series, Foundations for Spirit-Filled Christianity, is a timely intervention, one that will certainly help to fill this gap."

—**Cheryl Bridges Johns**, Global Pentecostal House of Study,
United Theological Seminary

"The Foundations for Spirit-Filled Christianity series rightly identifies the pivotal role of Pentecostal and Charismatic Christianity in shaping tomorrow's global Christianity and addresses the shortage of resources for training future leaders. The titles of the series will serve this Christian family's continuing growth by providing textbooks for its theological education."

—**Wonsuk Ma**, College of Theology and Ministry, Oral Roberts University

"The church and academy are finally ready for Foundations for Spirit-Filled Christianity, which relays the insights and perspectives of mature Pentecostal and Charismatic theologians and biblical scholars on a broad array of important theological topics, doctrinal loci, and practical realities. Pentecostal theologians from around the world are now ready to speak in their own accents in ways that will benefit the church catholic."

—**Amos Yong**, Fuller Theological Seminary

Introduction
to Spirituality

FOUNDATIONS FOR
SPIRIT-FILLED
CHRISTIANITY

SERIES EDITORS

Jerry Ireland, chaplain, US Navy

Paul W. Lewis, associate dean and professor of historical theology and intercultural studies, Assemblies of God Theological Seminary at Evangel University, Springfield, Missouri

Frank D. Macchia, professor of systematic theology, Vanguard University, and associate director of the Centre for Pentecostal and Charismatic Studies at Bangor University, Wales, United Kingdom

ADVISORY BOARD

Kim Alexander, director of academics and RSM online, Ramp School of Ministry

Roli Dela Cruz, Assemblies of God (USA) World Missions missionary serving as Greek and New Testament instructor at Asia Pacific Theological Seminary, Baguio, Philippines

Sarita Gallagher Edwards, practitioner-scholar and frequent speaker and writer on global Christianity, biblical theology of mission, and mission history

Robert L. Gallagher, professor of intercultural studies emeritus, Wheaton College Graduate School

Byron Klaus, professor of intercultural leadership studies, Assemblies of God Theological Seminary

Andy Lord, minister at All Saints' Didcot in the diocese of Oxford and visiting lecturer at the London School of Theology

Gary Tyra, professor of biblical and practical theology, Vanguard University

Nimi Wariboko, Walter G. Muelder Professor of Social Ethics, Boston University

Introduction *to* Spirituality

CULTIVATING A LIFESTYLE
OF FAITHFULNESS

GARY TYRA

B

Baker Academic
a division of Baker Publishing Group
Grand Rapids, Michigan

© 2023 by Gary Tyra

Published by Baker Academic
a division of Baker Publishing Group
www.bakeracademic.com

Printed in the United States of America

Library of Congress Cataloging-in-Publication Data
Names: Tyra, Gary, 1955– author.
Title: Introduction to spirituality : cultivating a lifestyle of faithfulness / Gary Tyra.
Description: Grand Rapids, Michigan : Baker Academic, a division of Baker Publishing Group, [2023] | Series: Foundations for Spirit-filled Christianity | Includes bibliographical references and index.
Identifiers: LCCN 2022046587 | ISBN 9781540965226 (paperback) | ISBN 9781540966575 (casebound) | ISBN 9781493441792 (ebook) | ISBN 9781493441808 (pdf)
Subjects: LCSH: Spirituality—Christianity.
Classification: LCC BV4501.3 .T96 2023 | DDC 248.4—dc23/eng/20221125
LC record available at https://lccn.loc.gov/2022046587

Baker Publishing Group publications use paper produced from sustainable forestry practices and post-consumer waste whenever possible.

23   24   25   26   27   28   29   7   6   5   4   3   2   1

This book is prayerfully and lovingly dedicated
to my parishioners and students: past, present, and future.
May each of you someday hear the Lord Jesus say to you,
"Well done, good and faithful servant!"

CONTENTS

SERIES PREFACE

The demographics of Christianity, along with those of the general world population, have changed and expanded significantly over the past few centuries. A key aspect of this expansion has been the influence and growth of the church internationally, especially in the Global South, which is largely composed of believers within Pentecostal and Charismatic streams of Christianity. Consequently, the changing face of global Christianity is becoming increasingly diverse and characterized by Pentecostal and Charismatic beliefs and praxis. Despite the massive increase in Pentecostal churches and educational institutions, there still exists a lacuna of textbooks that incorporate perspectives from Pentecostal and Charismatic streams of Christianity. The Foundations for Spirit-Filled Christianity series attempts to fill that void by offering high-quality introductory textbooks that include both global and Pentecostal streams of thought. These textbooks will explore primary topics of interest in the fields of biblical studies, church ministries and practical theology, church history, theology, and missions.

The global aspect of Christianity is reflected in the diversity and breadth of the series advisory board, and global perspectives have been intentionally highlighted by the series editors, who have been immersed in other cultural settings throughout their lives. Jerry Ireland and his wife, Paula, lived and worked in Africa, including in educational entities, for well over a decade; Paul Lewis and his wife, Eveline (a native Chinese Indonesian), lived and worked in East Asia, primarily in academic institutions, for almost two decades; and Frank Macchia and his wife, Verena (a native of Switzerland), lived in Europe while Frank studied at the University of Basel.

Each book in the series will also reflect the increasingly Pentecostal nature of global Christianity. The various authors will offer robust discussions and balanced appraisals of their topics while simultaneously situating Pentecostal perspectives alongside those traditionally showcased in introductory textbooks for evangelical Bible colleges and seminaries. These textbooks will also help students navigate the sometimes-controversial arguments surrounding some Pentecostal and Charismatic themes and concerns. Further, while remaining global in perspective, authors will locate their themes within a theologically conservative framework.

In summary, what distinguishes this series is, first, its primary focus on providing high-quality introductory college and seminary textbooks and, second, its resonance with contemporary students who are fully in tune with global Pentecostal and Charismatic theology and perspectives. Ultimately, the goal is to provide tools for the global church that represent the vast array of church expressions in order to set the stage for the next generation to continue to effectively and responsibly advance the good news of the gospel. To God be the glory!

ACKNOWLEDGMENTS

This book was a delight to write! It is fitting, therefore, for me to express my gratitude here to a few folks who contributed to this joyful and fulfilling experience.

I will begin by thanking the series editors, Jerry Ireland, Paul Lewis, and Frank Macchia, for the invitation extended to me to contribute to this series and the support they provided throughout the publication process. Thanks, guys, for the opportunity to be a part of this important and, I trust, influential book series.

I must also acknowledge how much I enjoyed working with everyone at Baker Academic, from Dave Nelson, who initially acquired the book; to Brandy Scritchfield, who took the ball and ran with it, providing all kinds of encouragement and careful leadership in the early stages of the publication process; to Julie Zahm, who as the project editor was an exquisite jewel and joy to partner with; and to all the anonymous folks who touched the book in each stage of its development. I also acknowledge Anna English and all the other dear ones in the marketing department who have already begun the hard work of making this entire enterprise a huge publishing success. In other words, my thanks to everyone at Baker Publishing! I very much enjoyed this experience and hope we can do it again soon.

Finally, I want to express my deep and sincere appreciation to my family for the patience they have shown for the past two years. Since this is their ninth visit to this rodeo, they knew what to expect: their husband and father being intensely focused on something other than his students, wife, kids, grandkids, and border collie (not necessarily in that order). And yet, they didn't simply acquiesce to my spending huge amounts of time studying and banging away on the computer, they encouraged and supported me every step of the way.

Thanks, Patti, Brandon, Megan, Lindsay, Jacob, Raelyn, Maisey, and Blue for loving and supporting me and what I do so generously. What a gift all of you are to me!

It is my sincere hope that this book will genuinely make a difference for good in the lives of many readers. If it does, and God is pleased, may everyone I've referred to in these acknowledgments sense his smile along with me. *We did this together!*

INTRODUCTION

What you are is God's gift to you; what you become is your gift to God.

—attributed to Hans Urs von Balthasar

For many years now, I have taught a theology course that aims at the spiritual formation of university students, regardless of their major. Recently, my practice has been to begin the course by requiring that each student create a brief "personal introduction video." Though most of those enrolled in this required course are *not* theology or ministry majors, I ask them to share with me their current thoughts regarding the importance of paying attention to the spiritual dimension of their lives. I have never had a student make the assertion that paying attention to one's spirituality is a waste of time. So far, virtually all of them—with varying degrees of intensity, of course—have indicated that being mindful of the spiritual aspect of their existence is important to them. While allowing for the possibility that at least some of these students may have been guilty of simply telling their professor what they assume he wants to hear, I get the feeling that most of them have been and are sincere. They really do want to learn how to pay more and better attention to their spirituality!

This interest in spirituality is a good thing since, as the late Christian philosopher Dallas Willard has reminded us, everyone is being formed spiritually, whether they recognize it or not. According to Willard, "The most despicable as well as the most admirable of persons have had a spiritual formation.

Terrorists as well as saints are the outcome of spiritual formation. Their spirits or hearts have been formed. Period."[1] But Willard goes on to explain that "we each become a certain kind of person in the depths of our being, gaining a specific type of character. And that is the outcome of a process of spiritual formation as understood in general human terms that apply to everyone, whether they want it or not. Fortunate or blessed are those who are able to find or are given a path of life that will form their spirit and inner world in a way that is truly strong and good and directed Godward."[2]

It is almost as if Willard was responding to the prompt I put to my students! Put simply, the reason why it is important for all of us to pay attention to the spiritual dimension of our lives is that doing so makes a huge difference in how our lives play out. In other words, one's spirituality matters immensely because it largely shapes the kind of person one becomes and the kind of life one leads. It all depends, says Willard, on the specifics of one's spiritual formation.

So, yes, I am heartened by the fact that nearly all my students seem to take their spirituality seriously. And yet, as I hope to illustrate in the pages that follow, just being open to the process of spiritual formation doesn't guarantee the direction in which it moves, the shape it takes, or the kind of person it creates. The most basic aim of this book is to encourage and enable its readers to make some good choices about the specifics of their spiritual formation.

First Things First: An Overview of the Spirituality Spectrum

The truth is that the introductory videos I survey each semester demonstrate the variety of ways one may understand what spirituality is and what it means to take it seriously. This suggests to me that a principal reason why so many of my university's nontheology majors can indicate at least a theoretical interest in spirituality is because they are not all talking about the same thing! Therefore, before we go any further in this project, we must acknowledge that some nuance is necessary.

Though there are many ways that spiritualities differ, three basics are worth noting. First, spiritualities can vary in their *focus*. Judging by what I see going on in the lives of my students, it is possible, on the one hand, to conceive of a nonmystical spirituality that has nothing to do with anything divine but

1. Dallas Willard, *Renovation of the Heart: Putting on the Character of Christ* (Colorado Springs: NavPress, 2002), 19–20.
2. Willard, *Renovation of the Heart*, 20.

focuses only on the actualization of the human spirit.[3] On the other hand, it is also possible for one's spirituality to take into account "*the human capacity to experience transcendent reality.*"[4] In other words, the focus here goes beyond the human spirit to the divine, to something that is out there, beyond one's own spirit or sense of self, and yet somehow foundational to it.

This leads to a discussion of the second way in which spiritualities differ: their *process*, or what people feel led to do about this crucial aspect of their existence. The truth is that, despite what they indicated in their introductory videos, some of my students will eventually demonstrate a reluctance to do anything more than acknowledge that their lives possess a spiritual dimension of some sort. At the same time, however, other students in the course will evidence a genuine willingness to do more—to become adept at *nurturing, cultivating, tending to* their spirituality. For these more motivated students, spirituality is not simply an acknowledgment; it is something they feel they need to perform or, as I like to say, *live into*.

Third, spiritualities can also differ with respect to their *motive*. For instance, early in the semester, some of my students describe an eagerness to do what is necessary to achieve a greater degree of personal integration or mindfulness—a mental state that they suspect will result in better health and more happiness and success in this life. At the same time, other students, usually those who hail from Christian homes, describe a "living into" process that is redolent of the quotation that served as the epigraph at the beginning of this introduction: "What you are is God's gift to you; what you become is your gift to God." For these students, the deliberate cultivation of their spirituality is not simply about experiencing some practical and temporal benefits—that is, serving themselves. Instead, it is motivated by a desire to know, please, and honor God.

Now, there is a reason why I have been referring here to the various ways my students conceive of and practice their spirituality. It is my sense that to a great degree they are indicative of what is going on not only in the local church but also in the culture at large.

The truth is that spirituality is big these days. Years ago, sociologists predicted that America would become thoroughly secular.[5] Just the opposite

---

3. See Sandra M. Schneiders, "Theology and Spirituality: Strangers, Rivals, or Partners?," *Horizons* 13, no. 2 (1986): 266, cited in Michael Downey, *Understanding Christian Spirituality* (Mahwah, NJ: Paulist Press, 1997), 14–15.

4. H. Newton Malony, introduction to *Spirituality and Psychological Health*, ed. Richard H. Cox, Betty Ervin-Cox, and Louis Hoffman (Colorado Springs: Colorado School of Professional Psychology Press, 2005), xv (emphasis original).

5. See Mary Tedeschi, review of *Religion in the Secular City: Toward a Postmodern Theology*, by Harvey Cox, *Commentary*, August 1, 2010, https://www.commentarymagazine.com/articles/mary-tedeschi/religion-in-the-secular-city-by-harvey-cox/.

has happened, however. North American culture has become increasingly fascinated with all things spiritual.[6] But, as with my students, this interest in spirituality in our culture at large doesn't necessarily mean that we are all making the same choices about the focus of our spirituality, how much effort we put into it, and why we are putting in this effort. Referring to the issue of focus in particular, one spirituality expert has observed that increasing numbers of people are actively searching for the spiritual but doing so in some increasingly diverse ways, ranging from a revived interest in the practice of voodoo to a passion for organic gardening.[7] So, yes, spirituality is alive and well not only in the minds of my students but also in our society as a whole. As Willard so poignantly reminds us, the decisions people make about their spiritual formation matter. The choices we make with respect to the focus, process, and motive of our spirituality will largely determine the kind of people we become.

Dialing In: The Specific Kind of Spirituality This Book Is About

I trust that the reader has begun to surmise that my aim is not to encourage and enable just any type of spirituality, but one in particular: the kind that strives to honor God. And yet further complicating things is the very real possibility that, just as God has preferences about the way we relate to one another (e.g., Mic. 6:8; cf. Matt. 23:23), he may also have an opinion about the way we conceive of and relate to him. It is for this reason that the aim of this work, even more specifically, is to facilitate the cultivation of *a biblically informed Christian spirituality*. And yet, even with qualifications such as these in place, I tell my students that when it comes to forging a spirituality that sufficiently honors the God revealed in the Christian Scriptures, even more levels of nuance are necessary!

Christian Spirituality: Simply Theistic or Theologically Real?

It is possible for a Christian spirituality to be *theistic*—to have room for God in it—but only in a philosophical, conceptual sense. We can, for example, limit our understanding of God to his role as the "first cause" or "prime mover"—that which is responsible for all the motion in the universe.

---

6. Jerry Adler, "In Search of the Spiritual," *Newsweek*, August 28, 2005, http://www.news week.com/id/147035.

7. For a description of some of the current trends in spirituality, see Downey, *Understanding Christian Spirituality*, 6–13.

Or similarly, God can be thought of merely as our "ground of being"—the "isness" that underwrites our existence.

For sure, the Scriptures do portray God as the first cause (Gen. 1:1) and the causal source of all that is (see Gen. 1:1; Isa. 42:5; Acts 14:15; 17:24). But if we focus only on these passages and overlook what the rest of the Bible has to say about who God is and what he is about—passages that portray God as dynamic rather than static, fully involved in the world he created—we may end up with a spirituality that is theologically shallow. Such a spirituality allows for the existence of God but not for the possibility of humans interacting with him in personal and experiential ways. Some would say this is a problem. After all, the notion that our spirituality may be thought of as a way for us to forge a character we gratefully offer back to our Creator as a gift would not make much sense if all he is is "isness" itself.

There is, however, an alternative to a spirituality that is merely theistic in its orientation. Not all Christians believe that it is necessary or prudent to ground their spirituality *solely* in a static acknowledgment of God as the first cause or reality's ground of being. It is possible to possess a fully trinitarian understanding of God that is not only theistic but also *theologically real*. I will have more to say about "theological realism" below (and in chap. 1). Here it is incumbent on me to simply indicate the possibility of an "I-Thou" rather than "I-It" understanding of God. Such an understanding derives from the belief that because of the incarnation of Christ and the outpouring of the Holy Spirit on the day of Pentecost, it is possible for God's human image-bearers (Gen. 1:26; 9:6) to really *know* and *experience* their Creator in some real, phenomenal, life-story-shaping ways. In other words, their spirituality is not only an acknowledgment of God; it involves the cultivation of a personal, intimate, interactive, existentially impactful relationship with him as their heavenly Father. This is the first distinction that is necessary for us to keep in mind: the focus of this book will be on the cultivation of a fully trinitarian, Christian spirituality that is not just theistic but theologically real as well.

Christian Spirituality: Only Occasional or Actually Perpetual?

The second distinction to be made is between a Christian spirituality that is *occasional* in its orientation—centering on the performance of a set of discrete practices (spiritual disciplines)—and one that is more *perpetual* in the way it plays out. Both approaches possess a measure of biblical support, and the spiritual disciplines are, of course, important to any approach to Christian spirituality. I contend, however, that it is the latter, more perpetual, approach that does the best job of enabling a *lifestyle* earmarked by the spiritual, moral, and missional faithfulness the Bible clearly indicates that God the Father is looking for in the lives of those who claim to belong to him.[8] This is because the primary focus in the second approach is not on an *occasional* or *episodic* engagement in some discrete soul-nurturing, body-taming disciplines but on an *ongoing* sensitivity to and cooperation with the Spirit of Christ as he empowers us to embody the character of Jesus himself (see Gal. 5:22–23). Later, in chapter 3, I will have more to say about the importance Paul placed on spirituality that produced a God-pleasing lifestyle. Then, in chapter 9, I will indicate why a spirituality that centers almost exclusively on a performance of spiritual disciplines, even if this is done routinely, can actually end up being problematic rather than helpful. For now, the point to be made is that my focus in this work will be on the kind of Christian spirituality that, precisely because it is "I-Thou" rather than "I-It" in its orientation, plays out as a perpetual, lifelong pursuit of the empowering presence of Christ.

The Apostle Paul's Call for a Lifestyle Spirituality That Is Spirit Empowered

Some additional insight into the kind of Christian spirituality this book is about can also be discerned in the way the apostle Paul prayed for the church members in Colossae: "For this reason, since the day we heard about you, we have not stopped praying for you. We continually ask God to fill you with the knowledge of his will through all the wisdom and understanding that the Spirit gives, so that you may live a life worthy of the Lord and please him in every way: bearing fruit in every good work, growing in the knowledge of God" (Col. 1:9–10). I have become convinced that the practice of Christian spirituality can and should involve our learning how to live into this Pauline prayer. It is not just about obeying a particular list of rules, observing a particular collection of rituals, or engaging in a particular register of practices. The focus is, instead, on an ongoing Holy Spirit–enabled interaction with Christ the Son that results in a *lifestyle* or *way of being in the world* that pleases God the Father.

Additional biblical support for the notion that Paul's call was for Christians to devote themselves to the cultivation of a Spirit-empowered, genuinely transformational spirituality is scattered throughout his epistolary corpus. There are, for example, Pauline passages that explicitly indicate that Christian discipleship should go beyond sin management toward the experience

8. See, e.g., Josh. 24:14; Hosea 4:1; Eph. 1:1; Col. 1:2; Rev. 13:10.

of personal *transformation* (Rom. 12:1–2; 2 Cor. 3:18). In other places, Paul announces the possibility of church members experiencing a "new" (*kainos*) kind of life (Rom. 6:4; 2 Cor. 5:17) as they "put off" or "take off" their previous way of being in the world and "put on" or "clothe" themselves in a way more in keeping with the way of Christ (Eph. 4:22–24; Col. 3:7–10; cf. Rom. 13:12–14; Col. 3:12–14). Another Pauline notion is that Jesus, through his incarnation, atoning death, resurrection, and bestowal of his Spirit, not only models for his followers what it means to be truly human but actually heals our humanity and creates within himself a "new humanity" altogether— what some in the history of Christianity have referred to as a "third race" of human beings (in addition to Jews and gentiles) who may begin living now in anticipation of what life will be like in the new Eden (see Rev. 21:1–4; 22:1–5).[9]

There are also passages penned by Paul that encourage his readers to be careful to avoid a spirituality that is preoccupied with, driven by, or limited to the observance of religious festivals and celebrations linked to certain days, months, seasons, and years (Gal. 4:8–11; Col. 2:16). Instead, Paul insists, sincere prayer and worshipful thanksgiving can become habituated: they can become righteous, holiness-producing lifestyle habits (Rom. 6:19; Eph. 6:18; Phil. 4:6; Col. 3:17; 1 Thess. 5:16–18). Finally, in his letter to the Galatian Christians, Paul writes, "Since we live by the Spirit, let us keep in step with the Spirit" (Gal. 5:25).

Paul's call for his readers to keep in step with the Spirit certainly seems to suggest that, in his mind, the cultivation of a Christian spirituality will be an ongoing rather than occasional activity. Moreover, the context of this verse seems to indicate that keeping in step with the Spirit is key to the Spirit's work of producing within believers the nine *Christlike* traits Paul refers to as the "fruit of the Spirit" (Gal. 5:22–23). In other words, Paul seems to be suggesting that our experience of a transformation into an increasingly new, Christlike life depends on learning what it means to keep in step with the Spirit—and then actually doing so!

For all the reasons just referred to, the thesis of this work is that the Pauline exhortation to "keep in step with the Spirit" is foundational to the cultivation of a theologically real, Spirit-empowered, Christ-emulating, God-the-Father-pleasing Christian spirituality—a fully trinitarian spirituality that involves

9. See, e.g., F. F. Bruce, *The Epistles to the Colossians, to Philemon, and to the Ephesians* (Grand Rapids: Eerdmans, 1984), 296, 319–20; Charles H. Talbert, *Ephesians and Colossians* (Grand Rapids: Baker Academic, 2007), 81–82; R. Kent Hughes, *Ephesians: The Mystery of the Body of Christ* (Wheaton: Crossway, 1990), 92–93, 97–102, 105, 262. For a discussion of the ministry implications of the "new humanity" teaching presented in the New Testament, see Gary Tyra, *A Missional Orthodoxy: Theology and Ministry in a Post-Christian Context* (Downers Grove, IL: IVP Academic, 2013), 240–48.

more than an episodic engagement in a set of disciplines. For sure, Paul encourages the readers of his letters to engage in various spiritual practices (e.g., worship, prayer, the study of Scripture, community building, service), but the cardinal discipline is prayer, a practice he refers to fifty-seven times! The way he keeps insisting that all these practices, especially prayer, can and should be performed perpetually rather than occasionally (see, e.g., Rom. 12:12; Eph. 6:18; Phil. 4:6; Col. 4:2; 1 Thess. 5:17) is the reason why the spirituality he promotes should be viewed as a lifestyle rather than as a mere component of one's walk with Christ.

The key to this lifestyle, according to Paul, is the dynamic of keeping in step with the Spirit. Thus, it is fair to say that Paul's call is for Christ's followers to devote themselves to the cultivation of a Spirit-empowered, genuinely transformational lifestyle spirituality.

The Book's Blueprint

On the one hand, this book's special emphasis (i.e., the need for Spirit empowerment if one's spirituality is going to result in genuine personal transformation precisely because it plays out as a lifestyle rather than an occasional activity) will set it apart from many other books belonging to the genre. At the same time, the structure of the work is based on the generic observation that any type of spirituality is composed of three basic components. The foundational *convictions* (beliefs) a person has about the nature of God will produce a set of *commitments* or fervently held notions regarding what it means to please God, which, in turn, issue forth in a collection of *customs* or practices whereby the desired connection with God is achieved. In keeping with this observation, I have divided this book into three main sections.

A Preview of Part One

Part 1 focuses on several theological *convictions* that form the foundation or *root system* for the kind of lifestyle spirituality Paul enjoins upon his readers. The writings of Paul contain several references to a Spirit-enabled *mindset* that is necessary for Christ's followers to live in a way that pleases God.[10] The historical context of these passages makes clear that the renewing of the mind that Paul had personally experienced and then prescribes for others had to do with some new paradigm-impacting theological beliefs that

10. See Rom. 8:6; 12:2; 1 Cor. 2:16; Eph. 4:20–24; Phil. 3:17–21; Col. 2:18; 3:1–4, 7–8; 1 Tim. 6:3–5. See also 1 Pet. 4:7; 5:8.

were generated by his own life-changing experience with the risen Christ and the Holy Spirit (see Acts 9:1–22). In other words, as it relates to a lifestyle spirituality productive of a truly God-pleasing life, our foundational beliefs about who God is and what he is about matter big time!

In a nutshell, chapter 1 will delve more deeply into the "theological realism" I have alluded to already. Rather than conceiving of God as merely a philosophical notion (e.g., a first cause or one's ground of being), the Christian Scriptures portray the Creator as a very real, hyperpersonal, and ultrarelational divine being who, because of the incarnation of Christ and the outpouring of his Spirit, can be personally known and experienced in ways that are quite real and tremendously transformative. Going further still, I will argue that a Christian version of theological realism will necessarily be a "trinitarian realism" in that it also requires realist rather than nonrealist understandings of and personal experiences with Christ and the Holy Spirit. The conviction that Christians should expect to experience the Holy Spirit in ways that make possible an ongoing, mentoring relationship with the risen Jesus is nothing less than a game changer with respect to Christian spirituality.

Chapter 2 will go on to discuss three specific existential realities that have to do with God. These three realities can be referred to in a couple of ways. We can think of God's relational, holy, and sending *nature*, or we can talk about his cardinal *characteristics*: his charity, sanctity, and missionality. In sum, the message of this chapter is that these three foundational attributes, when sufficiently reckoned with (or *real*ized), will result in a spirituality that seeks to please rather than placate or manipulate what we Christians are convinced is the "ultimate reality." Such a spirituality is a million miles away from one that is focused merely on our own health, happiness, and success. The goal instead is a spirituality that produces a lifestyle earmarked by a spiritual, moral, and missional faithfulness before a loving, holy, sending God.

A Preview of Part Two

Part 2 of the book is composed of three chapters that treat the most fundamental lifestyle *commitments* entailed in the spirituality I am proffering in this work. If the convictions referred to above constitute the root system of a lifestyle spirituality, the commitments they generate can be considered the *shoot system*.

Since I have already referred several times in this introduction to the three salient commitments I have in mind, I will articulate them here in a slightly different manner. Influencing the shape of a Christian spirituality that is ongoing rather than occasional in nature are these three fervently held and interrelated commitments: to be continually filled with and led by the Holy Spirit;[11] to cultivate a passionate, perpetual pursuit of Christ's empowering presence; and to engage in a lifelong facilitation of God's missional purposes for his creation. Specifically, chapter 3's focus is on the apostle Paul's realist understanding of the Holy Spirit. His "pneumatological realism," if you will, is evidenced by the importance he places on the Spirit in Christian discipleship, the specific way in which he connects the Spirit with Christian spirituality, and the urgency of his call for his readers to learn what it means to keep in step with the Spirit and then actually do it.

The emphasis on the Holy Spirit in this book about Christian spirituality really should not surprise anyone. The British churchman and biblical scholar John Stott once remarked, "The Christian life is essentially life in the Spirit, that is to say, a life which is animated, sustained, directed, and enriched by the Holy Spirit. Without the Holy Spirit, true Christian discipleship would be inconceivable, indeed impossible."[12] Likewise, in one of his later works, the eminent Swiss theologian Karl Barth evidenced his own (latent) commitment to a pneumatological realism when he advised, "As a foolish church presupposes his presence and action in its own existence, in its offices and sacraments, ordinations, consecrations, and absolutions, so a foolish theology presupposes the Holy Spirit. . . . Only where the Spirit is sighed, cried, and prayed for does he become present and newly active."[13] In other words, like the apostle Paul, both Stott and Barth insist that we must take the Spirit seriously in order to live the Christian life. Making the commitment to a lifetime of keeping in step with the Spirit is what a Pauline lifestyle spirituality is all about!

In chapter 4, I will discuss the christological realism that a pneumatological realism engenders. Nearly twenty years ago, I participated in an intensive, two-week-long doctor of ministry seminar taught by Dallas Willard, titled Spirituality and Ministry. Our prereading for the course amounted to multiple volumes and thousands of pages. My deep dive into the writings of Christian spiritual masters, ancient and contemporary, convinced me that at the heart of a biblically informed and Spirit-empowered Christian spirituality is the pursuit of a moment-by-moment mentoring relationship with the risen Christ. In chapter 4, I provide a pungent summary of what this pursuit involves and the support it enjoys from both the Bible and the writings of many Christian

11. For more on the importance of being continually filled with the Spirit, see Francis Foulkes, *Ephesians*, Tyndale New Testament Commentaries (Downers Grove, IL: InterVarsity, 1983), 152.

12. John R. W. Stott, *The Message of Romans* (Downers Grove, IL: IVP Academic, 2001), 216.

13. Karl Barth, *Evangelical Theology: An Introduction* (Grand Rapids: Eerdmans, 1979), 58.

spiritual masters. My aim here is to encourage readers to make the pursuit of Christ's empowering presence one of the core commitments at the heart of their approach to spiritual formation. I am confident that both Willard and the apostle Paul would concur! Indeed, in one of his books, *The Spirit of the Disciplines*, Willard asserts that "the heart of Paul and his message lies in one area—in the continuous appropriation of the 'real presence' of Christ himself within the experiential life of the believer."[14]

Chapter 5 then delves deeply into the nature of the God-the-Father-pleasing lifestyle that a realist understanding and experience of God issues in. Having already argued that to please God requires that we prove faithful not only spiritually and morally but missionally as well, this chapter broaches the topic of a missional orthodoxy, which is the product of Christians being careful to keep *contending* for the faith that was once for all entrusted to the saints (Jude 3) even as they keep *contextualizing* that faith for new people groups (1 Cor. 9:19–23). Though it is not easy to do, maintaining a steadfast commitment to both of these tasks at the same time is key to an *incarnational* contextualization of the Christian gospel.

To be sure, Christ's incarnation was one of a kind. But I explain here that the goal of an incarnational approach to ministry on the part of Christ's followers is to replicate the *identification-differentiation-transformation* dynamic that was spectacularly at work in Jesus's own missional endeavor. The good news presented in chapter 5 is that we can do this! Why? Precisely because empowering Christian disciples to engage in Christian mission faithfully and fruitfully is one of the main aims of the Holy Spirit (Acts 1:8).

Indeed, with this notion of an empowerment for mission in mind, the chapter will also introduce the notion of a *missional spirituality*—one that is practiced in a contextually sensitive manner with the aim of successfully encouraging our pre- and post-Christian cultural peers to "taste and see" or "come and see" for themselves who Jesus really is and what he is about (see Ps. 34:8; John 1:46). In an increasingly postmodern, post-Christian ministry context, the apologetic (or means whereby we interest folks in the gospel) must be *relational* and *experiential* as well as *intellectual* in nature. It is by inviting pre- and post-Christians to "hang" with us as we engage in prayer, worship, Scripture study, small group fellowship, and service to the poor that we allow the Holy Spirit to do his best convincing and convicting work in their lives.

Once again, the main message of this chapter is that this is doable! A lifestyle spirituality that is sufficiently informed both biblically and theologically

14. Dallas Willard, *The Spirit of the Disciplines: Understanding How God Changes Lives* (New York: HarperOne, 1988), 96.

will be missional in nature and thus will be deliberate about the way it impacts not only the Christian disciple but also his or her family members, friends, neighbors, and coworkers who are not currently walking with Christ. This is a big part of how we live lives worthy of the Lord and please him in every way (Col. 1:10).

A Preview of Part Three

The primary aim of part 3 is to provide three no-nonsense discussions of the spiritual formation *customs* (or practices) that derive from the convictions and commitments treated in the first two sections of the book. If part 1 constitutes the *root* of a lifestyle spirituality and part 2 the *shoot*, then part 3 represents its *fruit*.

Thus, chapter 6 elaborates on what is involved in actually keeping in step with the Spirit on a daily basis. In the process, the discussion will highlight the devotional and missional value of one pneumatologically real spirituality practice in particular: what Paul and Jude refer to as "praying in the Spirit."

The focus of chapter 7 is on what some spiritual masters past and present have had to say about the nuts and bolts of pursuing Christ's empowering presence. It is often said that "the devil is in the details." Not so in this case. Rather than playing out as discouraging or as dry and boring, the "how-tos" presented to us by the spiritual masters will prove to be inspirational in the extreme.

Chapter 8 delves more deeply into the missional spirituality introduced in chapter 5. If we intend to practice our spirituality in a contextually sensitive manner with the aim of encouraging our pre- and post-Christian peers to experience the reality of Christ, it is vital that we are routinely experiencing this reality ourselves. Thus, in this chapter we will explore the *purpose*, *particulars*, and *practice* of a missional spirituality.

Chapter 9, the final chapter, will zero in on the important, enabling role all the spiritual disciplines—classical, contemporary, and other—play in the cultivation of a God-the-Father-pleasing lifestyle spirituality. In the process, we will consider the need for us to engage in all spiritual disciplines in a way that is *functional, theologically informed, theologically real, pneumatologically real*, "*pursuit prioritizing*," and *mission minded*. In addition, I will briefly address how Christian liturgy, Christian praxis, and just about every activity we engage in at the prompting of the Spirit of mission—from belonging to the Rotary Club to imbibing pop culture—can be thought of as a legitimate spirituality practice. The upshot of the discussions presented in this crucial final chapter is this: when it comes to just about everything related to the cultivation of a trinitarian, Christian lifestyle spirituality, there is no end to the need for nuance.

The Big Picture

I have spent many years as a pastor and professor ministering to people of all ages. One of the most significant lessons I have learned is the importance of the big picture. Without a holistic perspective, an attempt to understand any topic or accomplish any task is destined to founder. Thus, I have found myself repeatedly encouraging anxious, frustrated parishioners and students to stop, take a breath, and seek to prayerfully enlarge their frame of reference with respect to the task at hand. I have found that gaining a fresh sense of the big picture of an endeavor will be not only clarifying but energizing.

In a sense, this book is my attempt to help readers (students and church members) gain a *bigger* picture about the nature and importance of their own spiritual formation and that of those they may be called to care for. Again, given the missionary nature of God, I am convinced that a biblically informed and Christ-honoring spirituality cannot help but impact the lives of Christians in a *missional* manner. That said, I also contend that learning to keep in step with the Spirit, and thereby experiencing a moment-by-moment mentoring relationship with the risen Christ, will function in our lives not only as a missional spirituality but as a *mental health* spirituality (Rom. 8:15; 2 Tim. 1:7), a *warfare* spirituality (Eph. 6:10–20), a *holiness* spirituality (Heb. 12:14), a *faithfulness* spirituality (Matt. 25:21, 23), and ultimately an eschatological *readiness* spirituality as well (Matt. 22:44).

In other words, a lifestyle spirituality is required if we are to render to God the threefold (spiritual, moral, and missional) faithfulness he desires and deserves and if we are to someday hear Jesus say to us, "Well done, good and faithful servant!" (Matt. 25:21, 23). Hearing it put this way, who wouldn't feel the need to treat their own spiritual formation with the seriousness it deserves and then want to serve as a resource to others? This is the power of the big picture!

Time to Choose

Once again, the good news is that *we can do this*! I have not only researched, preached, taught, and written about the convictions, commitments, and customs that make up the approach to spiritual formation this book is about; I have practiced them as well. As I'm wont to tell my students, I'm still a million miles away from all that I can and eventually will be in Christ (Phil. 1:6), but I'm certainly *not* the same person I was before I began to take seriously Paul's call to a lifestyle spirituality.

The question is, *Will we do this?* And if so, *when will we begin?* One well-worn adage says, "Today is the first day of the rest of your life." Another reminds us that "the journey of a thousand miles begins with a single step." I am suggesting that the first step in cultivating a lifestyle spirituality is to take Galatians 5:25 seriously and commit ourselves to a lifetime of keeping in step with the Spirit of Jesus. It is a simple step and yet so profoundly important!

In the opening scenes of the movie *The Matrix*, the main character, Neo, is presented with a choice: red pill or blue pill. The blue pill represents a return to business as usual—that is, to believing and living (so to speak) as he has before. The red pill represents a journey into Wonderland—a journey that will begin with a baptism of sorts into a new reality and then will initiate a spiritual formation process that will forever alter his life and the lives of many others. You get where I'm going with this. It's time for all of us to choose.

So, enough introduction. Let's get the journey started and see just how deep the rabbit hole goes!

PART ONE

The *Convictions* (Root) of a Christian Lifestyle Spirituality

1

THE TRINITARIAN REALISM
THAT UNDERWRITES
A LIFESTYLE SPIRITUALITY

> While these charismatic evangelicals continued talking about a personal rela-
> tionship with Jesus and seeking ecstatic experiences in worship, they never-
> theless made faith formation about commitment to the idea of Jesus, stripping
> formation, ironically, of its transcendent encounter with divine action, making
> conversion an epistemological shift rather than an ontological encounter.
>
> —Andrew Root, *Faith Formation in a Secular Age*

There is a huge night-and-day difference between a mere nodding of one's head at the notion of a deity and a personal, experience-informed, trust-based relationship with him. Near the end of Job's saga, we hear him confess to God: "My ears had heard of you but now my eyes have seen you" (Job 42:5).

Unfortunately, it is possible for someone's faith in God to never progress from mental assent (*assensus*) to existential trust (*fiducia*). Put differently, there is believing that remains merely intellectual in nature, and then there is believing that is existentially impactful because it leads to trusting, investing, and going "all in"—believing in God so thoroughly that it influences just about everything you believe, say, and do. You may already have a sense about where I am going with this. With respect to the Christian faith, it is apparent that the New Testament calls for Christ's followers to exhibit both mental assent and existential trust (John 20:30–31; Rom. 15:13; cf. Rom. 2:23–25).

And yet there is a version of Christianity that, because it focuses on belief as mental assent, essentially reduces the life of faith to an intellectual endeavor that has virtually no room in it for any type of trust-engendering experience. In this case, God becomes an idea or concept we must assent to and remain mindful of rather than a divine entity we can personally encounter.

The epigraph for this chapter suggests that even Charismatic evangelicals (who are known to be open to spiritual experience) can be guilty of overly conceptualizing God and therefore downplaying the importance of "encounter" to both Christian conversion and spirituality. One way to state the concern I am alluding to here might be to ask, Could it be that too many Christians, even Charismatics, are guilty of praying to, worshiping, and serving the idea of God rather than interacting with God himself?

The apostle Paul would be shocked at the very possibility. For him, God was much more than an intellectual concept. Paul's own spirituality, and the one he enjoined upon the readers of his letters, was intensely "I-Thou" rather than "I-It" in nature. He had always thought of God as personal, but the Jewish rabbi known as Saul of Tarsus became the apostle Paul precisely because, after his dramatic *encounter* with the risen and ascended Jesus on the road to Damascus, his understanding of God became trinitarian, radically realist, and even more personal. According to Paul, God the Father, as experienced through Christ the Son by means of the Holy Spirit, is much more than a philosophical concept that possesses some explanatory power. He is instead a very real spiritual but personal being who can be interacted with in real, personal, life-shaping ways. The overarching message of this chapter is that these new convictions functioned for the apostle Paul as both the foundation and lifeblood of his faith and the spirituality that flowed from it.

I will have more to say in subsequent chapters about the specifics of how Paul's "I-Thou" (rather than "I-It") relationship with God affected his spirituality. The aim here is to explore the realist (rather than nonrealist) way Paul experienced God and how Paul's embrace of a particular form of "theological realism" tremendously impacted his understanding of who God is and what he is about. This preliminary discussion is made necessary by the fact that the several realisms elaborated upon in this chapter are not only game changing but critical to our ability to imitate the apostle Paul's lifestyle spirituality. Though I have endeavored to make the discussion as clear as possible, it may still strike some as a bit "nerdy" or technical. But be encouraged: there is some spiritual *honey* here (see Prov. 24:13–14) that has the potential to *brighten our eyes* (see 1 Sam. 14:27, 29) if we do our due diligence with it.

Philosophical Realism in a Nutshell

Swiss theologian Karl Barth once warned, "The great temptation and danger consists in this, that the theologian will actually become what he seems to be—a philosopher."[1] Though I take this warning seriously, I still feel the need to present here what I hope will be a helpful overview of the philosophical perspective that has greatly influenced the way many theologians explain their commitment to a realist rather than nonrealist understanding of God.[2]

In his book *Realism and Christian Faith*, Andrew Moore explains that philosophical realism puts forward three main assertions. The first assertion is that there is a reality external to human minds existing independently of the ways we conceive of it. This means that reality is what it is regardless of how we perceive it, feel about it, or will it to be. As Moore puts it, "Reality is there to be discovered as it objectively is; it is not subjectively invented, constructed, or projected."[3] You are probably familiar with the brainteaser that asks, If a tree falls in a forest and there is no one around to hear it, does it make a sound? Though often trivialized by pop-cultural references to it, this query is at the heart of a serious philosophical discussion concerning the independent reality of the world. A technical, science-informed response to the brainteaser would likely involve a technical discussion of the sonic vibrations created by the tree's crash and the need for ears nearby to interpret those vibrations aurally. Still, at the end of the day, the realist answer to this philosophical query would be an adamant "Yes!" It would make a sound, because that is what tree-crashing vibrations do. The real world with all its phenomena is what it is, irrespective of any creature's subjective perception or assessment of it.

A second assertion made by the proponents of philosophical realism is that it is possible for human beings to come to know reality as it really is rather than simply how it appears to be.[4] Now, this is where things become a bit complicated. Modern Western philosophy has been preoccupied for literally hundreds of years now with the question of whether, and the degree to which, we humans can know reality in an objective rather than subjective manner. Taken at face value, the assertion that "it's possible for human beings to come to know reality as it really is" could connote the idea that reality can be known

---

1. Karl Barth, "Fate and Idea in Theology," in *The Way of Theology in Karl Barth: Essays and Comments*, ed. H. Martin Rumscheidt (Eugene, OR: Pickwick, 1986), 29.

2. For a much more erudite, book-length treatment of these topics, see Andrew Moore, *Realism and Christian Faith: God, Grammar, and Meaning* (Cambridge: Cambridge University Press, 2003).

3. Moore, *Realism and Christian Faith*, 1.

4. Moore, *Realism and Christian Faith*, 1.

by humans in a way that is absolutely objective and therefore abjectly certain. This view is often referred to as *direct, scientific,* or *naive realism.*

The tendency among modern philosophers, however, is toward a strident skepticism with respect to this prospect. Indeed, the position of not a few philosophers is diametrically opposed to the idea that we humans can possess any knowledge of the way things are in the world that is not thoroughly and utterly perspectival in nature. Often referred to as *anti-realism*, this view holds that while "realists see scientific inquiry as *discovery*," "anti-realists see it as *invention.*"[5] In other words, according to anti-realism, everyone's worldview—the unique way each person sees the world—is an interpretation, a construction, and therefore an illusion. Everyone's perspective of reality is thoroughly determined by their cultural location. For all intents and purposes, there is no real world to bother about!

Adding yet another voice to the conversation are the proponents of a perspective known as *critical realism.* As a kind of realism, this mediating view holds that there is a mind-independent reality that is external to us and waiting to be discovered. But it is a crucial kind of realism in that it goes on to acknowledge that because we humans lack omniscience and the appearance of things can sometimes be deceiving, we should never assume that our knowledge of this or that aspect of reality is impeccable, faultless, incapable of improvement. At the same time, critical realists hold that even though our knowledge of reality may be approximate rather than perfect, we should never stop pursuing it. I will have more to say about the relationship between critical realism and theological realism below. At this point, the big takeaway of this mediating position is this: One doesn't have to choose between a pristine, impeccable, perfect knowledge of reality (naive realism) and no knowledge at all (anti-realism). It is possible to possess a "good-enough" knowledge of reality while at the same time always being on the lookout for even better ways of understanding the way things are (critical realism).

A third assertion states that it is unnecessary to completely give up on the idea that it is possible to *speak of, refer to, talk about* reality as it really is. An anti-realist argument holds that human language is much too messy and imprecise for it to adequately represent reality to us. After all, language is composed of words that are merely signs that point to reality while never really making contact with it. I explain this argument in the classroom by pointing to the piece of furniture at which the first row of students is seated and asking what it's called. "Table," someone volunteers. Then I inquire what it's called

---

5. Henry Folse, "The Realism vs. Anti-realism Debate," accessed July 3, 2021, http://people .loyno.edu/~folse/Realism1.html (emphasis original).

in Español. Someone will indicate that the Spanish word is *mesa*. Then I ask, "But which is the correct word? Which word does the best job connecting us to the reality behind 'tableness'?" Students look at me quizzically for a few moments, and then more than one at the same time will offer that neither word is more accurate. I go on to explain that this is the problem with language from the anti-realist perspective. All words are arbitrary symbols that refer to things they really are not in touch with at a metaphysical level. Why should we think, then, that any collection of words can accurately mirror to us any sort of reality?

A commonsense version of philosophical realism, however, contends that this anti-realist critique of the sufficiency of language, while appearing coherent, does not hold. Yes, language is messy, but real-life experience argues against the postmodern contention that language is an impregnable barrier between humans and reality. It's theoretically possible, says the critical realist, for human words "to refer successfully to, and so make (approximately) true statements about, reality."[6]

Perhaps it would be helpful at this juncture to point out that some cogent support for a critically realist approach to understanding the world in which we live has been put forward by the scientist and philosopher Michael Polanyi (1891–1976). At the risk of some oversimplification on my part, I'll offer here that Polanyi describes the phenomenon of *tacit knowledge*—an implicit, inherent, reflexive awareness of reality—that is acquired as we bump around within and adapt to the physical and social worlds in which we dwell. One implication of this is that everyone possesses more knowledge than they are consciously aware of—an awareness of reality that functions below the radar or in the background rather than in the foreground of their deliberation. Another implication is that this adaptive, interactive *maturation process* results in a worldview that is to some degree acquired rather than simply received and is influenced by both personal experience and the worldview categories and constructs communicated to us via language. In other words, it is possible through our interactions with and within reality for us to acquire the cognitive frameworks necessary to assimilate a trustworthy, "good-enough" knowledge of the way the world works and how to best navigate in it.[7] Think of the way babies, then infants, become adept through both experience and instruction at figuring out some very important stuff!

6. Moore, *Realism and Christian Faith*, 1.

7. Thomas F. Torrance, "The Place of Michael Polanyi in the Modern Philosophy of Science," *Ethics in Science and Medicine* 7 (1980): 60, cited in Elmer Colyer, *How to Read T. F. Torrance: Understanding His Trinitarian and Scientific Theology* (Downers Grove, IL: InterVarsity, 2001), 335.

Once again, the upshot seems to be that when it comes to worldview matters, we should beware of the false antithesis presented to us by those who argue that we must choose between an epistemology (view of human knowledge) that is earmarked by an arrogant dogmatism, on the one hand (naive or direct realism), and one that is riddled with a cynical skepticism, on the other (anti-realism). There is a third alternative: a chastened and therefore humble critical realism.

Theological Realism in General

As for how this discussion of philosophy relates to theology, Moore goes on to indicate that some parallels exist between the assertions that form the core philosophical realism and those put forward by a realism that is theological in nature. Though there are various versions of theological realism, not all of which focus specifically on the God of the Bible, it is safe to say that most, if not all, versions would claim at a minimum that (1) a transcendent divine being (i.e., God) really does exist, and he does so independently of whether we are willing to acknowledge him or not; (2) human beings really can know this divine being/God—that is, it is possible, despite his otherness and our fallen noetic (intellectual) limitations, for people of faith to acquire a "good-enough" knowledge of who God is and what he is about; (3) this acquisition of knowledge is made possible by the fact that "human language is *not* an utterly inadequate or inappropriate medium for truthful speech about God."[8] Thus, there is at least the possibility that a text (or group of texts) considered sacred by a given religion or faith tradition (with varying degrees of accuracy) speak truthfully about God.

Christian (Trinitarian) Realism in Particular

Building on the work of Michael Polanyi, the Scottish theologian T. F. Torrance (1913–2007) put forward a version of theological realism that is specifically Christian (and trinitarian) in orientation. At the heart of Torrance's proposal is the conviction that it is possible for humans to arrive at real, dependable knowledge of God precisely because he has revealed himself through the incarnation of Christ the eternal Son and the revelatory—inspiring and illuminating—work of the Holy Spirit. In his own words, Torrance explains,

8. Moore, *Realism and Christian Faith*, 1–2 (emphasis added).

> Everything hinges on the *reality* of God's *self*-communication to us in Jesus Christ, in whom there has become incarnate, not some created intermediary between God and the world, but the very Word who eternally inheres in the Being of God and is God, so that for us to know God in Jesus Christ is really to know him as he is in himself. It is with the same force that attention is directed upon the Holy Spirit, whom the Father sends through the Son to dwell with us, and who, like the Son, is no mere cosmic power intermediate between God and the world, but is the Spirit of God who eternally dwells in him and in whom God knows himself, so that for us to know God in his Spirit is to know him in the hidden depths of his divine Being.[9]

It is important to note that, according to Torrance, it is both the *incarnation of Christ* and the *indwelling of his Spirit* that make a theological realism—a real, trustworthy knowledge of our triune God—possible. Thus, Torrance's theological realism might also be referred to as trinitarian realism; that is how crucial both the Son and the Spirit are to it!

According to Torrance, as the members of a Christian community indwell or "bump around" within the "world" presented to us in the pages of the Spirit-inspired Scriptures,[10] it is possible for them to undergo an existentially impactful "enculturation" experience. Not only do they begin more and more to see the world the way the biblical characters did; slowly but surely the Holy Spirit enables the acquisition of a "cognitive framework" that, I suggest, the apostle Paul referred to as the "mind of Christ" (1 Cor. 2:16)—a Spirit-enabled capacity to know the deep things of God (1 Cor. 2:10–11).

What is required, then, for a *real* knowledge of God and what he is up to in the world is an ongoing indwelling of the Spirit-inspired Scriptures. It is through a Christ-centered, Spirit-empowered indwelling of the biblical narrative that we find access to spiritual wisdom—a profoundly helpful understanding of the way the world God created works and how to best navigate our way in and through it (see Prov. 2:1–6). For sure, our current knowledge of these things will not be perfect (see 1 Cor. 13:12), but a critical (epistemologically humble rather than arrogant), realist understanding of God and his economy will serve us well as we journey through this life as Christ's disciples.

Trinitarian Realism and Christian Spirituality

The emphasis Paul placed in 1 Corinthians 13 on the Christian virtue of love suggests that a theological realism will do more than facilitate knowledge

---

9. Thomas F. Torrance, *Reality and Evangelical Theology: The Realism of Christian Revelation* (1982; repr., Eugene, OR: Wipf & Stock, 2003), 23 (emphasis added).

10. Torrance, *Reality and Evangelical Theology*, 83–84. See also Colyer, *How to Read T. F. Torrance*, 352–53, 356–57; Torrance, *Reality and Evangelical Theology*, xv, 48–49.

(cf. 1 Cor. 8:1). Ideally, it will facilitate a growth in character as well. Do we have reason to believe that the embrace of trinitarian realism is indeed critical to a Christian disciple's spiritual, moral, and ministry formation? We do.

So far, our focus in this chapter has been on the *epistemological impact* of trinitarian realism. But given the theme of this book, we need to press on to consider its *existential significance* as well. What I am referring to here is the way in which a trinitarian realism makes it possible for human beings to not only *know* God but also *experience* him in existentially impactful (i.e., transformational, life-story-shaping) ways. This is what makes a trinitarian realism so very important to Christian spirituality: there is such a thing as a trinitarian spirituality, and the difference it can make in people's lives is huge!

At the heart of most treatments of trinitarian spirituality is the notion that one of the primary attributes of God is his relationality. The Godhead—Father, Son, and Holy Spirit—has existed for all eternity in a loving, trusting, mutually preferring community. This implies that all the members of the Trinity are personal rather than impersonal divine beings profoundly capable of and deeply committed to the dynamic of communion.

As I explained in this book's introduction, the distinction between a God who is personal and one who is impersonal is extremely relevant to the cultivation of a Christian spirituality. And, at the risk of making this discussion even more nerdy, I will point out that the distinction is supported by a theological construct many theologians refer to as the "social Trinity." According to this concept, God

> is conceived as a relational community of equality and mutuality within which the distinctive identity of each person of the Trinity is fully maintained as Father, Son, and Spirit. There is an irreducible otherness within God in relation to each person of the Trinity. This deep interrelated communion of the three persons of the Trinity is often expressed by the word *perichoresis*, which refers to the mutual indwelling within the threefold nature of the Trinity. All three persons of the divine community mutually indwell one another in a relational unity while maintaining their distinct identities.[11]

The upshot is that this understanding of the inner life of the Trinity provides some rather powerful support for the conviction that God, rather than being essentially impersonal, is actually a hyperpersonal, ultrarelational, *unified community* of divine being(s) with whom his human image-bearers can interact in real, personal, transformative, life-story-shaping ways.

11. Craig Van Gelder and Dwight J. Zscheile, *The Missional Church in Perspective: Mapping Trends and Shaping the Conversation* (Grand Rapids: Baker Academic, 2011), 54.

Obviously, this realist, hyperpersonal, ultrarelational, trinitarian conception of God will have huge implications for a Christian spirituality that is also distinctively realist and trinitarian. First, such spirituality will necessarily be "I-Thou" rather than "I-it" in its orientation. It is not the idea, concept, or doctrine of God that we Christians are to worship, petition, serve, or commune with, but God himself!

In his book *I and Thou*, Jewish philosopher Martin Buber (1878–1965) expounded on the interpersonal, relational nature of reality.[12] According to Buber, human existence is essentially *dialogical*, defined by the manner in which each of us *dialogues* with other persons, the world, and, most importantly, God. Buber emphasizes the hugely significant difference between an "I-Thou" and "I-It" relationality. "I-Thou" is a relation of subject to subject, while "I-It" is a relation of subject to object. Most basically, this means that in an "I-Thou" relation I recognize the other as a whole, complex, wonder-filled, personal being I can never fully comprehend much less manage or control. It is a relation of profound respect and is earmarked by humility and, hopefully, love. An "I-It" relation differs greatly. Here, I am not interacting with a whole, complex, personal being but with a *thing*—something I can deconstruct, analyze, comprehend, master, control.

It matters greatly if our approach to God is "I-Thou" rather than "I-It." The eternal *Thou* is not an object we merely experience or conceive of. He is someone we *encounter*. Moreover, there is an immediacy between us and the eternal *Thou*. Thus, it is possible for us to speak directly to God, to relate to him in a way that is personal—intimate, interactive, and existentially impactful (life-story shaping).[13]

Second, the ultrarelational nature of God also explains why a realist Trinitarian spirituality will be *experiential* and *interactive* as well as cognitive and reflective. This means that real transformational encounters with God made possible by the redemptive work of Christ and effected by the Holy Spirit (see 2 Cor. 3:17–18) are both anticipated and sought after. We don't simply engage in spiritual disciplines because Jesus did, we do so for the same reasons as he—to honor, commune with, and be guided and empowered by our heavenly Father. Hearing and honoring the heart of God the way Jesus did

---

12. Martin Buber, *I and Thou*, trans. Ronald Gregor Smith (New York: Touchstone Books, 1971).

13. I've adapted this overview of Buber's concept of *I and Thou* from an essay titled "Martin Buber's *I and Thou*. See Alex Scott, "Martin Buber's *I and Thou*," accessed 8/20/22, https://www.angelfire.com/md2/timewarp/buber.html#:~:text=In%20the%20I-2DThou%20relation%20between%20the%20individual%20and%20God,can%20speak%20directly%20to%20God.

is the highest priority for those who, like Jesus, take seriously their "I-Thou" relation with him. Christ's Spirit can be counted on to enable us to experience transformational encounters with the living God.

Third, a realist trinitarian spirituality will be pursued in a *perpetual* rather than occasional manner. Jesus's spirituality (communion with the Father) was actually not episodic but chronic—that is, ongoing (John 8:29). Likewise, when the apostle Paul referred in his writings to the spirituality of his readers, his tendency was to use words like "always," "continually," "in all circumstances," "on all occasions," and "in every situation" (see 1 Thess. 5:16–18; Eph. 6:18; Phil. 4:6). Put simply, Paul promoted a *lifestyle* of interacting with God the Father, through Christ the Son, in the power of the Holy Spirit.

Fourth, a realist trinitarian spirituality will not only *effect* an ongoing mentoring relationship with the risen Christ in the power of the Spirit; it will also *affect* the relational capacity of his apprentices. According to Buber, God is the eternal *Thou*, the source of *all* being and becoming.[14] Since we've never locked eyes with someone who doesn't innately bear God's image, we must recognize the *Thou* in everyone we interact with. For us Christians, this underwrites Christ's radical call for his followers to not only love their neighbors as themselves (Matt. 19:19; 22:39) but their enemies as well (Matt. 5:43–44). Jesus was really good at loving God supremely and at loving his neighbors as himself (see Matt. 22:34–40). Could it be that one of the primary goals of Christian discipleship is a growth on our part to do the same? If so, this raises a question: How might or should this emphasis on our relationship with God and others impact the motive and manner in which we engage in spiritual disciplines (cf. Matt. 6:1–18)? Christian spirituality not only affects one's relation to God but also impacts the way we interact or "dialogue" with everyone and everything that God, the Eternal Thou, has made.

Theologian and professor of spirituality Michael Downey provides support for each of these earmarks of a trinitarian spirituality: "Christian spirituality is an invitation to participate in the very life of God through communion with the Incarnate Word by the power of the Holy Spirit who is love. Such participation brings the Christian into the heart of the mystery of God's own life. The call to ever deeper communion with God is at the same time the call to ever deeper communion with others."[15]

14. See Scott, "Martin Buber's *I and Thou*."
15. Michael Downey, *Understanding Christian Spirituality* (Mahwah, NJ: Paulist Press, 1997), 147.

Toward a *Fully* Trinitarian Realism

The way this book emphasizes the vital need for a theological realism will, by itself, set it apart from other works that promote a trinitarian spirituality. That said, yet another distinguishing feature is my suggestion that, given the critical importance of Christ's incarnation and the outpouring of the Spirit to a biblically informed theological realism, two other "realisms" also need to be embraced. I contend that a fully trinitarian theological realism not only infers but also requires a realist rather than nonrealist *pneumatology* and *Christology*.

The Need for a Pneumatological Realism

A close reading of the New Testament leads me to believe that Christ's followers should expect to experience the Spirit of God in ways that are real—that is, personal, interactive, and phenomenal—rather than merely theoretical, conceptual, or ritualistic. Moreover, the sincere Christian disciple should expect that these interactions with the Spirit can and will prove to be assistive. They will be *epistemologically helpful*, meaning revelatory in terms of God's love, will, and purposes (1 Cor. 2:6–16; Eph. 1:17; 3:16–19), and *existentially impactful*, meaning transformative, morally formational, and ministry engendering (1 Cor. 12:7–11; Gal. 5:19–23; Col. 1:9–10).

Unfortunately, however, not a few theologians have commented on the "pneumatological deficit" they associate with some theologies and ministries in the contemporary era.[16] Because of a tendency in some theologies to overly conceptualize the Holy Spirit and truncate the role he plays in the Christian life, it is not uncommon for contemporary church members to view the Holy Spirit as a sanctifying force they simply *presume* to be at work in their lives because they have engaged in this or that religious ritual (e.g., water baptism,

---

16. See, e.g., Timothy Tennent, *Invitation to World Missions: A Trinitarian Missiology for the Twenty-First Century* (Grand Rapids: Kregel Academic, 2010), 94; Roger Olson, *The Story of Christian Theology: Twenty Centuries of Tradition and Reform* (Downers Grove, IL: IVP Academic, 1999), 521, 523; and Veli-Matti Kärkkäinen, *Pneumatology: The Holy Spirit in Ecumenical, International, and Contextual Perspective* (Grand Rapids: Baker Academic, 2002), 17–18. Moreover, Jürgen Moltmann provides not only a nuanced discussion of the reason for the "reserve in the doctrine of the Holy Spirit" within the established churches in Europe during the modern era but also an eloquent critique of the tendency among some evangelicals to conflate Word and Spirit and to conceive of the Spirit only in an intellectual manner. See Jürgen Moltmann, *The Spirit of Life: A Universal Affirmation* (Minneapolis: Fortress, 1992), 2–3. For a more in-depth discussion of how the pneumatological imbalance Moltmann refers to can impact the spiritual formation process, see Kenneth Boa, *Conformed to His Image: Biblical and Practical Approaches to Spiritual Formation* (Grand Rapids: Zondervan, 2001), 291, 316–21.

confirmation, the laying on of hands). It is also possible to refer to the Holy Spirit when reciting the creed or when singing hymns or worship songs while at the same time possessing an attitude of *presumption* (or even *indifference*) toward the third person of the Trinity. What is missing in an ecclesial environment influenced by an overly scholastic or ritualistic—essentially nonrealist—pneumatology is an adequate understanding of

- the Holy Spirit's personhood and relationality,
- how important the Spirit is to absolutely every aspect of the Christian life,
- why Christ's followers can and should expect to experience the Spirit in ways that are sometimes *phenomenal* in nature (i.e., immediate and evident to the senses), and
- why church members can, through the Spirit, hope to interact with the risen Christ in genuinely life-story-shaping ways.

I will have more to say about each of these points in chapter 3. I will also go into some detail there regarding the pneumatological realism that I consider to be central to the apostle Paul's theological paradigm. For now, the important point is that, given what we have already learned about the importance of a realist understanding and experience of the Holy Spirit, we already possess some good reasons to believe that a full-throated affirmation and wholehearted practice of a pneumatological realism is simply integral to a fully trinitarian realism and the lifestyle spiritualty that is shaped by it.

The Crucial Import of a Christological Realism

Someone reading this chapter might wonder why I addressed the need for a pneumatological realism before discussing the importance of a christological realism. The reason for this sequencing is functional. It is based on my interpretation of what we find Jesus saying in John 14 and 16 about the role the Holy Spirit will play in enabling his disciples to heed the call located in chapter 15 to "continue," "abide," "remain," and "stay connected" to him. Taken together, we discover in John 14 and 16 that the Holy Spirit is "another" *advocate, counselor,* or *mentor (paraklētos;* John 14:15–18) and that his role is to bring to the minds of Jesus's disciples everything that Jesus has taught them (John 14:26) and wishes (in an ongoing way) to teach them (John 16:13). In sum, what I am proposing is that a careful consideration of the pneumatology presented in John 14–16 provides support for the notion that one of the primary tasks of the Holy Spirit is to make it possible for Christian disciples to experience the ongoing mentoring relationship with Christ that John 15 exhorts us toward![17]

It is not just a memory or an example of Christ that will drive a vibrant Christian spirituality but the real, risen Jesus, raised from the dead and interacting with his followers in real, personal, life-story-shaping ways. A christological realism means that when we pray to or worship Christ, we are careful to reckon with his real presence. In this way, we avoid merely talking at or singing toward the idea of him. In addition, when we call out to Christ, asking him to help us in this or that endeavor, we genuinely expect a response. In sum, a christological realism creates an attitude or posture of *expectancy* with respect to him. He might at any time, through the Spirit, break into our reality, bringing comfort or providing us with some crucial wisdom or guidance.[18] It is not that we have the power to conjure or command his presence as if he were a genie residing in a lamp. On the other hand, he really does seem to be perpetually available to us. We have come to know and experience him as risen, real, and really committed to being with us day in and day out, 24-7, in a sometimes encouraging, sometimes challenging, always empowering manner. Apparently, he meant it when he promised to be with us always (Matt. 28:20; cf. Rev. 3:20).

My contention that a trinitarian realism necessarily entails not only a theological realism writ large but also a pneumatological and christological realism is supported by the way Paul prayed for the Ephesian and Colossian Christians. A careful reading of the prayers quoted below reveals that Paul not only referred to all three members of the Trinity when praying for his readers but also seemed to attribute to the Holy Spirit a primary role in helping them *experience* an ever-deepening connection with God the Father and the Lord Jesus Christ! Here are Paul's prayers:

> For this reason, ever since I heard about your faith in the *Lord Jesus* and your love for all God's people, I have not stopped giving thanks for you, remembering you in my prayers. I keep asking that the *God* of our *Lord Jesus Christ*, the *glorious Father*, may give you the *Spirit of wisdom and revelation*, so that you may know him better. I pray that the eyes of your heart may be enlightened in order that you may know the hope to which he has called you, the riches of his glorious inheritance in his holy people, and his incomparably great power for us who believe. (Eph. 1:15–19)

17. Moreover, some explicit support for this assertion can be discerned by comparing Matt. 10:19–20 and Luke 21:14–15. For more on this, see Gary Tyra, *Christ's Empowering Presence: The Pursuit of God through the Ages* (Downers Grove, IL: IVP Books, 2011), 99. See also Tyra, "Proclaiming Christ's Victory over Sinful Personal Desires," *Enrichment Journal*, accessed July 3, 2021, https://ministry.journeyonline.org/proclaiming-christs-victory-over-sinful-personal-desires/.

18. See, e.g., Acts 18:9–11; 22:17–21; 23:11; 26:15–18; 2 Tim. 4:17.

For this reason I kneel before the *Father*, from whom every family in heaven and on earth derives its name. I pray that out of his glorious riches he may strengthen you with power *through his Spirit* in your inner being, so that *Christ* may dwell in your hearts through faith. And I pray that you, being rooted and established in love, may have power, together with all the Lord's holy people, to grasp how wide and long and high and deep is the love of *Christ*, and to know this love that surpasses knowledge—that you may be filled to the measure of all the fullness of *God*. (Eph. 3:14–19)

For this reason, since the day we heard about you, we have not stopped praying for you. We continually ask *God* to fill you with the knowledge of his will through all the wisdom and understanding that the *Spirit* gives, so that you may live a life worthy of the *Lord* and please him in every way: bearing fruit in every good work, growing in the knowledge of *God*, being strengthened with all power according to his glorious might so that you may have great endurance and patience, and giving joyful thanks to the *Father*, who has qualified you to share in the inheritance of his holy people in the kingdom of light. (Col. 1:9–12)

I have strenuously suggested in the preceding pages that the kind of Christian spirituality that will facilitate a high-octane "I-Thou" relationship with our triune God, which the apostle Paul enjoyed, will eagerly embrace a realist rather than nonrealist understanding of God the Father, Christ the Son, and the Holy Spirit. The precise way these three realisms function within a trinitarian spirituality will be explained in the chapters that make up part 2 of this book. However, before I conclude this discussion of foundational convictions, one more biblical and theological matter demands our attention.

Yet Another Reality a Lifestyle Spirituality Must Reckon With

I must press on in this initial, foundation-laying chapter to suggest that yet another spiritual reality must be taken seriously if we are to do justice to what the New Testament has to say about the cultivation of a lifestyle spirituality. Ironically, this additional "realism" has to do *not* with our triune God but with the reality of an entity the New Testament mentions more than 238 times, most often as *Satan* (37 times), the *devil* (35 times), and the *evil one* (34 times).

Though many contemporary scholars, religious as well as secular, simply dismiss the idea of a real "evil one" at work in our world, the New Testament indicates that Jesus, Paul, Peter, John, James, and the author of the Letter to the Hebrews all reckoned otherwise. For heaven's sake, one of the petitions in the paradigmatic prayer Jesus taught his disciples has us beseeching God to deliver us from evil or the evil one (Matt. 6:13). I think I know why.

While I will refrain from proposing here the need for a "demonological realism," the New Testament warns us time and again that we most certainly do have a real spiritual enemy who is committed to sabotaging our spiritual formation. Throughout my four-plus decades of pastoral and professorial ministry activity, I have been careful to keep reminding church members and students of the need to keep reckoning with the devil's reality lest he succeed at using the adverse circumstances that come their way to drive a wedge between them and God. Moreover, my study of the New Testament also suggests that the devil is strategically and deliberately seeking to corrupt the Christian's theologically real engagement in the four cardinal components of Christian discipleship: worship, nurture, community, and mission.[19]

But the devil's attempt to corrupt our engagement in worship, nurture, community, and mission need not succeed. Once again, to be forewarned is to be forearmed. Thus, my counsel to church members, students, and readers of this book is this: We must never forget that it is never just us and God. This reminder is incredibly important. I have discovered over the years that when church members and students are encouraged to keep this reality in mind, they are enabled to cooperate with our triune God in a way that is devil defeating.

C. S. Lewis (1898–1963) once observed that "there are two equal and opposite errors into which our race can fall about the devils. One is to disbelieve in their existence. The other is to believe, and to feel an excessive and unhealthy interest in them. They themselves are equally pleased by both errors and hail a materialist or a magician with the same delight."[20] Clearly Lewis believed there is a third alternative: it is possible to believe in the devil, even to take him seriously, without also obsessing over him. This is the type of "realism" with respect to the devil and spiritual warfare that I will recommend here and there in the remainder of this work. For sure, experiencing the dark side of reality (evil) can be frightening, disconcerting, even infuriating. However, the proper response, says Paul, is not to whistle at it, trying to convince ourselves it is not real, or to become mesmerized by it because of some sense of inordinate fear or perverse fascination. No, having acknowledged the reality of evil in this or that situation, Paul calls Christ's apprentices to "live as children of light" (Eph. 5:8).

I am happy to be able to report that, if we let it, the lifestyle spirituality Paul was careful to commend will help us do just that. The cumulative effect of a

---

19. For more on this dynamic and how to defeat it, see Gary Tyra, *The Dark Side of Discipleship: Why and How the New Testament Encourages Christians to Deal with the Devil* (Eugene, OR: Cascade Books, 2020), 61–160.

20. C. S. Lewis, *The Screwtape Letters* (1942; repr., New York: HarperOne, 2015), ix.

trinitarian realism (theological, pneumatological, and christological) is simply stunning in its significance. This is how we render to God "a long obedience in the same direction."[21] This is how we cultivate a spiritual, moral, and missional faithfulness before him. And what's more, this is how we participate responsibly and fruitfully in God's evil-ending agenda.

The next chapter will focus on some other spirituality-shaping theological convictions: three divine attributes or cardinal characteristics that will also tremendously impact the shape and effect of a realist, trinitarian, "I-Thou" spirituality. Are you a fan of theology, or do you just genuinely love and want to please God? In either case, by all means, read on.

TOPICS FOR REVIEW

1. How would you explain the difference between naive realism, anti-realism, and critical realism?

2. What three claims are at the heart of most all versions of theological realism?

3. How would you explain what this chapter suggests is the process by which Christians can acquire real knowledge of God and what God is up to in the world?

4. What are the four implications that a realist, hyperpersonal, ultrarelational, trinitarian conception of God will have for a Christian spirituality that is distinctively realist and trinitarian?

5. According to this chapter, what two other realisms does a fully trinitarian realism require? Why?

6. How would you explain why this chapter insists that taking what the New Testament has to say about Satan seriously is also important to lifestyle spirituality? Do you agree or disagree? Why?

---

21. This phrase—first used in print by one of Christianity's fiercest critics, Friedrich Nietzsche (1844–1900) and later utilized by Christian pastor and author Eugene Peterson (1932–2018) as the title of one of his books—is one of my favorite ways of referring to the faithfulness Jesus is looking for in the lives of his followers. See Friedrich Nietzsche, *The Essential Nietzsche: Beyond Good and Evil and the Genealogy of Morals* (New York: Chartwell Books, 2017), 88; Eugene H. Peterson, *A Long Obedience in the Same Direction: Discipleship in an Instant Society* (1980; repr., Downers Grove, IL: IVP Books, 2021).

2

GETTING THERE FROM HERE

Paul's "I-Thou" Spirituality

Since the life of prayer consists in an ever-deepening communion with a Reality beyond ourselves, which is truly there, and touches, calls, attracts us, what we believe about that Reality will rule our relation to it. We do not approach a friend and a machine in the same way. We make the first and greatest of our mistakes in religion when we begin with ourselves, our petty feelings and needs, ideas and capacities.

—Evelyn Underhill, *The School of Charity*

Numerous TV episodes and movies have depicted the same humorous scenario: a bewildered traveler asks a local how to get to a certain place. The local scratches his head and then responds dryly, "You can't get there from here!"

The response of the local to a befuddled traveler desperately looking for some direction is humorous precisely because of how ludicrous it is. Common sense tells us that the response is a simplistic exaggeration. Just because there is no *direct* route from here to there doesn't mean you can't get there. That said, the point is taken—when it comes to journeys or endeavors, starting points matter!

Imagine hearing the words "Sorry, but you can't get there from here" at the conclusion of a first meeting with a potential physical therapist, marriage counselor, career coach, or financial planner. Clearly, getting such a response after answering the expert's initial questions would be disconcerting, perhaps even exasperating. But what if it were also apparent that the observation had been made by the expert with the intent of encouraging in us a profound, fundamental change in our *mindset*—a change that would put us on an entirely different trajectory with respect to our physical, marital, career, or financial health? In that case, the reply "You can't get there from here" wouldn't be ludicrous at all, but potentially life-changing instead! The hard truth is that sometimes we can't get there from here, but it is not so much about *where* we are at the beginning of the journey or endeavor as about *who* we are—that is, our mindset.

As previously alluded to in this book's introduction, the apostle Paul kept referring in his writings to a Spirit-enabled *mindset, attitude*, or *renewed way of thinking* that is essential to a Christian life well lived.[1] Here are a couple of passages where we see Paul making this point:

Do not conform to the pattern of this world, but be transformed by *the renewing of your mind*. Then you will be able to test and approve what *God's will* is—his good, pleasing and perfect will. (Rom. 12:2)

You were taught, with regard to your former way of life, to put off your old self, which is being corrupted by its deceitful desires; *to be made new in the attitude of your minds*; and to put on the new self, created to be *like God* in true righteousness and holiness. (Eph. 4:22–24)

Commenting on these twin passages, biblical scholars Bruce Barton, David Veerman, and Neil Wilson explain,

The Greek word for "transformed" (*metamorphousthe*) is the root for the English word *metamorphosis*. Believers are to experience a complete transformation from the inside out. And the change must begin in the *mind*, where all thoughts and actions begin. . . . One of the keys, then, to the Christian life is to be involved in activities that renew the mind. *Renewing* (*anakainōsei*) refers to a new way of thinking, a mind desiring to be conformed to God rather than to the world. We will never be truly *transformed* without this *renewing* of our mind.[2]

In other words, according to the apostle Paul, one's mindset matters. The lifestyle transformation a genuine Christian discipleship can effect requires that we "be made new in the attitude of our minds." Otherwise, it's true: we can't get there from here!

---

1. See Rom. 8:6; 12:2; 1 Cor. 2:16; Eph. 4:20–24; Phil. 3:17–21; Col. 2:18; 3:1–4, 7–8; 1 Tim. 6:3–5; see also 1 Pet. 4:7; 5:8.

2. Bruce B. Barton, David Veerman, and Neil S. Wilson, *Romans*, Life Application Bible Commentary (Wheaton: Tyndale House, 1992), 231 (emphasis original).

In this chapter, we will explore how critical three things are to the cultivation of a Pauline ("I-Thou") lifestyle spirituality: (1) a theocentric *starting point*; (2) a theo-sensitive *ultimate concern*; and (3) a *theological mindset* that approximates how the apostle understood who God is and what he is about. In other words, this chapter is an introduction to the renewed thinking that is necessary if Christians are to get from *here* to *there*.

The Critical Importance of a Theocentric Starting Point

The quotation that serves as the epigraph for this chapter supports the Pauline notion that where one starts with respect to the Christian life is all-important. Specifically, Evelyn Underhill (1875–1941) explains, the life of prayer (one's spirituality) is bound to founder if we begin with ourselves rather than God.[3] This may seem patently obvious, yet it is possible for even committed church-goers to possess a starting point that is not sufficiently informed by the reality and character of God. When this happens, it brings to mind the much-quoted line from the movie *Apollo 13*: "Houston, we have a problem!"

In a nutshell, the problem is that a spirituality which either ignores or misunderstands God, beginning instead with the self's "petty feelings and needs, ideas and capacities," tends to become *narcissistic* and *utilitarian* in essence and is approached with a *consumeristic* mentality in place. As a result, such a spirituality cannot help but fail what I refer to as the "threefold faithfulness test." Only a mindset that is theologically *rich* (rather than *bankrupt* or even *impoverished*) has what it takes to engender within church members the *spiritual*, *moral*, and *missional faithfulness* God is looking for.

In his primer titled *Understanding Christian Spirituality*, Michael Downey lends his voice to the concerns I am raising here about starting points and the mindsets that produce them. First, Downey reminds us that some approaches to spirituality essentially ignore the divine and focus only on the actualization of the human spirit. The aim in these approaches has nothing to do with communing with and pleasing God. Instead, the goal is self-transcendence—determining for oneself a grand goal, purpose, or *ultimate concern* and then fully living into it, experiencing a sense of personal integration in the process.[4]

To be sure, I affirm the notion of self-transcendence as a divinely endowed capacity resulting from humans having been created in the image of God (Gen.

3. Evelyn Underhill, *The School of Charity: Meditations on the Christian Creed* (1934; repr., Wilton, CT: Morehouse, 1991), 6–11.

4. Michael Downey, *Understanding Christian Spirituality* (Mahwah, NJ: Paulist Press, 1997), 14–15.

1:26–27). This ability to transcend or overcome the givens of our existence (nature and nurture) and progress toward becoming the very best versions of ourselves—who and what we were created to be—is one of the things that distinguishes us from animals (Gen. 1:28). The problem is that missing from the lives of many of our cultural peers, religious or not, is any serious consideration of what it means to bear God's image. Thus, such people lack any divine direction regarding what the best version of themselves might or should look like. It's no wonder then that, as Downey puts it, "in some circles spirituality has become virtually synonymous with self-help, self-fix. The spiritual journey can become nothing more than a narcissistic ego trip wrapped in the rhetoric of the sacred."[5]

This is a bold critique, but Downey proceeds to double down on it:

> Similarly, in many approaches to spirituality today there is a kind of shopping around from one brand of spiritual experience to another, from workshops on self-improvement, to varieties of herbal medicines and organic diets, to blends of Celtic and Native American spiritualities, to stargazing and colored stones, to the cults of Wicca and the practices of witchery. . . .
>
> More problematic still is the tendency in many approaches to spirituality today to seek results, to look for changes in our personality or in our ability to relate to others. Many adopt spiritual disciplines and practices because it helps their day go better. If this doesn't work, then it's dropped and another one taken up. The pragmatic mentality is deeply ingrained.[6]

Downey's conviction regarding the importance of theology for spirituality is crystal clear. For spirituality to be something other than narcissistic, commercialistic, and utilitarian—a set of practices we engage in because we find them useful toward the goal of living our best lives now—it must be about God rather than us. We must be taken with *him*, devoted to *him*, alive in *him*. In other words, *God* must be our starting point. Downey, a Christian theologian, concludes his discussion this way: "The only reason for embarking on the way of spirituality is for the sake of the sacred itself. . . . The reason for living the spiritual life is . . . simply because God is God."[7]

The Apostle Paul's Theo-sensitive Ultimate Concern

I have already hinted at the fact that, in addition to a theological rather than anthropological starting point, also required is an *ultimate concern* that tran-

5. Downey, *Understanding Christian Spirituality*, 20.
6. Downey, *Understanding Christian Spirituality*, 20–21.
7. Downey, *Understanding Christian Spirituality*, 21.

scends the goal of self-transcendence. In other words, the ultimate concern that drives and orients our spirituality must be *theo-sensitive* rather than determined by what our culture would suggest the best version of ourselves will look like.

That the starting point for the apostle Paul's "I-Thou" spirituality was theocentric is obvious. The good news is that it is also possible to zero in on the ultimate concern that animated his life and ministry. The Pauline corpus leads us to believe that the apostle was thoroughly convinced that, rather than focusing on the actualizing of the self, the Christian's ultimate concern must be to *please God* (Rom. 12:1–2; 2 Cor. 5:9; Col. 1:10; 1 Thess. 4:1).

Moreover, Paul's letters also support the notion that he equated *pleasing God* with *proving faithful* (see 1 Cor. 4:2, 17; Gal. 5:22; Eph. 1:1; 6:21; Col. 1:2, 7; 4:7, 9; 1 Tim. 2:7). Passages such as these prompt me to suggest, more specifically, that Paul's ultimate concern, and the one he sought to inculcate in the hearts and minds of his readers, was the theo-sensitive conviction that a vibrant Christian spirituality will be one that engenders within its adherents a Christ-emulating, Spirit-empowered, God-the-Father-pleasing lifestyle that is earmarked by a spiritual, moral, and missional faithfulness. God, rather than Paul himself, was Paul's starting point, and pleasing God by means of a thoroughly faithful lifestyle was the apostle's ultimate concern.

The Infrastructure of Paul's Theological Paradigm

To fully appreciate (and thus to emulate) Paul's theo-sensitive ultimate concern, we have to possess at least a rudimentary understanding of how Paul understood God's nature and intentions. This is possible because of the consistent way the apostle referred to these theological themes in his writings.

I suggest here that Paul wanted his readers to conceive of *charity*, *sanctity*, and *missionality* as three *prime traits* of the God of the Bible. The idea here is that when Paul wrote to church members asserting that a prerequisite to authentic life transformation was a mental renewal—being made new in the attitude of their minds—he had in mind the same kind of theological paradigm shift he had experienced because of his encounters with Christ and the Holy Spirit. It is not that the concepts of charity, sanctity, and missionality were unknown to Paul before his life-changing encounter with Christ, but the way they could be *understood* and *lived into* in a theologically real manner was a radically new development. Paul wanted the church members he was responsible for to experience the same kind of life renewal he had experienced. Paul had become convinced that genuine transformation is possible but that it required an entirely new theological perspective (cf. 2 Pet. 1:3–4). In other words, this is how you get *there* from *here*.

The first step in our approach to understanding and emulating the understanding of God that formed the foundation of Paul's "I-Thou" lifestyle spirituality, along with his theological realism, will be to identify those passages in the apostle's letters where he emphasizes the three divine traits referred to above: charity, sanctity, and missionality. My premise is that it is because these three cardinal characteristics were especially significant (primary) to the way Paul came to understand who God is and what he is about that his writings are replete with references to them. Specifically, the focus here will be on relevant Pauline passages where we find the apostle

- *reflecting* on his own spiritual and ministry journey (i.e., his personal experience of God's charity, sanctity, and missionality);
- *exhorting* his readers to think, believe, or act in ways that are in keeping with these cardinal characteristics; and
- *informing* his readers about how he is *praying* for them with these divine traits in mind.

When it seems appropriate to do so, I will also refer to some passages outside the Pauline corpus that seem to provide additional apostolic encouragement for the readers of the New Testament to cultivate a spirituality that is driven by these three prime divine traits.

Warning: Pauline Theology Ahead—Proceed Ponderingly!

While the spirituality Paul promoted involved the *contemplation* of God, the goal was not to empty his mind of all temporal, worldly distractions so he could focus solely on God in the same manner as the angels.[8] Instead, Paul's contemplation involved a prayerful pondering of what the Bible has to say about *who God is* and *what he is about*. What's more, we know that Paul did more than muse: he also acted on his new theological understanding and encouraged his readers to do likewise. I am hopeful that our own prayerful contemplation of the divine traits that, I believe, served as the primary foci of the apostle Paul's *contemplation* and *praxis* might impact us in the same transformational, faithfulness-producing manner as it did him. Again, this is how we get *there* from *here*.

---

8. See George Lane, *Christian Spirituality: An Historical Sketch* (Chicago: Loyola, 1984), 11–17.

Cardinal Characteristic 1: God's Charity

We have already learned that one of the fundamental qualities of God is his *relationality*. More precisely, we have come to understand how it is legitimate to think of God as being both *hyperpersonal* and *ultrarelational*. We will look in vain, however, for Pauline passages that use these precise terms to describe God's character. For this reason, I encourage readers to keep God's personal and relational characteristics in mind as we focus on a closely related primary characteristic that is applied to him in a much more explicit manner: his *charity*.

It is well known that the King James Version used the word "charity" to refer to *agapē*—God's unconditional, gratuitous love. As a cardinal characteristic, then, God's charity refers to how he is *loving, kind, merciful, gracious,* and *forgiving.* Paul's letters are filled with references to all these attributes, and it should be immediately acknowledged that Paul not only ascribed them to God but also encouraged his readers, who had experienced these divine attributes in and through Christ, to speak and act into the lives of others in loving, kind, merciful, gracious, and forgiving ways. For instance, not only did Paul ascribe *agapē* to God (e.g., Eph. 2:4–5); he also exhorted his readers to love others with that same kind of love (e.g., Eph. 5:2). Indeed, so significant in Paul's renewed thinking was the phenomenon of God's *agapē* love that he devoted an entire discussion to it in one of his letters (see 1 Cor. 13). It is simply impossible to overstate the impact that Paul's experience of the *agapē* of God in Christ had on his theological mindset.

And yet Paul's use of the word "love" doesn't exhaust the various ways in which he refers to God's charitable nature. Apparent to anyone familiar with Paul's writings is the fact that they are rife with references to God's grace (*charis*) as well. What's more, the "gospel"—referred to eighty-three times in Paul's letters—is a translation of the Greek word *euangelion*, which literally means "good message" and is often translated "good news." Thus, Paul's main message was something *good*, something grounded in the *agapē* and *charis* of God.

Specifically, Paul makes it very clear in his proclamation of the good news that the eternal salvation everyone desperately needs is not something we can merit, earn, or effect in our own strength. Instead, our salvation, owing entirely to God's mercy and grace (his *charity*), has been made possible by Jesus Christ and is experienced by faith, which is, itself, a gift from God (see Eph. 2:4–5, 8; Titus 3:4–7). In his letter to his ministry protégé, Titus, Paul explains the gospel in a manner rich with theological significance: "But when the *kindness* and *love* of God our Savior appeared, he saved us, not because of righteous things we had done, but because of his *mercy*. He saved us through the washing of rebirth and renewal by the Holy Spirit, whom he poured out on us *generously* through Jesus Christ our Savior, so that, having been justified by his *grace*, we might become heirs having the hope of eternal life" (Titus 3:4–7).

Moreover, Paul's writings also make clear how very impactful the experience of God's grace was for him personally. In the passages where he describes his own spiritual journey, he is consistently careful to indicate how his conversion, call to apostleship, and subsequent success in ministry were all astonishing indications of the unfathomable depth of God's grace, mercy, and patience.[9] In an especially poignant passage of this type, Paul humbly asserts,

> I thank Christ Jesus our Lord, who has given me strength, that he considered me trustworthy, appointing me to his service. Even though I was once a blasphemer and a persecutor and a violent man, I was shown *mercy* because I acted in ignorance and unbelief. The *grace* of our Lord was poured out on me abundantly, along with the faith and love that are in Christ Jesus.
>
> Here is a trustworthy saying that deserves full acceptance: Christ Jesus came into the world to save sinners—of whom I am the worst. But for that very reason I was shown *mercy* so that in me, the worst of sinners, Christ Jesus might display his immense *patience* as an example for those who would believe in him and receive eternal life. (1 Tim. 1:12–16)

Paul also shares with his readers the way he was graciously enabled by God to eventually interpret and respond to a significant season of suffering in his life (2 Cor. 12:7–10). After three unsuccessful attempts through prayer to have God remove a "thorn"—a severe personal trial perpetrated by Satan but apparently allowed by God (cf. Job 2:1–6)—Paul says he finally heard from the Lord in a theologically real "I-Thou" manner. According to Paul, God declined to remove the thorn, explaining, "My grace is sufficient for you, for my power is made perfect in weakness" (2 Cor. 12:9a). Paul's response to God and this painful trial simply doesn't make sense apart from an infusion of divine grace into his life. He explains to the Corinthian Christians, "Therefore I will boast all the more gladly about my weaknesses, so that Christ's power may rest on me" (2 Cor. 12:9b). The point is that grace was much more than a theological concept for Paul; it was, instead, a very personal, situation-specific, life-story-shaping and ministry-empowering endowment provided to him by the living God.

---

9. See, e.g., Rom. 1:5; 1 Cor. 3:10; 15:10; 2 Cor. 1:12; 4:1; 12:9; Gal. 1:5; 2:9; Eph. 3:7–8.

The fact that a postconversion experience of God's charity can be so existentially impactful explains the passages at the beginning and end of many of
Paul's letters where he wishes upon his readers a fresh encounter with God's
grace and *mercy*, as well as the profound sense of *peace* that flows from such
a bestowal.[10] Pondering these passages in a prayerful, contemplative manner
causes me to wonder: Given Paul's theological and pneumatological realism, is
there a possibility that these epistle-beginning and -ending benedictions were
not simply a mere formality in Paul's mind but were communicated with the
hope that a sacramental experience of God's grace and peace might result
(cf. 2 Tim. 4:22; Philem. 25)?

Especially pertinent to this discussion of the impact of God's gracious
being on the lifestyle of Christ's followers are the many passages where we
find Paul exhorting his readers to respond to God's charity by being careful
to *continue in it*.[11] It is passages such as these that suggest the need for what
I refer to as a *spiritual faithfulness*.

For Paul, faith in Christ functions as a doorway leading the believer into a
new kind of relationship with God: "Therefore, since we have been justified
through faith, we have peace with God through our Lord Jesus Christ, through
whom we have gained access by faith into this grace in which we now stand.
And we boast in the hope of the glory of God" (Rom. 5:1–2). According to
this passage, it is through faith in Jesus that we move from a state of being
"under the law" to a state of grace.[12] Though grace means that one's right
standing is not determined by an impeccable obedience to or observance
of the Jewish law (both moral and ceremonial), believers are nevertheless
responsible for "continuing" in grace by continuing in the *faith* by which it
is accessed. This explains those several passages in which Paul, in ways both
explicit and implicit, links the experience of *grace* to *faith*.[13]

This strong connection between grace and faith in Paul's theology is key to
understanding what was, perhaps, the bedrock of the apostle's understanding
of the Christian disciple's *spiritual faithfulness* before God. To be spiritually
faithful is to "continue" in Christ and one's faith in him as God's messiah
(see, e.g., Rom. 11:22; Col. 1:21–23; 2:6–7). Thus, Paul's writings not only

10. See Rom. 1:7; 1 Cor. 1:3; Gal. 1:3; 1 Tim. 1:2; 2 Tim. 1:2; 4:22; Philem. 25.

11. See, e.g., 1 Cor. 15:2; 16:13; 2 Cor. 6:1; Gal. 5:4; Eph. 6:10–13; Col. 1:21–23; 1 Tim.
1:18–19; 6:12; 2 Tim. 2:1.

12. Paul uses the phrase "under the law" multiple times to depict the disciple's former
state of being before their experience of grace in and through Christ: see Acts 13:39; Rom.
2:12; 3:19; 6:14, 15; 1 Cor. 9:20; Gal. 3:23; 4:4, 5, 21; 5:18. We should note that in his Letter to
the Romans, Paul formally contrasts being "under the law" with being "under grace" (Rom.
6:14, 15).

13. See, e.g., Rom. 1:5; 4:16; 5:2; Eph. 2:8; 1 Tim. 1:2, 14; 6:20–21; Titus 1:4; 3:15.

contain passages that exhort his readers to remain in Christ but also warn against the very real danger of apostasy.[14]

Finally, we must not forget how Paul's prayer for the readers of his Epistle to the Ephesians seems to indicate that the Christian life requires not only a Spirit-enabled communion with Christ "through faith" but also a (Spirit-enabled) growth in one's ability to "grasp" and "know" (live into) the love of Christ. All of this moves toward the grand goal of being filled with the "fullness of God"—that is, becoming a completely God-saturated, God-controlled, and therefore God-pleasing Christ follower. This powerful prayer is pregnant with significance for a realist, trinitarian lifestyle spirituality:

> For this reason I kneel before the Father, from whom every family in heaven and on earth derives its name. I pray that out of his glorious riches he may strengthen you with power through his Spirit in your inner being, so that Christ may dwell in your hearts through faith. And I pray that you, being rooted and established in love, may have power, together with all the Lord's holy people, to grasp how wide and long and high and deep is the love of Christ, and to know this love that surpasses knowledge—that you may be filled to the measure of all the fullness of God. (Eph. 3:14–19)

These are just a few ways in which a contemplation of and a "living into" God's *charity* can deeply affect one's spirituality. According to Paul, the appropriate response on the part of God's people to God's personal, relational, gracious being is a spiritual faithfulness. A realist, trinitarian spirituality will be intentional about those practices that enable a steady growth in one's faith (in the sense of both mental assent and existential trust) and the ability to commune with the Father, in the Spirit, the way Jesus did. It will also be intentional about enabling Christ's followers to keep growing in their willingness and ability to share the love of God with others in a Christlike, cruciform (self-sacrificial) manner. This is what a spiritual faithfulness involves, and it takes a Pauline "I-Thou" lifestyle spirituality to get us there.

Even more will be said about this version of faithfulness before God in chapters 3 and 6. But for now, we must press on to consider another essential earmark of God's character that was foundational in the theology of the apostle Paul.

---

14. See Rom. 11:17–22; 1 Cor. 9:24–10:12; 15:1–2; 16:13; 2 Cor. 1:24; 11:2–3; Gal. 4:8–20; 5:2–6; Col. 1:21–23; 1 Thess. 3:5; 1 Tim. 1:18–19; 3:6–7; 4:1–10; 5:8; 6:9–12, 20–21; 2 Tim. 2:11–13, 16–21, 24–26; 4:7–8.

Cardinal Characteristic 2: God's Sanctity

Another prime trait of God that Paul refers to often is how God is *holy* and *wholly committed to justice*. The Scriptures indicate that our Creator is a moral being who has preferences about the ways his image-bearers relate to him, themselves, one another, and the rest of creation. It is this cardinal characteristic that suggests that another product of a Christ-emulating, Spirit-empowered, God-the-Father-pleasing spirituality will be a *faithfulness* that is *moral* in nature.

Various passages make clear that Paul understood God to be *holy, just*, and *wholly committed to justice* and that the Creator expects his image-bearers to "live into" this characteristic while at the same time keeping in mind the need to love with mercy (see Mic. 6:8). Whereas the apostle Peter seems to have quoted one of the many Old Testament passages that portrays God declaring his own holiness (1 Pet. 1:16; cf. Lev. 11:44–45), Paul chose to refer to God's holiness in less direct ways. Consider, for example, the many passages (too many to cite here) in which Paul refers to the Spirit of God as *holy*. Especially worthy of note is Romans 1:4, where Paul refers to the "Spirit of holiness." Thus, the word "Holy" when applied to God's Spirit can be considered an adjective. This means that the term "Holy Spirit" is not simply a title but a description as well. Likewise, Paul goes on to describe many other things that are associated with God as *holy*: the *Scriptures*, the *law*, God's *temple*, God's *apostles and prophets*, Christ's *church*, God's *angels*, and finally God's *people*. All of these passages indirectly ascribe holiness to God.[15]

Not only does Paul refer to God's people as holy in an *indicative* manner, he also issues some *imperatives* with this divine characteristic in mind. According to Paul, it is God's will that church members be *holy* and that they become, with the help of the risen Christ and the Holy Spirit, *pure and blameless*.[16] In keeping with this, Paul encourages his readers to *pursue* such things as *holiness, sanctification, righteousness, purity, compassion, kindness, humility, gentleness, patience*, and *godliness*.[17] What's more, he also

---

15. On the Scriptures, see Rom. 1:2; 2 Tim. 3:15. On the law: Rom. 7:12. On God's temple: Eph. 2:21. On God's apostles and prophets: Eph. 3:5. On Christ's church: Eph. 5:25–27. On God's angels: 1 Thess. 3:13; cf. Matt. 25:31; 2 Thess. 1:7. On God's people: Rom. 11:16; 2 Cor. 1:1; Eph. 1:1, 18; 3:18; 5:3; Phil. 1:1; Col. 1:2, 12; 3:12; 2 Thess. 1:10; Philem. 5.

16. On church members and holiness, see, e.g., Rom. 1:7; 12:1; 1 Cor. 1:2; Eph. 1:4; Col. 1:22; 1 Thess. 4:4, 7; 2 Tim. 1:9; Titus 1:8. On purity and blamelessness: Eph. 1:4; 5:27; Phil. 1:10; 2:15; 1 Thess. 3:13; 5:23.

17. On holiness, see, e.g., Rom. 6:19, 22; 1 Cor. 1:30; 2 Cor. 7:1; Eph. 4:24; 1 Thess. 3:13; 1 Tim. 2:2; 2 Tim. 2:21. On sanctification: Rom. 15:16; 1 Thess. 4:3. On righteousness: 1 Cor. 1:30; Eph. 4:24. On purity: 2 Cor. 7:1; cf. Titus 2:14. On compassion, kindness, humility, gentleness, and patience: Col. 3:12. On godliness: 1 Tim. 2:2.

associates other lifestyle virtues with holiness. Thus, according to Paul, if one is holy, then one is necessarily *self-controlled*, *upright*, and *disciplined* as well (see, e.g., Titus 1:7–8).

In several of his letters, the apostle encourages the recipients (as members of God's family) to *greet one another* in a way that is holy.[18] In keeping with this are a couple of passages in which Paul alludes to himself as someone who modeled for the churches what it is to act toward others in a holy, pure, blameless manner (e.g., 2 Cor. 6:3–6; 1 Thess. 2:10).

Veteran Bible readers are aware that the final chapters of Paul's letters tend to be "hortatory" in nature. This is where Paul devotes his attention to the task of exhorting his readers to act in ways that are in keeping with the theological truths communicated in preceding portions of the letter. A classic example of this is Ephesians 4:17–6:20. Since in Ephesians 4:22–24 Paul indicates that the new "self" he is advocating for is "created to be like God in true *righteousness* and *holiness*," there is a sense in which all the exhortations in this lengthy hortatory section of the epistle can be viewed as a Pauline promotion of the need for his readers to pursue a moral faithfulness before God that is profoundly informed by the Creator's innate holiness.

Finally, we should take note of how God's sanctity influenced the way the apostle prayed for his readers. In 2 Corinthians 13:7, we read, "Now we pray to God that you will not do anything wrong." And for the believers in Philippi, Paul prays, "This is my prayer: that your love may abound more and more in knowledge and depth of insight, so that you may be able to discern what is best and may be *pure and blameless* for the day of Christ, filled with the fruit of *righteousness* that comes through Jesus Christ—to the glory and praise of God" (Phil. 1:9–11). Similarly, it is with God's sanctity in mind that Paul prays that the church members in Colossae might "live a life *worthy of the Lord* and *please* him in every way" (Col. 1:10) and that the Thessalonian disciples would "be *blameless* and *holy* in the presence of our God and Father when our Lord Jesus comes with all his *holy* ones" (1 Thess. 3:13).

The sheer number of the passages cited above testifies to the fact that Paul considered God's holiness to be a theological attribute worth contemplating and then living into.[19] However, that is only half the story. Coinciding with God's innate holiness is his being *just* and *wholly committed to justice*. In 2 Thessalonians 1:6, Paul boldly and explicitly asserts that "God is just." But, once again, we find that Paul sometimes makes the same point in less direct ways. For instance, I am thinking of a Pauline passage that brings attention to

---

18. See Rom. 16:16; 1 Cor. 16:20; 2 Cor. 13:12; 1 Thess. 5:26.
19. Note the references in Ps. 119:99–100 to *meditating* and then *obeying*.

God's innate righteousness and radical commitment to justice in a poignant though nuanced manner. I am referring to Romans 3:24–26, which suggests that the substitutionary, atoning work of Christ on the cross was made necessary by the confluence of God's uncompromising commitment to remain just himself and his equally radical desire to graciously justify guilty sinners.[20] In this one passage, we find Paul alluding to both the sanctity and the charity of God in a breathtaking manner. Have a fresh look at this powerful passage with that idea in mind: "All are justified freely by his grace through the redemption that came by Christ Jesus. God presented Christ as a sacrifice of atonement, through the shedding of his blood—to be received by faith. He did this to demonstrate his righteousness, because in his forbearance he had left the sins committed beforehand unpunished; he did it to demonstrate his righteousness at the present time, *so as to be just and the one who justifies* those who have faith in Jesus" (Rom. 3:24–26).

Moreover, we know that Paul also addresses in his letters the need for *fairness* and *peace* in human relationships, especially those that are uneven in power. The apostle has much to say about the relationships between Jews and gentiles, husbands and wives, parents and children, masters and slaves, the rich and the poor.[21] Invariably, Paul calls for a fairness that is rooted in a mutual respect for one another and that ultimately derives from the Christian disciple's *reverence for God* (e.g., Eph. 5:21; Col. 3:22), the *"new self"* Paul kept advocating for (Eph. 4:24; Col. 3:10–15), and the *egalitarianism* that one Pauline passage in particular is so suggestive of: "There is neither Jew nor Gentile, neither slave nor free, nor is there male and female, for you are all one in Christ Jesus" (Gal. 3:28).

Can there be any doubt that Paul took the need for a moral faithfulness seriously? The author of the Letter to the Hebrews boldly emphasizes how important it is to God that his children share in his holiness, indicating in the process that this holiness possesses both a vertical significance (vis-à-vis God) and a horizontal significance (vis-à-vis others) (Heb. 12:10, 14). The best way, therefore, to explain why Paul infused his letters with so many references to and calls for holiness (and justice) is not only with regard to his understanding of the Creator's own sanctity but also with regard to his

---

20. For more on the notion that Christ's death satisfied the cosmic demand for justice that derives from the being of the holy and just Creator of the cosmos, see Gary Tyra, *The Dark Side of Discipleship: Why and How the New Testament Encourages Christians to Deal with the Devil* (Eugene, OR: Cascade Books, 2020), 262–63.

21. On Jews and gentiles, see, e.g., Rom. 3:29; 1 Cor. 12:12; Gal. 2:8–9; Eph. 2:11–22. On husbands and wives: Eph. 5:22, 25; Col. 3:11, 18–19. On parents and children: Eph. 6:1, 4; Col. 3:20–21. On masters and slaves: Eph. 6:5–9; Col. 3:22–25; cf. 4:1; Philem. 8–21. On the rich and the poor: Gal. 2:10; 1 Tim. 6:17–18.

awareness of what God desires for and from his people. Christ, himself, embodies a moral faithfulness before the Father that, because it is grounded in Micah 6:8, possesses both a vertical and a horizontal significance (cf. Matt. 5:43–48; 23:23). If we let him, he will enable his followers to do the same. Such a discipleship dynamic cannot help but inform what a Pauline "I-Thou" lifestyle spirituality will involve.

More will be said about this form of faithfulness in chapters 4 and 7. But now we must turn to yet another feature of Paul's theological infrastructure.

Cardinal Characteristic 3: God's Missionality

So far, we have surveyed the way Paul's writings provide ample evidence for the notion that he viewed God's *charity* and *sanctity* as prime attributes or cardinal characteristics. This brings us to my third suggestion. Because Paul had been made privy to God's overarching intention with respect to his creation,[22] the apostle also had much to say about God's calling, sending, and commissioning nature—that is, his *missionality*.

Crucial to the idea of God's missionality is his intentionality. So let's begin with an acknowledgment of the passages in which Paul refers to God's plan for the cosmos he created. In a nutshell, Paul indicates that God's overarching intention is, through Christ, to "reconcile to himself all things, whether things on earth or things in heaven" (Col. 1:20), and in so doing to "bring unity to all things in heaven and on earth" (Eph. 1:10). This is God's world. It may be fallen, but it is not forgotten. God has a plan to redeem and reconcile his creation to himself (cf. Rom. 8:19–22).

This leads us to consider what Paul had to say about God's calling, sending, commissioning nature. It is my contention that all theology should be missional in nature because God, by nature, is a missionary God. A renowned missional theologian has suggested that there is a "sendingness of God" that is "evident within the trinity itself."[23] The Scriptures portray God sending both the Son and the Spirit into the world to fulfill his redemptive purpose. The apostle Paul alludes to the "sendingness" inherent in the Trinity in the following passage: "But when the set time had fully come, God *sent* his Son,

---

22. See Rom. 16:25; 1 Cor. 2:10; 2 Cor. 12:1–4, 7; Gal. 1:12; 2:2; Eph. 3:3, 5.

23. George R. Hunsberger, "Starting Points, Trajectories and Outcomes in Proposals for a Missional Hermeneutic: Mapping the Conversation," Gospel and Our Culture Network, January 28, 2009, https://gocn.org/library/the-gospel-and-our-culture-eseries-no-2/. See also Craig Van Gelder and Dwight J. Zscheile, *The Missional Church in Perspective: Mapping Trends and Shaping the Conversation* (Grand Rapids: Baker Academic, 2011), 52–53; John G. Flett, *The Witness of God: The Trinity, Missio Dei, Karl Barth, and the Nature of Christian Community* (Grand Rapids: Eerdmans, 2010), 5.

born of a woman, born under the law. . . . Because you are his sons, God *sent* the Spirit of his Son into our hearts, the Spirit who calls out, 'Abba, Father'" (Gal. 4:4–6, italics for *Abba* as shown in the NIV). Paul also dared to assert that he himself had been *sent* from God (2 Cor. 2:17), having been also *called* by him into apostolic ministry (see Rom. 1:1; 1 Cor. 1:1; Gal. 1:15). He refers to himself as having been *appointed* to and *commissioned* or *entrusted* with not only a ministry responsibility but a ministry authority as well.[24]

That Paul conceived of his ministry assignment as being essentially *missional* in nature is apparent from many passages.[25] Also indicative of Paul's sense that his ministry was something he was called to are his many references to the *suffering*, *persecutions*, *trials*, and *distress* he endured on Christ's behalf.[26]

So it is apparent that Paul conceived of God as a calling, sending, missionary God. But how does God's missional nature affect those of us who, unlike Paul, have not been called to be one of the "apostles and prophets" who functioned in the first century as the foundation of Christ's church (Eph. 2:20)? Do we have reason to believe that God has called us not only to *believe* (Gal. 1:6; 1 Cor. 7:22), *belong* (Rom. 1:6), and *be holy* (Rom. 1:7) but to *serve* as well (i.e., to play a role in God's redemptive purposes)? We do, and Paul was all over this!

I will begin by citing a passage that refers to a calling from God that is overarching in scope: "And we know that in all things God works for the good of those who love him, who have been *called* according to his purpose" (Rom. 8:28). More specifically, Paul infers that the readers of his various letters have been called not only to belong to God but also to serve, bear fruit, engage in doing good, and even share in the apostle's sufferings on Christ's behalf![27]

Though Paul doesn't refer to seeker-sensitive worship gatherings per se, he does encourage those in the Corinthian congregation to keep in mind the dynamic of *mission* as well as *nurture* and *community* when they gather for *worship* (1 Cor. 14:22–25). In the process, Paul implies that every member can play a role in what we might refer to as a missional worship gathering. This single verse reads, "What then shall we say, brothers and sisters? When you come together, each of you has a hymn, or a word of instruction, a revelation,

---

24. See 1 Cor. 4:1–2; 2 Cor. 10:8, 13; 13:10; Eph. 3:2; Col. 1:25–26; 1 Thess. 2:6; 4:2; 1 Tim. 1:11–12; 2:7.

25. See, e.g., Rom. 1:5, 16; 15:15–16; Eph. 3:6–9; 2 Tim. 1:9–11.

26. See 2 Cor. 1:5; 11:23–29; Eph. 3:13; Phil. 3:10; Col. 1:24; 1 Thess. 2:2; 3:3, 7; 2 Tim. 1:8, 11–12; 2:8–10; 3:10–11.

27. On the call to service, see, e.g., 1 Cor. 12:5; Gal. 5:3; Eph. 4:12; 6:7–8; 1 Thess. 1:9; cf. 1 Pet. 4:10. On bearing fruit: Rom. 7:4. On doing good: Eph. 2:10; 1 Tim. 6:18; Titus 3:1. On sharing in suffering, Rom. 8:17; 2 Cor. 1:7; Phil. 1:29–30; 1 Thess. 1:6; 2:14; 2 Thess. 1:4–5; 2 Tim. 1:8.

a tongue or an interpretation. Everything must be done so that the church may be built up" (1 Cor. 14:26). What if this bit of instruction were to be treated with the seriousness the apostle Paul seems to have had in mind? Would it not presume a theologically and pneumatologically real "I-Thou" spirituality?

Going further, we have reason to believe that Paul's concern for the church's impact on those "outside" the faith, alongside his own rather radical commitment to contextualize the gospel (1 Cor. 9:20–22), might have influenced the way he encourages church members to be circumspect in the way they interact with and minister to those who have not yet said yes to the faith.[28] By the way, we see this same missional concern for the reputation of the church before outsiders in the apostle Peter's writings as well (e.g., 1 Pet. 2:12–17; 3:15–16).

We can also sense Paul's personal commitment to mission in his repeated calls for his readers to pray for his own ministry faithfulness and fruitfulness.[29] A classic example of this type of passage reads like this: "Devote yourselves to prayer, being watchful and thankful. And pray for us, too, that God may open a door for our message, so that we may proclaim the mystery of Christ, for which I am in chains. Pray that I may proclaim it clearly, as I should" (Col. 4:2–4).

In other passages, we find Paul either *commending* the ministry faithfulness and fruitfulness his readers had already rendered[30] or *exhorting* them in that regard.[31] I wonder how many readers of Paul's Letter to the Colossians have, over the years, had their life story impacted by the seemingly innocuous reminder that we find at the end of the epistle: "Tell Archippus: 'See to it that you complete the ministry you have received in the Lord'" (Col. 4:17; cf. 2 Tim. 1:6–7)?

And then there is the way Paul prays for the churches with the theme of ministry in mind. For the Colossian Christians, Paul prays that they might be "bearing fruit in every good work" (Col. 1:10). Moreover, Paul's prayer for the Thessalonian believers also warrants inclusion here: "With this in mind, we constantly pray for you, that our God may make you worthy of his calling, and that by his power he may bring to fruition your every desire for goodness and your every deed prompted by faith. We pray this so that the name of our Lord Jesus may be glorified in you, and you in him, according to the grace of our God and the Lord Jesus Christ" (2 Thess. 1:11–12). This is a prayer for a missional faithfulness. It is beyond question that Paul's mindset was informed

28. See, e.g., Eph. 5:15–16; Col. 4:5–6; 1 Thess. 4:12; Titus 2:3–10; cf. 1 Tim. 5:14; 6:1.
29. See, e.g., Rom. 15:30–31; Eph. 6:19–20; Col. 4:3–4; 2 Thess. 3:1.
30. See, e.g., Rom. 1:8; 2 Cor. 9:12–15; Phil. 1:3–5; Col. 1:6; 1 Thess. 1:2–3, 7–8.
31. See, e.g., Gal. 6:9–10; 1 Cor. 15:58; Phil. 1:4–6.

by the missionality of God and that the apostle was committed to passing this awareness on to the members of the churches that were in his purview.

Of course, we can presume that his devotion to the cause was due to his ministry calling, but I contend we can also chalk it up to his having become acutely aware of the missionary nature of God the Father, Christ the Son, and the Holy Spirit. This is why Paul's letters render inconceivable the possibility that he would have ever flirted with the idea of "taking it easy" or "phoning it in," much less of "going off mission." He was absolutely committed not only to "finishing" the race (2 Tim. 4:7) but to getting "the prize" as well (1 Cor. 9:24). For Paul, this meant not only keeping the faith (a spiritual faithfulness) and living into God's holiness and justice (a moral faithfulness) but completing the mission God had entrusted to him as well. It is for this reason that even more will be said about the "what" and "how" of a missional faithfulness in chapters 5 and 8.

I will close this chapter by reminding readers that its aim has been to introduce you to the renewed thinking that is necessary if Christians are to successfully heed Paul's call for an "I-Thou" lifestyle spirituality. The upshot is that Paul's approach to spirituality had God as its *starting point* and as an *ultimate concern* that was informed by a specific understanding of him. More precisely, Paul's theological paradigm or mindset seemed to focus on three prime traits: God's *charity*, *sanctity*, and *missionality*. Moreover, Paul was convinced that to please God is to prove faithful and that the cardinal characteristics of God suggest that it is actually a threefold faithfulness that God is looking for: a spiritual, moral, and missional faithfulness. These are the convictions that form the root system of a theologically real, trinitarian "I-Thou" lifestyle spirituality. This is the renewed thinking Paul asserts is necessary for Christ's followers to experience genuine spiritual transformation. This is the theological mindset required for us to get *there* from *here*.

In part 2 of this work, we will turn to three important spirituality *commitments* that the theological *convictions* surveyed in part 1 entail. These are commitments crucial to the cultivation of a Christ-emulating, Spirit-empowered, God-the-Father-pleasing lifestyle spirituality. Hang on as we journey even deeper into the rabbit hole that leads to what Paul thought of as Wonderland.

TOPICS FOR REVIEW

1. How would you explain to someone what it means for spirituality to possess a theocentric starting point? Why this is so very important?

2. How would you explain to someone the theo-sensitive ultimate concern that influenced the spirituality of the apostle Paul and how he sought to inculcate this in the hearts and minds of his readers?

3. How would you articulate what Paul had in mind when he asserted in his writings that a prerequisite to authentic life transformation is a mental renewal?

4. What is your primary personal takeaway from this chapter's discussion of the ways in which a contemplation of, and a "living into," God's *charity* can deeply affect one's spirituality?

5. What is your primary personal takeaway from this chapter's discussion of how a thoughtful contemplation of, and a "living into," God's *sanctity*—his being holy, just, and wholly committed to justice—will impact one's spirituality?

6. What is your primary personal takeaway from this chapter's discussion of how a thoughtful contemplation of, and a "living into," God's *missionality* will impact one's spirituality?

PART TWO

The *Commitments* (Shoot) of a Christian Lifestyle Spirituality

3

KEEPING IN STEP WITH THE SPIRIT

Merely Nice or Utterly Necessary?

Life in the Spirit is not passive submission to the Spirit to do a supernatural work in one's life; rather, it requires conscious effort, so that the indwelling Spirit may accomplish his ends in one's life.

—Gordon Fee, *God's Empowering Presence*

It happens all too often: even veteran Christians will use personal pronouns when referring to God the Father and Christ the Son but then refer to the Holy Spirit in an impersonal way as "it." But this is simply a slip of the tongue, right? Not always. In an essay provocatively titled "Evangelicals, Heresy, and Scripture Alone," Matthew Block refers to a Lifeway Research project published in 2014 that reported a significant number of evangelicals actually "deny the personhood of the Holy Spirit, with 56 percent saying he is a 'divine force but not a personal being.'"[1]

Over against this deliberate denial of the personhood of the Spirit, I will pose a question: What if the relationality of God we took note of in the

1. Matthew Block, "Evangelicals, Heresy, and Scripture Alone," *First Things*, October 4, 2016, https://www.firstthings.com/blogs/firstthoughts/2016/10/evangelicals-heresy-and-scripture-alone. For a more granular look at the data, see the original Lifeway Research report: "Theological Awareness Benchmark Study," http://research.lifeway.com/wp-content/uploads/2014/10/Ligonier-Theological-Awareness-Final-Online-Report.pdf, 136–38.

previous chapter meant that life in the Spirit was relational as well? Such a reality would be a game changer with respect to Christian discipleship. Indeed, if our experience of the Holy Spirit is like our relationship with God and Christ—that is, personal and interactive rather than impersonal and automatic—it would mean that we must learn to discern the Spirit's leading and then decide time and again whether we will cooperate with him.

I contend that the Pauline epistolary corpus supports this supposition. In the fifth chapter of his Letter to the Galatians, Paul discusses the dramatic difference between being influenced by one's flesh (fallen nature) and being influenced by the Holy Spirit. He begins the discussion with this assertion: "For the flesh desires what is contrary to the Spirit, and the Spirit what is contrary to the flesh. They are in conflict with each other" (Gal. 5:17). Paul then proceeds in Galatians 5:19–21 to provide an incomplete but frank list of sinful behaviors that our fallen fleshly nature is predisposed to generate within us: "The acts of the flesh are obvious: sexual immorality, impurity and debauchery; idolatry and witchcraft; hatred, discord, jealousy, fits of rage, selfish ambition, dissensions, factions and envy; drunkenness, orgies, and the like. I warn you, as I did before, that those who live like this will not inherit the kingdom of God."

Then in Galatians 5:22–24 the apostle identifies those lifestyle virtues that evidence success in the Holy Spirit's determination to put the kibosh on the acts of the fleshly nature and engender within the Christian disciple the very character of Christ instead: "But the fruit of the Spirit is love, joy, peace, forbearance, kindness, goodness, faithfulness, gentleness and self-control. Against such things there is no law. Those who belong to Christ Jesus have crucified the flesh with its passions and desires."

After looking at these two lists, I will sometimes ask my ministry-bound theology majors to apply this discussion to their own lives by posing the following questions:

- Honestly, to what degree are you, in your current walk with Christ, able to recognize when you're being influenced more by your flesh than by the Holy Spirit?
- In those critical, Spirit-enabled moments of self-awareness, what do you do?

The second question is a doozy, isn't it? I've found that, regardless of how my students answer the first query, their response to the second is most often a wide-eyed stare. Indeed, it is my sense that it has never occurred to many Christian university students and church members that the Holy Spirit's work of forming the character of Christ in them requires that they keep making the quality decision to cooperate with him! Here is how Paul puts it: "Since we live by the Spirit, let us *keep in step* with the Spirit" (Gal. 5:25).

All this is to say that each of the three chapters that make up part 2 of this book will focus on one of three *commitments* crucial to the cultivation of the kind of spirituality we see Paul promoting in his writings. And based on what we have seen so far in this chapter, it should come as no surprise that the first commitment centers on our taking seriously the exhortation in Galatians 5:25 to "keep in step" with the Holy Spirit.[2]

Precisely *how* such a commitment might be honored on a day-to-day basis will be explored in part 3 of this book (chap. 6). At this point in our journey, the key questions are these: How can we be sure that the importance I am attaching to Paul's call to keep in step with the Spirit is justified? Is it as important to a Pauline lifestyle spirituality as I am suggesting?

What follows is a careful consideration of Paul's pneumatology and its impact on Christian spirituality, one that aims at being theologically and biblically informed. Specifically, we will discuss two topics in turn: (1) the pneumatological realism inherent in Paul's theology and (2) the way Paul's pneumatological realism intersects with Christian spirituality.

In large part, the exploration will be aided by the scholarship of a Pauline scholar whose grasp of Paul's theology of the Spirit is, in my opinion, unparalleled. If I may be so bold, I believe we will find in the work of New Testament theologian Gordon Fee (1934–2022) some fairly strong support for the contention that, as it relates to the cultivation of a Pauline spirituality, keeping in step with the Spirit is not merely nice, but utterly necessary!

The Apostle Paul's Realist Understanding of the Holy Spirit

In chapter 1 of this book, I referred in passing to a phenomenon theologians refer to as a "pneumatological deficit" and the way it produces in some churches an attitude of *presumption* or even *indifference* toward the Spirit instead of a posture of *expectancy*. Over against this pneumatological deficit, I am convinced the apostle Paul would have us recover a robust pneumatology

---

2. For two important discussions that together explain why Paul would not have endorsed the harsh mistreatment of one's "body" as the way to "crucify" one's "flesh," see George Ladd's treatment of Paul's differentiation between the sinful flesh (*sarx*) and the physical body (*sōma*) in *A Theology of the New Testament* (Grand Rapids: Eerdmans, 1993), 506–17, and George Lane's suggestion that the attempt, even among some Christians, to nurture the soul by mistreating the body was and is owing more to a dualist philosophical tradition (that pits spirit against matter) than to the teaching of sacred Scripture in *Christian Spirituality: An Historical Sketch* (Chicago: Loyola, 1984), 12–17.

that is composed of several Spirit-related realities, all of which support my contention that latent in Paul's theology overall was a vital and vigorous pneumatological realism.

The Personhood and Agency of the Holy Spirit

Rather than view the Holy Spirit as an impersonal force, the apostle Paul encourages us to understand and experience him as a divine person who exercises personal agency (i.e., he initiates action). Fee explains, "Even though Paul does not speak directly to the question of the Spirit's person, several converging pieces of evidence assure us that he understood the Spirit in personal terms, intimately associated with both the Father and the Son, yet distinct from them."[3] One of the primary and, for me, most compelling lines of evidence for the personhood of the Spirit is the way Paul ascribes behaviors to the Spirit that "demand a personal agent."[4] For example, according to Paul, the Spirit

- searches (1 Cor. 2:10)
- knows (1 Cor. 2:11)
- teaches (1 Cor. 2:13)
- dwells (Rom. 8:11; 1 Cor. 3:16; 2 Tim. 1:14)
- accomplishes (1 Cor. 12:11)
- gives life (2 Cor. 3:6)
- cries out (Gal. 4:6)
- leads (Rom. 8:14; Gal. 5:18)
- bears witness (Rom. 8:16)
- desires (Gal. 5:17)
- helps (Rom. 8:26)
- intercedes (Rom. 8:26–27)
- works (Rom. 8:28)
- strengthens (Eph. 3:16)
- grieves (Eph. 4:30)[5]

Given the way the apostle Paul refers to the Spirit, it is clear that Paul did not view him as "merely an impersonal force or influence or power."[6] Accord-

3. Gordon D. Fee, *Paul, the Spirit, and the People of God* (Peabody, MA: Hendrickson, 1996), 25.
4. Fee, *Paul, the Spirit, and the People of God*, 27.
5. Fee, *Paul, the Spirit, and the People of God*, 27.
6. Fee, *Paul, the Spirit, and the People of God*, 22.

ing to Fee, for Paul, "the Spirit is not thought of as 'it,' but as 'person.'"[7] In other words, Paul considered the Holy Spirit a "Thou"—a personal divine being with whom Christ's followers can cultivate an interactive "I-Thou" relationship. Such an observation lends theological support for the notion that learning to keep in step with the Spirit is indeed a crucial commitment at the heart of a Pauline lifestyle spirituality.

The Full *Divinity of the Holy Spirit*

Also concerning is the way the polling referred to above indicates that a surprising number of evangelical churchgoers denied not only the personhood of the Spirit but his *full* divinity as well. According to 28 percent of the evangelicals interviewed in that study, "The Holy Spirit is a divine being, but is not equal with God the Father or Jesus."[8]

The question I am posing here is this: How did the apostle Paul view the Holy Spirit's ontological status vis-à-vis the Father and the Son? Fee addresses this issue when he draws attention to the sixteen times Paul refers to the Holy Spirit as the "Spirit of God" or its equivalent and the several times he likewise has the Holy Spirit in mind when he refers to the "Spirit of Christ" or its equivalent.[9] The point is this: if the Holy Spirit can be so easily identified as the "Spirit of God" and the "Spirit of Christ," what sense does it make to marginalize the Holy Spirit with respect to the Father and the Son? It would certainly seem that, according to Paul, the Holy Spirit is not only a personal being but also equal in divinity to the other members of the Holy Trinity. This observation provides even more theological support for taking Galatians 5:25 very seriously.

The Importance of the Holy Spirit to Christian Discipleship

A careful study of Paul's writings reveals how very important he considered the Holy Spirit to be for the disciple's walk with Christ. This is another very strong indication of Paul's latent pneumatological realism.[10] As we are about

---

7. Fee, *Paul, the Spirit, and the People of God*, 28.

8. Block, "Evangelicals, Heresy, and Scripture Alone," citing from the Lifeway Research report, "Theological Awareness Benchmark Study," 145–47.

9. Fee, *Paul, the Spirit, and the People of God*, 28. For the several ways Paul associates the Holy Spirit with the Spirt of Jesus, see Acts 16:7; Rom. 8:9; Gal. 4:6; Phil. 1:19.

10. For a treatment of this topic that is rigorously annotated and includes scriptural support from passages outside the Pauline corpus, see Gary Tyra, *Getting Real: Pneumatological Realism and the Spiritual, Moral, and Ministry Formation of Contemporary Christians* (Eugene, OR: Cascade Books, 2018), 125–28.

to discover, the roles Paul ascribes to the Spirit are many, and the biblical support from his pen is significant!

According to Paul, it is the Holy Spirit's job to

- enable an intimate relationship with both God the Father and Christ the Son (Eph. 2:18, 22; 3:16–17);
- assure us that we have become God's children (Rom. 8:15–16; Gal. 4:6);
- serve as a guarantee of our heavenly inheritance (2 Cor. 1:22; 5:5; Gal. 4:6–7; Eph. 1:13–14; 4:30);
- inspire a vital, joyful, prophetic, communal, theologically real worship experience (Eph 5:18–20);
- manifest the risen Christ's presence and power in our lives in various edifying, community-building, ministry-engendering ways (1 Cor. 12:4–8; 14:24–25);
- empower us to obey God's moral commands (Rom. 8:1–4) by enabling us to overcome our habituated sinful tendencies (Gal. 5:16–21) and by producing within us the character traits and ethical virtues of Jesus instead (Gal. 5:22–25);
- intercede for us and through us according to the will of the Father (Rom. 8:26–27);
- empower us to boldly bear witness to the risen Christ (Acts 1:8; cf. Eph. 6:1–20);
- provide an amazingly precise degree of ministry guidance (Acts 13:1–3; 16:6–10);
- motivate us to stand firm in the faith and to intercede for others in this regard (Eph. 6:10–18; 2 Tim 1:13–14); and
- endow us with a dynamic, despair-defeating sense of hope (Rom. 15:13).

Here is the big takeaway: according to Paul, the Holy Spirit is vital to just about *every* aspect of our walk with Christ! How can we *not* consider it crucial that our spirituality enables us to discern the Spirit's working in our lives and that we then cooperate with the Spirit?

Paul and the Realist Ways Christians Experience the Holy Spirit

Finally, Fee seems to go out of his way to indicate the emphasis the apostle Paul put on the relational and interactive character of the Holy Spirit. In so doing, Fee provides some significant support for my contention that churchgoers should indeed *expect* to *experience* the Spirit in ways that are *phenom-enal* in nature and *empowering* in effect.[11]

Indeed, somewhat striking is the way Fee portrays Paul as someone who was thoroughly convinced of the *existential significance* of the indwelling of the Holy Spirit in the believer's life. Fee explains, "The Spirit is God's way of being *present, powerfully present*, in our lives and communities as we await the consummation of the kingdom of God. Precisely because he understood the Spirit as *God's personal presence*, Paul also understood the Spirit always in terms of *an empowering presence*; whatever else, for Paul the Spirit was *an experienced reality*."[12] Frankly, it is hard to imagine a more telling indication of Paul's latent pneumatological realism!

And then Fee goes on to offer these definitive, somewhat provocative, almost strident observations:

> This dynamic, evidential dimension of life in the Spirit probably more than anything else separates believers in later church history from those in Paul's churches. Whatever else, the Spirit was *experienced* in Paul's churches; *he was not simply part of a phrase in the creed.*[13]

> *One reads Paul poorly who does not recognize that for him the presence of the Spirit, as an experienced and living reality, was the crucial matter for Christian life, from beginning to end.*[14]

For what it's worth, Fee unquestionably understands Paul's pneumatology to have been realist rather than nonrealist. Passages such as Galatians 3:2–5; 1 Corinthians 12:7–11; 14:24–25; and 1 Thessalonians 1:4–6; 5:19–21 are just a few of the dozens of Pauline passages that indicate that the indwelling and subsequent working of the Spirit in the lives of the apostle's readers were experienced by them in real, phenomenal, life-story-shaping ways.

Thus, given the four pneumatological realities referred to above, it would certainly seem that Paul would endorse in our day a full-throated affirma-tion and wholehearted practice of a pneumatological realism. According to Gordon Fee, "In the final analysis, in every aspect of this theology—at least what is basic to his theology—the Spirit plays a leading role. To be sure, the Spirit is not *the* center for Paul—Christ is, ever and always—but the Spirit stands close to the center, making Christ known and empowering all genuinely

---

11. See Rom. 8:15 (cf. Gal. 4:6); 1 Cor. 12:7–11; 14:16 (cf. Eph. 5:18–20); 1 Thess. 1:5–6 (cf. Acts 13:52; Rom. 15:13).

12. Fee, *Paul, the Spirit, and the People of God*, xxi (emphasis original).

13. Fee, *Paul, the Spirit, and the People of God*, 144 (emphasis original).

14. Fee, *Paul, the Spirit, and the People of God*, xiii (emphasis original).

Christian life and experience. For this reason, the Spirit must play a much more vital role in our thinking about Paul's theology than tends to be the case."[15]

How Paul Connects a Pneumatological Realism with Christian Spirituality

Pressing on, it's one thing to be convinced that there is a pneumatological realism at work in Paul's theology, but it's another to see how this realism impacted the way Paul encourages his readers to cultivate a Christ-emulating, God-the-Father-pleasing spirituality.

There are several ways to understand this connection. Let's take a quick look at three of them.

The Holy Spirit and Paul's Primary Spirituality Practices

One way to argue for the importance of a pneumatological realism with respect to Christian spirituality is to identify the spirituality practices that Paul most often emphasizes and then point out how important the Holy Spirit is to them. It is apparent from the number of times Paul refers to his own *praying* and *giving of thanks*, as well as from the frequency with which he encourages his readers to do likewise, that he considered these to be primary practices.

But we should take special note of how many times Paul specifies that the praying and thanksgiving of Christian disciples should be *ongoing* rather than occasional. One of the shortest verses in the Pauline corpus is 1 Thessalonians 5:17, which reads, "Pray continually." Paul says something similar in his Letter to the Romans, where he encourages his readers to be "faithful in prayer" (Rom. 12:12). Another related passage has Paul exhorting the Ephesian Christians to pray "on all occasions" (Eph. 6:18). And in Philippians 4:6, we read that prayer should occur "in every situation."

With respect to the practice of giving thanks, Paul speaks of disciples "always giving thanks to God the Father for everything" (Eph. 5:20) and giving thanks "in every situation" (Phil. 4:6). The apostle also lets his readers know that thanksgiving should be present in "whatever you do, whether in word or deed" (Col. 3:17), offered "in all circumstances" (1 Thess. 5:18) and "for all people" (1 Tim. 2:1). Finally, in some passages Paul emphasizes that thanksgiving was "constantly" and "always" a part of his own incessant praying (2 Tim. 1:3; Philem. 4).

---

15. Fee, *Paul, the Spirit, and the People of God*, 180 (emphasis original).

How are we to understand these passages, which seem to prioritize prayer and thanksgiving, link these two practices together, and encourage their perpetual performance? Perhaps the answer lies in the Pauline concept of praying and giving thanks "in the Spirit." Well known is this comforting yet intriguing passage found in Paul's Letter to the Romans: "In the same way, the Spirit helps us in our weakness. We do not know what we ought to pray for, but *the Spirit himself intercedes for us through wordless groans*. And he who searches our hearts knows the mind of the Spirit, because the Spirit intercedes for God's people in accordance with the will of God" (Rom. 8:26–27). But it is in his Letter to the Ephesians where Paul links the concepts of ongoing, continual prayer with the enablement of the Spirit. The famous "armor of God" discussion in Ephesians 6 concludes with this final exhortation: "And *pray in the Spirit* on all occasions with all kinds of prayers and requests. With this in mind, be alert and always keep on praying for all the Lord's people" (Eph. 6:18).

As for giving thanks in the Spirit, Paul refers to this dynamic in one of his letters to the Corinthian church: "Otherwise when you are *praising* God *in the Spirit*, how can someone else, who is now put in the position of an inquirer, say 'Amen' to your *thanksgiving*, since they do not know what you are saying?" (1 Cor. 14:16).

I will have much more to say in chapter 6 about how important praying and giving thanks in the Spirit are to a lifestyle spirituality and how we can do these things in an ongoing rather than occasional manner. For now, the upshot is that (1) prayer and thanksgiving are, for Paul, primary Christian lifestyle and spirituality practices, and (2) he is especially keen on pneumatologically real versions of these twin practices that can be engaged in perpetually with great effect.

The Holy Spirit and a God-Pleasing Lifestyle

Another way to demonstrate the importance of a robust, realist pneumatology for Christian spirituality is to take a step back and focus on the big picture—how the apostle Paul conceived of a Christian life well lived—and then point out the significance of the Holy Spirit to this big picture. Michael Downey helps us here by asserting a theoretical connection between Christian living and Christian spirituality. He writes,

> Spirituality is not one dimension of the Christian life. It *is* the Christian life in the presence and the power of the Holy Spirit; being conformed to the person of Christ and united in communion with God and others.[16]

16. Michael Downey, *Understanding Christian Spirituality* (Mahwah, NJ: Paulist Press, 1997), 146 (emphasis original).

In contemporary perspective, Christian spirituality is concerned with the whole
Christian life. At issue here is the fullness of life in Christ by the presence and
power of the Holy Spirit, being conformed to the person of Christ and united
in communion with God, others, and all creation.[17]

Of course, it is one thing to simply assert a connection between Christian
living and Christian spirituality; it is another to provide biblical evidence for
such a connection. Not to worry; I believe such evidence is available.

First, let's recall that, for Paul, the *ultimate concern* of the Christian life—
and therefore that which should drive a Christian spirituality—is the ambition
to please God. Paul summarizes for the church members in Thessalonica his
ministry message to them when he writes, "As for other matters, brothers and
sisters, we instructed you *how to live in order to please God*, as in fact you
are living. Now we ask you and urge you in the Lord Jesus to do this more
and more" (1 Thess. 4:1).

Second, as we have already seen, the vital role the Holy Spirit plays in
enabling Christians to live well before God is explicitly indicated in Paul's
prayer for the Colossian Christians. In the opening paragraphs of his letter
to them, the apostle explains, "For this reason, since the day we heard about
you, we have not stopped praying for you. We continually ask God to fill you
with the knowledge of his will through all the wisdom and understanding
that *the Spirit gives*, so that you may *live a life worthy of the Lord and please
him in every way*" (Col. 1:9–10). Moreover, it is my contention that when
Paul wrote this introductory passage, he already had in mind the series of
exhortations we find in Colossians 3:5–17—a litany or "laundry list," if you
will, of actions and attitudes God is looking for in the lives of Christ's followers. This passage is worthy of being considered in full:

> Put to death, therefore, whatever belongs to your earthly nature: sexual im-
> morality, impurity, lust, evil desires and greed, which is idolatry. Because of
> these, the wrath of God is coming. You used to walk in these ways, in the
> life you once lived. But now you must also rid yourselves of all such things as
> these: anger, rage, malice, slander, and filthy language from your lips. Do not
> lie to each other, since you have taken off your old self with its practices and
> have put on the new self, which is being renewed in knowledge in the image
> of its Creator. Here there is no Gentile or Jew, circumcised or uncircumcised,
> barbarian, Scythian, slave or free, but Christ is all, and is in all.
>
> Therefore, as God's chosen people, holy and dearly loved, clothe yourselves
> with compassion, kindness, humility, gentleness and patience. Bear with each

17. Downey, *Understanding Christian Spirituality*, 90.

other and forgive one another if any of you has a grievance against someone. Forgive as the Lord forgave you. And over all these virtues put on love, which binds them all together in perfect unity.

Let the peace of Christ rule in your hearts, since as members of one body you were called to peace. And be thankful. Let the message of Christ dwell among you richly as you teach and admonish one another with all wisdom through psalms, hymns, and songs from the Spirit, singing to God with gratitude in your hearts. And whatever you do, whether in word or deed, do it all in the name of the Lord Jesus, giving thanks to God the Father through him. (Col. 3:5–17)

Now, if it is true that the summary of Paul's prayer for the Colossians (located in chap. 1 of the letter) anticipates the more detailed description of the God-the-Father-pleasing lifestyle (located in chap. 3 of the same letter), it can be assumed that the importance of the Holy Spirit for the way of life referred to in Colossians 1:10 also applies to the well-lived Christian life described in Colossians 3:5–17. In other words, it is through the Spirit that we cultivate a lifestyle that is "worthy of the Lord" and that pleases him "in every way."

The Holy Spirit and a Spiritual Faithfulness

In this book's introduction, I referred to Paul's lifestyle spirituality as a "faithfulness spirituality," one that can and will make it possible for Christ's followers to someday hear Jesus say to them, "Well done, good and faithful servant!" I have also made it clear that it is actually a threefold faithfulness that God is looking for, one that impacts the spiritual, moral, and missional aspects of one's life. Now, since a spiritual faithfulness is foundational to the other two aspects and because I will have more to say about a moral and missional faithfulness later in the book, the focus of this discussion is on the importance of Christ's Spirit to a spiritual faithfulness.

To begin, the phenomenon of spiritual faithfulness in the Old Testament required that the people of Israel remain loyal to the Mosaic covenant they had entered into with God (see Pss. 25:8–10; 78:32–37). Similarly, the New Testament also speaks of a covenant—a *new* covenant that centers on the sacrifice of Christ (see Luke 22:20; 1 Cor. 11:25; Heb. 8:6–13; 9:15–28). Thus, a faithfulness to this new covenant requires that disciples remain steadfast in their devotion to Jesus, God's Son.

Might it be otherwise? Apparently so. In his follow-up letter to the Corinthians, Paul confesses a concern: "I am jealous for you with a godly jealousy. I promised you to one husband, to Christ, so that I might present you as a pure virgin to him. But I am afraid that just as Eve was deceived by the serpent's cunning, *your minds may somehow be led astray from your sincere and pure devotion to Christ*" (2 Cor. 11:2–3).

As I indicated in chapter 2 of this book, apostasy—the abandonment of one's Christian faith—was a genuine Pauline concern. His writings contain several passages that encourage his readers to "hold firmly to," "stand firm in," and "fight the good fight for" their faith in Christ:

> By this gospel you are saved, *if* you *hold firmly to* the word I preached to you. Otherwise, you have believed in vain. (1 Cor. 15:2)

> Be on your guard; *stand firm in the faith*; be courageous; be strong. (1 Cor. 16:13)

> *Fight the good fight of the faith.* Take hold of the eternal life to which you were called when you made your good confession in the presence of many witnesses. (1 Tim. 6:12)

And because it is not merely a maintenance of mental assent that Jesus is looking for but one's existential trust in him as well, Paul's letters also refer to the need for his readers to *hang on to their hope* and *remain strong in their embrace of grace*:

> But now he has reconciled you by Christ's physical body through death . . . if you continue in your faith, established and firm, and *do not move from the hope held out in the gospel*. (Col. 1:22–23)

> You then, my son, *be strong in the grace* that is in Christ Jesus. (2 Tim. 2:1)

The upshot seems to be that at the heart of a spiritual faithfulness is an ongoing belief and trust in Christ that results in our rendering to him a long obedience in the same direction.[18]

Now, in this discussion I am going to point out that, while Paul emphasizes the pivotal role the Holy Spirit plays in the cultivation of a spiritual faithfulness, it is also important to him that his readers not expect the Spirit's empowerment in this regard to be autonomous and automatic. In other words, once again, a Pauline lifestyle spirituality requires us to nuance, this time between God's role in our remaining faithful to him and ours. Let me show you what I mean.

On the one hand, Paul makes it clear that, ultimately, our standing firm in Christ is God's doing rather than ours. Specifically, Paul states in 2 Corinthians 1:21–22 that God does this through the enabling work of the Holy Spirit in

---

18. See note 21 in chap. 1 of this book for background on the phrase "long obedience in the same direction."

our lives, beginning with an initial spiritual *experience* whereby our hearts are assured of our new standing before God and his radical commitment to us.[19] This passage reads, "Now it is God who makes both us and you stand firm in Christ. He anointed us, set his seal of ownership on us, and put his *Spirit* in our hearts as a deposit, guaranteeing what is to come" (2 Cor. 1:21–22). By itself, this passage can make it seem that our standing firm in Christ is something God's Spirit accomplishes in us in a way that is autonomous and automatic. On the other hand, passages such as Romans 8:15–16 and Galatians 4:6–7 suggest that the phenomenal, palpable, and therefore evidential experience referred to in 2 Corinthians 1:21–22 is to some degree interactive since it involves the Spirit praying through us. Moreover, the fact that Paul did not expect this initial experience with Christ's Spirit to be thought of as a one-off is indicated by other passages that clearly call for Christ's followers to continue interacting with the Spirit. These passages call us to live according to the Spirit (Rom. 8:5–13), keep in step with the Spirit (Gal. 5:24–25), be led by the Spirit (Gal. 5:18), and be filled with the Spirit (Eph. 5:18).

A couple of these exhortations merit a closer look because they emphasize the need for some *ongoing* surrender and cooperation on the part of the disciple with respect to the working of the Spirit. Commenting on the exhortation in Ephesians 5:18 to be filled with the Spirit, biblical commentator Francis Foulkes explains as follows:

> The tense of the verb, present imperative in the Greek, should be noted, implying as it does that the experience of receiving the Holy Spirit so that every part of life is permeated and controlled by Him is not a "once for all" experience. In the early chapters of the Acts of the Apostles it is repeated a number of times that the apostles were "filled with the Holy Spirit." The practical implication is that the Christian is to leave his life open to be filled constantly and repeatedly by the divine Spirit.[20]

And then, commenting on the implicit exhortation in Galatians 5:18 to be led by the Spirit, scholar Ronald Fung provides this clarification:

> This conditional sentence clearly shows that Paul does not regard the believer as a helpless spectator or an unwilling pawn in the fierce battle between the

19. Support for the notion that Paul thought of this work of the Spirit as a personal *experience* that was phenomenal (palpable, observable) in nature can be found in James D. G. Dunn, *Jesus and the Spirit: A Study of the Religious and Charismatic Experience of Jesus and the First Christians as Reflected in the New Testament* (Grand Rapids: Eerdmans, 1997), 201–2.

20. Francis Foulkes, *Ephesians*, Tyndale New Testament Commentaries (Downers Grove, IL: InterVarsity, 1983), 152.

flesh and the Spirit; the assumption is rather that the Christian can overcome the flesh by siding with the Spirit. Being "led by the Spirit" is in form passive; in its actual meaning, however, it is not entirely passive. The active leading of the Holy Spirit does not signify the believer's being, so to speak, led by the nose willy-nilly; on the contrary, he must let himself be led by the Spirit—that is, actively choose to stand on the side of the Spirit over against the flesh.[21]

As the epigraph for this chapter indicates, Gordon Fee insists Paul's view was that "life in the Spirit is not passive submission." Rather, a "conscious effort" on the part of the disciple is required if the work of the indwelling Spirit is to be accomplished in one's life.[22] The bottom line is that, for Fee, keeping in step with the Spirit is not merely nice but utterly necessary. Commenting on Paul's discussion of the flesh versus the Spirit in Galatians 5, Fee writes, "But for Paul all is not automatic. One must sow to the Spirit (6:8) and be led by the Spirit (5:18); indeed, 'if we live . . . by the Spirit,' we must therefore also 'accordingly behave by the Spirit' (v. 25)."[23]

What makes Paul's call for disciples to keep in step with the Spirit critical is seen in other places where Paul warns that the Spirit, as he works in our lives, can be *resisted* (Acts 7:51), *grieved* (Eph. 4:30), *rejected* (1 Thess. 4:8), and *quenched* (1 Thess. 5:19). The point is that all these passages, when viewed together, give the impression that a spiritual faithfulness in our walk with Christ, while Spirit effected, is anything but autonomous and automatic. Instead, the nuanced perspective of Paul seems to be that the spiritual faithfulness of the Christian disciple is ultimately produced by the work of the Spirit in our lives, but only to the degree we allow.

Once again, the realization that Christ's followers can experience an intimate, *interactive* relationship not only with Christ but with his Spirit as well changes everything with respect to the Christian life. We simply must stop viewing the Spirit as a sanctifying force that works in our lives without our expecting or inviting him to do so. A pneumatological realism encourages us to take very seriously the need to *surrender to, cooperate with*, and *pray in* the Holy Spirit—and to do these things in an ongoing rather than an occasional manner! It is because these spirituality moves are so fundamental to a Pauline "I-Thou" lifestyle spirituality that we will expound on them much more fully in chapter 6.

---

21. Ronald Y. K. Fung, *The Epistle to the Galatians*, New International Commentary on the New Testament (Grand Rapids: Eerdmans, 1988), 251–52.

22. Gordon D. Fee, *God's Empowering Presence: The Holy Spirit in the Letters of Paul* (Peabody, MA: Hendrickson, 1994), 433.

23. Fee, *God's Empowering Presence*, 370.

In his book *True Spirituality*, the very evangelical Francis Schaeffer (1912–84) writes, "If I woke up tomorrow morning and found that all that the Bible teaches concerning prayer and the Holy Spirit were removed, . . . what difference would it make *in practice* from the way we are functioning today? The simple tragic fact is that in much of the church of the Lord Jesus Christ—the evangelical church—there would be *no difference whatsoever*. We function as though the supernatural were not there."[24] I am struck by the way Schaeffer's words acknowledge the pneumatological deficit referred to at the beginning of this chapter and the way he associates prayer with the Holy Spirit. As we have seen and will see again, prayer is a primary practice in any Christian spirituality, especially one that aims to be perpetual rather than episodic. If Paul was convinced that prayer could and should be empowered by the Spirit, the same can be said about Christian spirituality as a whole.

For instance, what if we were to discover that Paul believed an *ongoing* mentoring relationship with the risen Jesus is possible *if* we cooperate with the Holy Spirit's work in our life? And what if we discovered that this idea shows up repeatedly in the writings of Christianity's spiritual masters? The next chapter will enable a deep dive into this proposal. Our trek to Wonderland via the rabbit hole continues!

TOPICS FOR REVIEW

1. According to this chapter, what would it mean if our experience of the Holy Spirit is like our relationship with God and Christ, personal and interactive rather than impersonal and automatic?

2. What are the four Spirit-related realities that contribute to a robust pneumatology and support the contention that latent in Paul's theology overall was a vital and vigorous pneumatological realism?

3. What does the author consider to be the primary takeaway from a careful consideration of what Paul had to say about the importance of the Holy Spirit to Christian discipleship?

4. What did you gain from the discussion of "Paul and the Realist Ways Christians Experience the Holy Spirit"?

5. What two spirituality practices did the apostle Paul apparently consider primary? How would you explain to someone why you agree or disagree

24. Francis Schaeffer, *True Spirituality* (Wheaton: Tyndale House, 1971), 150–51 (emphasis original).

with the notion that these two practices really are foundational to a Christian spirituality?

6. This chapter encourages readers to "stop viewing the Spirit as a sanctifying force that works in our lives without our expecting or inviting him to do so," and to instead "take very seriously the need to *surrender to*, *cooperate with*, and *pray in* the Holy Spirit." How would you explain to someone why you to tend to agree or disagree with these exhortations?

4

AN ONGOING MENTORING RELATIONSHIP WITH JESUS? YES PLEASE!

While a daily devotional hour is vital for saturating our minds with Christ, it is not enough.

—Frank Laubach, *Prayer: The Mightiest Force in the World*

I suspect some of us use the phrase to refer to too many things, but have you ever had an experience that really was "life changing"? I indicated in the book's introduction that part of my doctoral studies included an intensive course taught by the late Dallas Willard. The thousands of pages of prereading that were required and then the two weeks spent at a retreat center in the hills above Sierra Madre, California, studying the relationship between spirituality and ministry, were genuinely life and ministry altering.

My intention here and in chapter 7 is to condense much of what I learned from Willard and the writings of literally dozens of Christianity's spiritual masters into a pungent pair of essays that adequately communicate my contention that at the heart of a Pauline "I-Thou" lifestyle spirituality is a Spirit-enabled, moment-by-moment mentoring relationship with the risen Jesus. As the next few paragraphs should indicate, my goal in both chapters is not only to inform but also to inspire—to encourage and enable readers of this work to embrace the second commitment I contend is at the heart of the spirituality the apostle Paul so enthusiastically commended.

Imagining a Life Full of God

Years ago, I came across a short satirical piece authored by churchman Wilbur Rees that was designed to produce within Christian readers some serious self-examination. Apparently intending to provide a commentary on the spiritual complacency and consumerist mindset at work in the hearts of many contemporary churchgoing Americans, this concerned pastor writes,

> I would like to buy $3 worth of God, please, not enough to explode my soul or disturb my sleep, but just enough to equal a cup of warm milk or a snooze in the sunshine. I don't want enough of Him to make me love a black man or pick beets with a migrant. I want ecstasy, not transformation; I want the warmth of the womb, not a new birth. I want a pound of the eternal in a paper sack. I would like to buy $3 worth of God, please.[1]

To the degree that this tongue-in-cheek request really is indicative of the spiritual state of many churchgoers, it is no wonder that recent cultural developments suggest that the church in America has been far less than fully effective at functioning as spiritual salt and light in our contemporary era. What do you think: Was Rees right? Is there an attitude of spiritual complacency at work in the lives of too many churchgoing Americans? Could it be that this attitude is at least to some degree present in your church, your family, your own heart? Have you ever been guilty of desiring or settling for only three dollars' worth of God?

If we are being honest, everyone reading this book will acknowledge how easy it is for the best of us to become lukewarm in our walk with Christ (Rev. 3:15–16). But let's imagine now an alternative, what a life full of God might look like.

Dallas Willard and the Colossians 3 Kind of Life

In the previous chapter, I suggested that one Pauline passage in particular describes a Christian life well lived. That passage is Colossians 3:5–17. Willard made much of this passage, literally challenging those of us who participated

---

1. As relayed in Tim Hansel, *When I Relax I Feel Guilty* (Elgin, IL: David C. Cook Publishing, 1979), 49.

in his Spirituality and Ministry seminars to commit it to memory. His aim, I have come to believe, was to encourage his students to become convinced that, with God's help, these exhortations really could be lived into.

Since I have cited the passage in full already, I will simply summarize it here, pointing out that Willard was convinced the apostle Paul was dead serious when he calls for Christ's followers to *overcome* their tendencies toward

- sexual immorality, impurity, lust, evil desires, and greed (Col. 3:5);
- anger, rage, malice, slander, and filthy language (Col. 3:8);
- dishonest speech (Col. 3:9); and
- prejudicial attitudes toward people of other races and cultures (Col. 3:11).

But that is not all. Willard also took seriously the way Paul goes on in this passage to call for his readers to *become* the kind of people who are able to

- manifest compassion, kindness, humility, gentleness, and patience toward others (Col. 3:12);
- forgive others in the same way they have been forgiven (Col. 3:13);
- genuinely love their brothers and sisters in Christ (Col. 3:14);
- function as peacemakers (rather than troublemakers) in the church, grateful for the privilege just to belong (Col. 3:15);
- speak prophetically into the lives of others in encouraging, edifying ways and offer Spirit-inspired praise and thanksgiving to God (Col. 3:16; cf. Eph. 5:18–20); and
- honor Christ in everything they say and do, offering their entire lives to God as an act of grateful worship (Col. 3:17).

In other words, for Willard, this extended passage functions in the Pauline corpus as the sine qua non for Christian living—the fullest Pauline description of what a God-pleasing life will entail and the apostle's vision of the lifestyle that a fully trinitarian "I-Thou" spirituality can and will produce.

The Apostle Paul and the Empowering Presence of Christ

But this raises a question: From whence does the empowerment to live this kind of life come? Discerning the answer to this crucial query requires some biblical exegesis. We must seek to understand the Colossians 3:5–17 pericope in its historical and literary context. I will attempt to make this exegetical discussion as painless as possible.

Most biblical commentators agree that a heretical teaching mandating an adherence to certain religious rules and rituals, as well as some sort of devotion to angelic beings, had infiltrated the church in Colossae, threatening to disconnect the disciples there from Christ, the head of the church (Col. 2:16–19). Alarmed at this disturbing development, Paul's ultimate message to this confused and beleaguered community of faith was to stay focused on, rooted in, and connected to Christ (see Col. 2:1–12).[2]

In the process of encouraging the Colossian Christians to continue *living in Christ* (Col. 2:6), Paul offers a cogent critique of the heretical teaching to which they were being exposed, pointing out its powerlessness to do the very thing that its proponents had promised—that is, to help them overcome their human bent toward sensual indulgence (Col. 2:20–23). In other words, one of Paul's main messages in this letter is that the spirituality some of the Colossian disciples had embraced was at cross-purposes with his prayer that they might "live a life worthy of the Lord and please him in every way" (Col. 1:10; cf. Phil. 1:27). Christ's followers require something other than human philosophy or religiosity if they are to render to God a spiritual, moral, and missional faithfulness. This is where Paul's christological realism becomes abundantly apparent.

It is immediately after pointing out the complete inability of this false gospel to help its adherents experience any sort of genuine transformation in their lives that Paul offers his readers the critical counsel provided in Colossians 3:1–4. This pivotal passage reads like this: "Since, then, you have been raised with Christ, set your hearts on things above, where Christ is, seated at the right hand of God. Set your minds on things above, not on earthly things. For you died, and your life is now hidden with Christ in God. When Christ, who is your life, appears, then you also will appear with him in glory." In a nutshell, Paul seems to be suggesting here that the key to the Colossians 3 kind of life is a very important spirituality practice—an ongoing, prayerful, meditative communion with the risen Jesus.

More specifically, and at the risk of oversimplifying things, I will go on to suggest that this very basic counsel called for the Colossian Christians to do two simple things: (1) recognize the mystical union that exists between themselves and the risen Christ and (2) develop the habit of focusing their hearts and minds (affections and thinking) on things above, "where Christ is"—that

---

2. Douglas J. Moo, *The Letters to the Colossians and to Philemon*, Pillar New Testament Commentary (Grand Rapids: Eerdmans, 2008), 46–47.

is, on the risen Christ (rather than on philosophy, religiosity, or any number of angelic beings).

Paul then follows this very basic pastoral counsel with a vivid description of the kind of lifestyle that is "worthy of the Lord" and that will "please him in every way," a lifestyle that those who heed Paul's call to cultivate a prayerful communion with the risen Jesus will most certainly be able to achieve (Col. 3:5–17). In sum, the apostle Paul indicates here that those who follow his counsel will develop the ability to become new beings whose every word and action will reflect the mentoring influence of the one in whom all the fullness of divine wisdom and knowledge—and deity itself—dwells (Col. 3:17; cf. 2:3, 9). Put simply, it certainly seems as if Paul was encouraging the Colossian church members to cultivate and maintain a persistent, moment-by-moment mentoring relationship with the risen Christ—an intimate, interactive relationship that could and would empower them to live a Colossians 3 kind of life!

Furthermore, it is not just the rest of the New Testament that supports this interpretation of Colossians 3:1–4.[3] This interpretation also finds support in the devotional literature produced throughout the two-thousand-plus years of the Christian era.

The Spiritual Masters and the Empowering Presence of Christ

The two-week, intensive doctoral seminar I keep referring to in this chapter required its participants to read more than four thousand pages from various works authored by Christianity's spiritual masters, both ancient and contemporary. As I was fulfilling this pre-seminar reading assignment, I noticed a particular theme that kept recurring in the books I was studying, variations of one spiritual-life practice in particular. At the heart of many of the approaches to Christian spirituality that have been offered over the years is the idea that it is possible to learn to live moment by moment in the felt presence of the resurrected and ascended Jesus. It is possible to approach all the events in the course of a day with a sense that we are not alone: Christ is right there with us, loving us, encouraging us, enabling us to respond to this or that situation or person the way he would if he were we. Thus, in addition to everything else I learned from this reading of dozens of classic texts on Christian spirituality, I was exposed to the life-altering concept of Christ's empowering presence. This concept was later reinforced by the teaching of Dallas Willard in the seminar itself. The result was that by the time the two-week Spirituality

3. See, e.g., Matt. 18:19–20; 28:19–20; John 14:16–18, 23; 15:1–8; Rom. 13:12–14; Gal. 2:20; Eph. 3:17; Heb. 3:1; 12:1–3; Rev. 3:20.

and Ministry seminar was over, I had become absolutely convinced that it is Christ's empowering presence that enables the sincere Christ follower to live a Colossians 3 kind of life—and that the daily pursuit of Christ's empowering presence is at the very heart of Christian spirituality!

My aim in the remainder of this chapter is to explore in a cursory manner some of the support from the spiritual-life masters for the pursuit of Christ's empowering presence—that is, the *what* and the *why* of it. Then, later in the book (chap. 7), we will take a closer look at some practical how-tos.

What "the Pursuit" Involves

Let's take a look in this section at some ways in which the nature and purpose of this spirituality practice is treated in some of the classics of Christian devotional literature. For example, a work titled *The Practice of the Presence of God*, which is derived from some interviews with and the letters of a lay monk named Brother Lawrence (ca. 1610–91), leads us to believe that the pursuit of Christ's empowering presence calls for us to

- begin each day conversing with the risen Christ (the real Jesus, not just the idea of him), surrendering the entire day to him, asking him in advance to help us discern what he is up to in every part of it;
- keep an *internal* conversation with Christ going throughout the day, reckoning with his real presence, dedicating our work to him, seeking to serve and honor him in everything we say and do;
- express regret whenever we recognize that we have become distracted from "the pursuit" and have begun to respond to people and situations in our own strength rather than his;[4]
- keep returning to the pursuit of his presence, expressing gratitude for his grace and committing ourselves to both *knowing* his remarkable love and mercy and then *showing* it to others; and then
- conclude the day by taking stock of how well we fared in the pursuit, drifting off to sleep knowing that, Lord willing, we will awake in a few hours to begin the adventure of walking with Christ all over again.[5]

Of course, Brother Lawrence isn't the only spiritual master to advocate for the pursuit. Space will allow for only a sampling of quotations from the pens of some other ancient and contemporary spiritual masters.

4. I use the phrase "the pursuit" here and elsewhere in this work as a shorthand for the pursuit of Christ's empowering presence.
5. Brother Lawrence, *The Practice of the Presence of God with Spiritual Maxims* (Grand Rapids: Spire Books, 1967), 25.

For example, in the Christian classic titled *The Imitation of Christ*, a famous devotional work by Thomas à Kempis (1380–1471), we read,

> "The Kingdom of God is within you," says Our Lord. Turn to the Lord with all your heart, forsake this sorry world, and your soul shall find rest. Learn to turn from worldly things, and give yourself to spiritual things, and you will see the Kingdom of God come within you. For the Kingdom is peace and joy in the Holy Spirit; these are not granted to the wicked. Christ will come to you, and impart his consolations to you, if you prepare a worthy dwelling for Him in your hearts. All true glory and beauty is within, and there He delights to dwell. He often visits the spiritual man, and holds sweet discourse with him, granting him refreshing grace, great peace, and friendship exceeding all expectation.[6]

Another famous devotional work, *Introduction to the Devout Life*, was written by a Roman Catholic bishop and spiritual director named Francis de Sales (1567–1622). One of many excerpts from this highly quotable work reads, "I especially counsel you to practice mental prayer, the prayer of the heart, and particularly that which centers on the life and passion of our Lord. By often turning your eyes on him in meditation, your whole soul will be filled with him. You will learn his ways and form your actions after the pattern of his."[7]

Additional support for the pursuit can also be found in some spiritual-life authors nearer to us in time. For example, a twentieth-century missionary and mystic named Frank Laubach (1884–1970) offers this insight, part of which appeared in the epigraph for this chapter:

> While a daily devotional hour is vital for saturating our minds with Christ, it is not enough. All during the day, in the chinks of time between the things we find ourselves obliged to do, there are moments when our minds ask: "What next?" In these chinks of time, ask Him:
>
> "Lord, think Thy thoughts in my mind. What is on Thy mind for me to do now?"
>
> When we ask Christ, "What's next?" we tune in and give Him a chance to pour His ideas through our enkindled imagination. If we persist, it becomes a habit. It takes some effort, but it is worth a million times what it costs. It is possible for everybody, everywhere. Even if we are surrounded by throngs of people we can continue to talk silently with our invisible Friend. We need not close our eyes nor change our position nor move our lips.[8]

---

6. Thomas à Kempis, *The Imitation of Christ* (London: Penguin Books, 1952), 67–68.

7. Francis de Sales, *Introduction to the Devout Life* (New York: Doubleday, 1966), 81.

8. Frank C. Laubach, *Man of Prayer: Selected Writings of a World Missionary* (Syracuse: Laubach Literacy International, 1990), 245.

In his classic work *A Testament of Devotion*, American Quaker author Thomas Kelly (1893–1941) offers these words of encouragement: "There is a way of ordering our mental life on more than one level at once. On one level we may be thinking, discussing, seeing, calculating, meeting all the demands of external affairs. But deep within, behind the scenes, at a profounder level, we may also be in prayer and adoration, song and worship and a gentle receptiveness to divine breathings."[9]

In his book *The Transforming Friendship*, English churchman and theologian Leslie Weatherhead (1893–1976) poses the following question:

> Is it a real fact, practicable for everyday life in the twentieth century, that we may have communion with Jesus Christ as really as we have communion with our earthly friends? Can we know that same Jesus of Nazareth who walked about in Galilee two thousand years ago? I do not mean can we treasure His words, can we follow His way of life, can we, following His example, be heroic as He was, can we benefit by His ideas; I do not mean can we imaginatively reproduce a picture of Him clearly enough to form a substitute for His actual presence; but can we really meet Him, know Him, commune with Himself?[10]

He eventually answers his own question this way:

> What Jesus once was, He is eternally. He comes to us, not only in His temple, or in the room when the door is shut, but as He came to Mary and Martha in the midst of household tasks, and as He came to Peter mending his nets and doing his daily work; and He comes with the same offer, the offer of His transforming friendship. There are no conditions save the imaginative faith to believe that He is, and that fellowship with Him is possible.
>
> Can we enter into this friendship? We can. We can, as Brother Lawrence said, "practise the Presence of God," but the only way I know of practising the presence of God is by practising the presence of Jesus, who makes God credible and real, and entering into the transforming friendship which He offers.[11]

Contemporary author and speaker Jan Johnson portrays this key spiritual practice in this manner:

> An awareness of God can flow through our day the way blood circulates through the body, replenishing it with nutrients and oxygen. We pay attention to God, conscious that He may be speaking to us. His presence begins to permeate our lives—through thoughts, feelings, dreams, activities, and in-between moments.

9. Thomas Kelly, *A Testament of Devotion* (New York: Harper & Row, 1941), 35.
10. Leslie Weatherhead, *The Transforming Friendship* (Nashville: Abingdon, 1977), 29.
11. Weatherhead, *Transforming Friendship*, 35.

Practicing God's presence moves His companionship beyond church gatherings, before-meal graces, and quiet times to infiltrate the ordinary moments of life. Keeping company with God this way transforms tasks such as building circuit boards into acts of worship because we know at whose feet we sit for the rest of our lives.[12]

Finally, Dallas Willard himself lent his voice in support of the pursuit when he wrote the following passages:

> We therefore live in "hot pursuit" of Jesus Christ. "My soul followeth hard after thee," the psalmist called out (63:8, KJV). And Paul's panting cry was, "That I may know Him, and the power of His resurrection and the fellowship of His sufferings, being conformed to His death" in order to participate in the life of his resurrection (Phil. 3:10–11). What are we to say of anyone who thinks they have something more important to do than that?[13]

> Sometimes today it seems that our personal relationship with God is treated as no more than a mere arrangement or understanding that Jesus and his Father have about us. Our personal relationship then only means that each believer has his or her own unique account in heaven, which allows them to draw on the merits of Christ to pay their sin bills. Or possibly it means that God's general providence for his creation is adequate to provide for each person.
>
> But who does not think there should be much more to a personal relationship than that? A mere benefactor, however powerful, kind and thoughtful, is not the same thing as a *friend*. Jesus says, "I have called you friends" (John 15:15) and "Look, I am with you every minute, even to the end of the age" (Matt. 28:20, paraphrase; cf. Heb. 13:5–6).[14]

It is my hope that the collection of quotations presented in the preceding pages has not only adequately indicated what the pursuit involves—that is, a moment-by-moment mentoring relationship with the risen Christ—but also provided a measure of motivation. And yet, because my goal in this chapter is to inspire as well as inform, I'll press on to discuss another important topic.

Why the Pursuit Is Important

In this chapter's concluding section, I will do my best to provide some additional motivation to engage in the pursuit by once again quoting from the

12. Jan Johnson, *Enjoying the Presence of God: Discovering Intimacy with God in the Daily Rhythms of Life* (Colorado Springs: NavPress, 1996), 14.

13. Dallas Willard, *Renovation of the Heart: Putting on the Character of Christ* (Colorado Springs: NavPress, 2002), 42–43.

14. Dallas Willard, *Hearing God: Developing a Conversational Relationship with God* (Downers Grove, IL: IVP Books, 1999), 22.

writings of Christianity's spiritual masters. Scattered throughout the corpus of devotional literature can be found some rather glowing descriptions of the *benefits* that result from the practice of the presence of God. Like the more general references to this holy activity, these descriptions can be quite moving and informative.

In Brother Lawrence's view, the pursuit of Christ's empowering presence represents the most appropriate act of worship we can offer a gracious God. This godly monk challenged the readers of his letters to seriously consider this bold notion when he made this inquiry: "What offering is there more acceptable to God than thus throughout the day to quit the things of outward sense, and to withdraw to worship Him within the secret places of the soul?"[15] Ironically, Lawrence was also convinced that the pursuit of Christ's empowering presence plays a role in the Christian disciple's defeat of the devil. With this thought in mind, he went on to advise, "We must go about our labors quietly, calmly, and lovingly, entreating Him to prosper the works of our hands; by thus keeping heart and mind fixed on God, we shall bruise the head of the evil one, and beat down his weapons to the ground."[16]

According to Thomas à Kempis, the pursuit of Christ's empowering presence can make the difference between a heart that is hardened and disconsolate and one that is filled with comfort and delight. In his classic work, *The Imitation of Christ*, this good brother writes,

> When Jesus is with us, all is well, and nothing seems hard; but when Jesus is absent, everything is difficult. When Jesus does not speak to the heart, all other comfort is unavailing; but if Jesus speaks but a single word, we are greatly comforted. . . . Oh, happy the hour when Jesus calls us from tears to joy of spirit! How arid and hard of heart you are without Jesus! How foolish and empty if you desire anything but Jesus! Surely, this is a greater injury to you than the loss of the whole world.[17]

Frank Laubach claims the pursuit of Christ's empowering presence provides us with a remarkable sense of divine help in the present and hope for the future. If this is true, how does one put a value on this? Laubach explains,

> I feel simply carried along each hour, doing my part in a plan which is far beyond myself. This sense of cooperation with God in little things is what so astonishes me, for I never have felt it this way before. I need something, and turn round to find it waiting for me. I must work, to be sure, but there is God

15. Lawrence, *Practice of the Presence*, 71–72.
16. Lawrence, *Practice of the Presence*, 71.
17. Thomas, *Imitation of Christ*, 76.

working along with me. To know this gives a sense of security and assurance for the future which is also new to my life. I seem to have to make sure of only one thing now, and every other thing "takes care of itself," or I prefer to say what is more true, God takes care of all the rest. My part is to live this hour in continuous inner conversation with God and in perfect responsiveness to His will. To make this hour gloriously rich. This seems to be all I need think about.[18]

According to Leslie Weatherhead, the pursuit of Christ's empowering presence will eventually lead to the sanctifying of every part of life and the end of our spiritual wanderings. Notice the genuine sincerity and sense of excitement in this excerpt:

It is an amazing offer. It means that no single experience of life has ever to be faced alone. What would it mean to us if in the temptation to hasty temper, to meanness, contempt, jealously, impurity, avarice, we could pull ourselves up with the thought that this patient, kind, but inexorable Friend was near? What would it mean in sorrow, in bereavement, in pain, in loneliness? What would it mean in joy and laughter, in pleasure and fun? It would mean the sanctifying of every part of life. It is the experience our fathers called "being saved," for to be received into this friendship is to be at the end, not indeed of our journey but of all fruitless wanderings.[19]

Contemporary spiritual-life author Richard Foster expresses the view that the pursuit of Christ's empowering presence will enable us to possess a new "Center of Reference" that will bring a new and valuable sense of peace and serenity into our otherwise harried and hurried lives. Foster writes with compassion these words of encouragement:

I am sure you sense the desperate need for Unceasing Prayer in our day. We pant through an endless series of activities with scattered minds and noisy hearts. We feel strained, hurried, breathless. Thoughts dart in and out of our minds with no rhyme or reason. Seldom can we focus on a single thing for long. Everything and anything interrupt our sense of concentration. We are distracted people.

Unceasing Prayer has a way of speaking peace to chaos. We begin experiencing something of the cosmic patience of God. Our fractured and fragmented activities begin focusing around a new Center of Reference. We experience peace, stillness, serenity, firmness of life orientation.[20]

18. Frank C. Laubach, *Letters by a Modern Mystic* (Syracuse: New Readers, 1979), cited in Laubach, *Man of Prayer*, 21.
19. Weatherhead, *Transforming Friendship*, 35.
20. Richard Foster, *Prayer: Finding the Heart's True Home* (San Francisco: HarperSanFrancisco, 1992), 121.

According to the evangelical mystic A. W. Tozer (1897–1963), the pursuit of Christ's empowering presence will take us to a whole new level in our walk with God: "When the habit of inwardly gazing Godward becomes fixed within us we shall be ushered onto a new level of spiritual life more in keeping with the promises of God and the mood of the New Testament. The Triune God will be our dwelling place even while our feet walk the low road of simple duty here among men. We will have found life's *summum bonum* indeed."[21]

Finally, according to Dallas Willard, the ultimate benefit of the pursuit of Christ's empowering presence is that it is the one spirituality practice that really will effect a dramatic transformation in who and how we are in this world. Willard writes,

> The effect of standing before God by welcoming him before us will, by contrast, be the transformation of our entire life. All else that enters our mind, and especially the thoughts that first come to mind as we encounter various kinds of events that make up our lives, will be healthy, godly, and those in harmony with the realities of a good-God-governed universe, not the illusions of a godless or a me-governed universe, or one where man is supreme—or no one else. My patterns of thinking will conform to the truths of scriptural revelation, and I will extend and apply those truths, under the guidance of God's Holy Spirit, to all of the details of my daily life.
>
> Am I undertaking some task? Then I in faith do it with God, assuming and finding his power to be involved with me. That is the nature of his kingdom. Is there an emergency? I meet it with the knowledge that God is in the midst of it with me and will be calm in a center of intense prayer. Am I praised? My thoughts (and feelings) will move immediately to the goodness of God in my life. Am I condemned or reproached? I know that God is supporting and helping me because he loves me and has a future for me. Am I disappointed and frustrated? I rest in the knowledge that God is over all and that he is working things out—that "all things work *together* for good to those who love God and are called into the fulfillment of his purposes." And so forth.[22]

It is my hope that some time was taken to really drink in the wisdom and insight that effuses from the many quotations this chapter puts on display. This too can be part of the mind renewal that is necessary for genuine transformation (see Rom. 12:2; Eph. 4:22–24). Dallas Willard strongly encouraged his students and the readers of his books to "master the masters" as they attempt to live a Christ-focused life.[23] It just so happens that this practice provides a

---

21. A. W. Tozer, *The Pursuit of God* (Camp Hill, PA: Christian Publications, 1993), 90.

22. Willard, *Renovation of the Heart*, 109.

23. Dallas Willard, *Knowing Christ Today: Why We Can Trust Spiritual Knowledge* (New York: HarperOne, 2009), 157.

tremendous degree of support for the idea that at the heart of a Pauline "I-Thou" lifestyle spirituality is a *cardinal* practice that all the other practices (or spiritual disciplines) need, in one way or another, to contribute to.

Christ's Empowering Presence and a Moral Faithfulness

The notion that the pursuit of Christ's empowering presence is the cardinal practice at the heart of Christian spirituality is supported by the fact that it is generative of the threefold faithfulness God is looking for: spiritual, moral, and missional. That said, one cannot engage in a thoughtful pondering of Colossians 3:5–17 and avoid sensing how many of the exhortations Paul presents there relate to the cultivation of a *moral faithfulness* in particular.

Jesus of Nazareth is the model par excellence of someone committed to hearing and honoring the heart of the Father in their everyday life. While the Scriptures emphasize the important role the Holy Spirit is to play in our emulation of his moral message and manner,[24] the tendency today among even many churchgoers is to make important ethical decisions by using the Bible as a moral rule book in a pharisaical, rules-focused manner or by abandoning the Scriptures altogether and either going with their gut or taking their ethical cues from the surrounding culture in a results-driven manner. However, the ethical genius of Jesus, something we simply must strive to emulate, was in the way he combined a respect for rules, results, and virtues into a Spirit-empowered, God-the-Father-pleasing way of being in the world that left everyone around him thoroughly awash in both grace and truth. Here is the bottom line: Jesus was (and is) really good at loving God supremely and loving his neighbors in God-honoring ways (see Matt. 22:34–39). If we will let him, he can and will teach us how to do the same. Growing in our ability to render to God a moral faithfulness, as Jesus did, really is a big part of what Christian discipleship is about. An ongoing mentoring relationship with the risen Christ in the power of the Spirit is key!

For what it's worth, I have spent over twenty years engaged in the pursuit. It really has been a game changer. While I am still a million miles away from all I might be in Christ, I am also a long way from the person I used to be. The takeaway from this chapter is that real transformation is possible. We must never give up the goal of living a life that is worthy of the Lord and that pleases him in every way. However, this is going to require much more than

---

24. For more on this, see Gary Tyra, *Pursuing Moral Faithfulness: Ethics and Christian Discipleship* (Downers Grove, IL: IVP Academic, 2015), 181–204, 272–76.

three dollars' worth of God. What is desperately needed is the pneumatological and christological realism that makes possible a genuine experience of the empowering presence of Jesus in our everyday lives.

So far in part 2 of this work, we have explored two fundamental commitments that drive a lifestyle spirituality: keeping in step with the Spirit and pursuing thereby a moment-by-moment mentoring relationship with the risen Christ. The spiritual masters I have introduced in this chapter will provide us with some practical how-tos regarding the pursuit in chapter 7. But there is a third commitment we must focus on first: one that has to do with the *missional faithfulness* our missionary God is looking for and the *missional spirituality* that makes such a faithfulness fruitful. Heavy, right? Read on to find out just how much so!

TOPICS FOR REVIEW

1. Was Wilbur Rees right? Is there an attitude of spiritual complacency at work in the lives of too many churchgoing Americans? Could it be that this attitude is to some degree present in your church, your family, or your own heart? Have you ever been guilty of desiring, or settling for, only three dollars' worth of God?

2. What are your thoughts about the suggestion that Colossians 3:5–17 "functions in the Pauline corpus as the sine qua non for Christian living—the fullest Pauline description of what a God-pleasing life will entail and the apostle's vision of the lifestyle that a fully trinitarian "I-Thou" spirituality can and will produce?" What exhortation(s) in this biblical passage do you consider to be especially important to a Christian spirituality? Which one(s) are especially challenging?

3. To what degree do you concur with this chapter's suggestion that the daily pursuit of Christ's empowering presence is a spirituality practice the apostle Paul did (and would) support? Why?

4. Based on what this chapter has to say about "the Pursuit" of Christ, how would you explain to someone in just a sentence or two what his empowering presence involves?

5. Were any of the quotes from the spiritual masters (past and present) regarding "the Pursuit" especially informative or inspirational for you personally? If so, which ones? Why?

6. What is your assessment of the role an eager engagement in "the Pursuit" will play in the cultivation of a moral faithfulness? Give an honest assessment of your degree of eagerness for the "how to" discussion promised in chapter 7?

5

A MISSIONAL FAITHFULNESS
AND SPIRITUALITY

You Gotta Commit!

Mission is not just one of a list of things that the Bible happens to talk about, only a bit more urgently than some. Mission is, in that much-abused phrase, "what it's all about."

—Christopher J. H. Wright, *The Mission of God*

Have you ever been asked the question "How's your core?" If so, I would be willing to bet that the person posing it was either a physical trainer or a fitness devotee.

It is probably not a bad idea to be reminded occasionally of how important our core muscles are to our overall health and functionality. As it turns out, an online article titled "Importance of Core Training" informs us that "core training is a hot topic in the health and fitness world." The article goes on to explain that our core is made up of all the muscles in our "midsection," including "muscles in the front, sides and back." These muscles are important because they "work as stabilizers for the entire body and help the body function more effectively." The problem, however, is that "most people are unaware of the importance of strengthening the core muscles, and [they] tend to neglect them. This neglect can lead to injury and pain."[1] The bottom line, apparently, is that we are only as healthy and functional as our midsection—that is, the muscles that make up our core.

We are learning that one's spirituality has a core as well. At the center of a Pauline, trinitarian lifestyle spirituality are three core commitments. So far in this midsection of the book we have looked at the first two: (1) to keep in step with the Spirit and (2) to engage in a "hot pursuit" of Christ's empowering presence. In this chapter, a third *core commitment* enters our purview: one that has as its focus the cultivation of a God-the-Father-pleasing lifestyle.

Why Pleasing God Mandates Mission

Throughout this book, I have emphasized how important the threefold faithfulness is to the God of the Bible. Having associated the first core commitment (keeping in step with the Spirit) with the phenomenon of a *spiritual faithfulness*, and after alluding to the way the second core commitment (engaging in the pursuit of Christ's empowering presence) facilitates a *moral faithfulness*, in this chapter I will link the third core commitment (cultivating a God-the-Father-pleasing lifestyle) to a *missional faithfulness*.

This third association is not arbitrary. While the Scriptures clearly indicate that all three forms of faithfulness matter greatly to God, we have good reason to believe that a genuine missional faithfulness serves to indicate that all three are at work in someone's life. In other words, the three forms of faithfulness are interrelated in a critical way: a spiritual faithfulness underwrites the moral faithfulness, without which a missional faithfulness will founder. Put differently, a missional faithfulness before God derives from and evidences the presence and quality of the other two!

The conviction that a missional faithfulness is indispensable to a God-the-Father-pleasing lifestyle also finds some significant support from several types of New Testament texts. For instance, the Gospel of John seems to emphasize the fact that Jesus came "from the Father" (John 1:14) and that Jesus was not reluctant to assert this himself (John 16:28; cf. 17:1, 8). Moreover, the Fourth Gospel also indicates that Jesus was all about emulating, honoring, pleasing the Father rather than looking after himself or placating other people (see John 5:17, 19, 30; 8:29; 14:10, 24; 17:4–5). In other words, Jesus was self-conscious about being on mission (see John 4:34; 5:36; 6:38; 7:28–29; 12:49–50). We also know that Jesus was very intentional about "sending" his

---

1. "Importance of Core Training," Fight Club America, February 3, 2019, https://undemo cratic57.rssing.com/chan-31154853/latest-article9.php.

followers in the very same missional manner that the Father had "sent" him (see John 17:18; 20:21), and that this involved sending the Spirit, who has likewise come "from the Father" (John 15:26). Finally, also in Luke's Gospel and its sequel (i.e., the book of Acts), we find Jesus making a vivid connection between the coming of the Spirit into the lives of his followers and their being empowered thereby to please God in a missional manner (see Luke 24:45–49; Acts 1:8). All these passages make clear how important a missionally faithful lifestyle was to Jesus.

It was the same with Paul. We learned in chapter 2 that a big part of the infrastructure of the apostle's theological paradigm was the *missionality* of God. Just as was true of Jesus, the ultimate concern of the apostle Paul was to please this missionary, sending God (see 2 Cor. 5:9, 20). This being the case, we simply must have a serious talk about missional faithfulness. Because mission is dear to the *heart* of God, it must also be at the *heart* of a God-the-Father-pleasing lifestyle spirituality.

A Missionally Faithful Understanding of the *Missio Dei*

I do not mean to be alarmist when I point out that if we want to someday hear Jesus say to us, "Well done, good and faithful servant!" we simply must possess an accurate understanding of the mission that is important to him and that has been entrusted to us. It is impossible to be fully faithful while only partially aware of what our assignment is.

While this is not the place for a deep, dark discussion of the origin and development of the term *missio Dei* (the "mission of God"), we need to be aware that it is possible to have a truncated rather than holistic understanding of it. In other words, some on both sides of the conservative-versus-liberal theological spectrum would have us focus on only one of the following goals: disciple making, social action, or creation care. Over against this notion, I will argue that a missional faithfulness calls for Christ's followers to take a more holistic, comprehensive approach.[2]

Missiologist Christopher Wright seems to have the big picture of God's mission in view when he makes this proposal: "Fundamentally, our mission (if it is biblically informed and validated) means our committed participation as God's people, at God's invitation and command, in God's own mission within

2. For a more thorough discussion of this topic, see Gary Tyra, *The Holy Spirit in Mission: Prophetic Speech and Action in Christian Witness* (Downers Grove, IL: IVP Academic, 2011), 22–27; Tyra, *A Missional Orthodoxy: Theology and Ministry in a Post-Christian Context* (Downers Grove, IL: IVP Academic, 2013), 53–54, 310–17.

the history of God's world for the redemption of God's creation."[3] Some support for the way this wide-angle-lens perspective of God's mission focuses on the redemption of God's creation can be found in the way Genesis 1:26–28 and 2:15 can be interpreted to mean that God expects human beings to care for and develop the creation, to cooperate with him in his work of creating a world that reflects his original plans and intentions for the planet (Gen. 1:30). Furthermore, Romans 8:21 indicates that though a fall has occurred, estranging creation from its Creator, a future liberation awaits not only human beings but creation itself. Likewise, Colossians 1:15–20 specifies that God's plan is for "all things" (all creation) to be eventually reconciled in Christ. And finally, Revelation 21:5 boldly declares that God will someday make "everything" new. Taken together, these passages can at least infer that God's redemptive concern ultimately extends beyond the salvation of individual souls to human cultures, to the planet—indeed, to the welfare of the cosmos as a whole.

With this thought in mind, I believe it is possible to envision a missionally faithful lifestyle as one that endeavors to care for rather than despoil the good world God created and made his image-bearers responsible for (Gen. 1:26–28; 2:15). Though the worship of creation itself is strictly forbidden (e.g., Rom. 1:18–25), the way multiple passages from both Testaments keep reminding us that the earth belongs to God certainly gives the impression that, despite the effect of the fall upon his creation, he still "owns" and is invested in it.[4] The fact that God will someday create a new earth[5] doesn't give his human image-bearers the license to stop caring for this one! I appreciate the way one emergent author connects creation care with Jesus's call for us to love our neighbors. Says Brian McLaren,

> Clearly, if our thinking extends beyond "me, myself, and I" to our neighbors (human and nonhuman) as the gospel teaches us, we will realize that our neighbors downstream suffer from our water pollution, downwind from our air pollution, and downhill from our erosion. And when we consider our neighbors in time as well as space, we start thinking differently about our children, grandchildren, and more distant descendants. What toxins are we sending downstream in time to poison them? What kind of world do we want to bequeath to those downstream from us in time? . . . The more we as Christians follow Jesus by thinking of our neighbors "downstream" in space and time, the more we will take our stewardship of creation seriously.[6]

3. Christopher J. H. Wright, *The Mission of God: Unlocking the Bible's Grand Narrative* (Downers Grove, IL: IVP Academic, 2006), 22–23.

4. See Exod. 9:29; 19:5; Job 41:11; Pss. 24:1; 50:12; 1 Cor. 10:26.

5. See Isa. 65:17; 66:22; 2 Pet. 3:13; Rev. 21:1.

6. Brian McLaren, *A Generous Orthodoxy* (Grand Rapids: Zondervan, 2004), 242.

We must also reckon with the many biblical passages, from both the Old and New Testaments, that sound a call for God's people to promote justice in the communities they currently indwell.[7] This vigorous stream of prophetic admonitions provides some strong scriptural support for a bold assertion made by Christian political scientist Dennis McNutt: "Working for justice in the legal system is an act of high spirituality every bit as much as fasting, praying, paying tithes, or going to the mission field, for this is one way we can love our neighbor."[8] That McNutt envisions the pursuit of justice as a spirituality practice seems appropriate to this discussion since what we are currently exploring is the connection between spirituality and the missional concerns of God: a God who, as we have already learned, self-identifies as holy and wholly committed to justice. It is legitimate, therefore, to conclude that the *missio Dei* includes a call for Christ's followers to engage in Christian praxis—intentionally putting our theological beliefs into practical action, doing our best here and now to shape a community of faith that can image for the entire world, even if imperfectly, the reality and nature of the kingdom of God come and coming.

Long before the name George Floyd possessed social significance, McNutt offered this admonishment: "'Pietistic' spirituality may lead us to withdraw from the world of daily activities and seek God's face in a quiet place. . . . 'Applied spirituality' involves acting in all our relationships with other humans in ways that show we love them 'as ourselves.' I know how to love myself. When my breathing is restricted, I fight for air. . . . If the Scripture passage about loving my neighbor as myself means what it says, I must do the same for my neighbor."[9] However, since there is such a thing as "sinful praxis"— human reflection-action that is self-directed and therefore self-serving rather than God-honoring[10]—I will have more to say in the next chapter about the need for engagement in "applied spirituality" to be truly Christ emulating. For now, the point to be taken is simply this: God's mission involves social action as well as creation care.

That said, I must also acknowledge the degree to which I resonate with the understanding of the *missio Dei* that is inherent in the definition of the Christian gospel provided by Scot McKnight in his book *Embracing Grace*.

---

7. See, e.g., Deut. 16:20; Pss. 11:7; 106:3; Prov. 28:5; 29:7; Isa. 56:1; Jer. 21:12; Amos 5:15, 21–24; Zech. 7:9–10; Matt. 23:23; Luke 11:42.

8. Dennis McNutt, "Politics for Christians (and Other Sinners)," in *Elements of a Christian Worldview*, ed. Michael D. Palmer (Springfield, MO: Logion, 1998), 418.

9. McNutt, "Politics for Christians," 415.

10. Cheryl Bridges Johns and Vardaman W. White, "The Ethics of Being: Character, Community, Praxis," in *Elements of a Christian Worldview*, ed. Michael D. Palmer (Springfield, MO: Logion, 1998), 303–4.

McKnight defines the gospel as "the work of God to restore humans to union with God and communion with others, in the context of a community, for the good of others and the world."[11] McKnight's emphasis on the "gospel" as the "work of God" suggests that gospel proclamation and demonstration is at the very heart of God's mission. Moreover, this definition seems to succeed at holding disciple making, social action, and creation care in a healthy tension.[12] Long story short, I suggest that those who truncate God's mission by emphasizing *only* disciple making *or* social action *or* creation care need to take a step back and consider the possibility that, in truth, it includes a concern for all three endeavors. Since God's mission possesses a multifaceted focus, a God-the-Father-pleasing lifestyle spirituality will need to do so also.

The Primacy of Preaching or Sharing the Gospel

At the same time, I am convinced that an engagement in the proclamation or sharing of the gospel (good news) concerning Jesus Christ toward the making of disciples should be considered primary and essentially foundational to the prosecution of God's mission. The missionary and missional theologian Lesslie Newbigin (1909–98), who is considered by many to be the founder of the missional church movement, provides us with this important clarification regarding the importance of traditional disciple making: "The concept of *missio Dei* has sometimes been interpreted so as to suggest that action for justice and peace as the possibilities are discerned within a given historical situation *is* the fulfillment of God's mission, and that the questions of baptism and church membership are marginal or irrelevant. That way leads very quickly to disillusion and often to cynical despair."[13]

11. Scot McKnight, *Embracing Grace: A Gospel for All of Us* (Brewster, MA: Paraclete, 2005), xiii (emphasis original).

12. For more on this comprehensive take on the mission of God, see Lesslie Newbigin, *The Gospel in a Pluralist Society* (Grand Rapids: Eerdmans, 1989), 119, 123, 128–140; Alan J. Roxburgh and M. Scott Boren, *Introducing the Missional Church: Why It Matters, How to Become One* (Grand Rapids: Baker Books, 2009), 54, 87; Ed Stetzer and David Putnam, *Breaking the Missional Code: Your Church Can Become a Missionary in Your Community* (Nashville: B&H, 2006), 30–42, 79–81, 83–84; and Darrell L. Guder, ed., *Missional Church: A Vision for the Sending of the Church in North America* (Grand Rapids: Eerdmans, 1998), 12, 238, 247. See also Michael Frost and Alan Hirsch, *The Shaping of Things to Come: Innovation and Mission for the 21st-Century Church* (Peabody, MA: Hendrickson, 2003), 11; Dan Devadatta, "Strangers but Not Strange: A New Mission Situation for the Church (1 Peter 1:1–2 and 17–25)," in *Confident Witness—Changing World: Rediscovering the Gospel in North America*, ed. Craig Van Gelder (Grand Rapids: Eerdmans, 1999), 111–12, 121–24; James Davison Hunter, *To Change the World: The Irony, Tragedy, and Possibility of Christianity in the Late Modern World* (New York: Oxford University Press, 2010), 226.

13. Newbigin, *Gospel in a Pluralist Society*, 138 (emphasis original). Stetzer and Putnam speak to this issue also, commenting on the inappropriate, unnecessary manner in which some

What's more, the New Testament also clearly indicates how important it is for us to *proclaim* the gospel through preaching it or sharing it. First, the Gospels give attention to the preaching ministry of Jesus, his proclamation as well as demonstration of the good news concerning the kingdom of God.[14] Second, the New Testament refers dozens of times to the fact that there is a "message" that is central to gospel ministry, a message that must be shared and received.[15] Third, the apostle Paul asserts that God wants "all people to be saved and to come to a knowledge of the truth" (1 Tim. 2:4), the truth Paul goes on to summarize in the form of a message: "For there is one God and one mediator between God and mankind, the man Christ Jesus" (1 Tim. 2:5). Finally, the Great Commission emphasizes the making of disciples (Matt. 28:19–20) through the preaching of the gospel to all creation (Mark 16:15; cf. 13:10 and Acts 1:8).

This is not to say that gospel sharing, by itself, composes the entirety of God's mission, but it does mean that any version of the *missio Dei* that either ignores or downplays the making of disciples through gospel *proclamation*, as well as demonstration, simply lacks biblical support. Thus, while a holistic, comprehensive understanding of the *missio Dei* is called for, a missional faithfulness also requires that we take special care *not* to diminish the preaching or sharing of the Jesus story and its central importance to God's plan for all creation.

A Missional Faithfulness Implies a Missional Orthodoxy

Pressing on, to be missionally faithful we must also take care that the gospel we are preaching is true to the one that was "once for all entrusted to God's holy people" (Jude 3), while at the same time emulating the apostle Paul's commitment to contextualizing the good news for various people groups (1 Cor. 9:19–23). In other words, a missional faithfulness requires that we do justice to two critical tasks at the same time: the *contending* task (Jude 3) and the *contextualization* task (1 Cor. 9:19–23). It is the balancing of these two tasks that keeps us from *overcontextualizing* the gospel (altering the heart of the Christian message to make it palatable, acceptable to a new people group) on the one hand and *undercontextualizing* the gospel (not doing what

---

missional advocates feel the need to speak in a completely disparaging manner of the church growth and church health movements. See Stetzer and Putnam, *Breaking the Missional Code*, 49–50.

14. See Matt. 4:17, 23; 9:35; 11:1; Mark 1:14, 38; Luke 8:1; 20:1.

15. See Matt. 10:7; John 17:20; Acts 2:41; 4:4; 10:36, 44; 11:14; 13:26; 14:3; 15:7; 16:14; 17:11; 26:23; Rom. 10:8, 17; 16:25; 1 Cor. 1:18; 2:4, 6; 2 Cor. 5:19; Gal. 2:6; Eph. 1:13; Col. 1:5; 3:16; 4:3; 1 Thess. 1:6, 8; 2 Thess. 3:1; 2 Tim. 4:17; Titus 1:9; 1 Pet. 2:8; 2 Pet. 1:19; 1 John 1:5; 2:7; 3:11.

is necessary to minister the gospel in a way that is both coherent and compelling for as many people as possible) on the other hand.[16]

A Closer Look at the Contending Task

Going beyond Jude 3, the New Testament has much to say about the need for church members to be discerning regarding the version of the gospel they embrace and proclaim to others. There are passages that warn against false teachers putting forward false doctrines and teachings that are destructive rather than constructive with respect to the cultivation of the threefold faithfulness God is looking for.[17] Other passages encourage readers to focus solely on the gospel that was put forward by Jesus's true apostles.[18] Paul himself was concerned about this. Though he acknowledged that the timing of his call to apostleship was delayed (1 Cor. 15:8), he insisted that it was real and, therefore, diligently warned the readers of his missives to remain faithful to the gospel he had received by way of revelation and had faithfully delivered to them.[19]

This is an important point, since some contemporary scholarship questions whether the New Testament presents us with a "definitive articulation of the gospel" or "single attempt to summarize the gospel story as a whole."[20] Over against this assertion, I contend that passages such as 1 Corinthians 15:1–11 do just that. At the very least, this passage indicates that, for Paul and the other apostles, the historical facts of Jesus's death, burial, and resurrection were at the center of the gospel message they had proclaimed.[21]

Keeping in mind this and other passages that denote who Jesus is and what he is about, I have put forward what I refer to as four christological verities—four Christ-related doctrines I am convinced constitute the very heart of the Christian faith. These four crucial christological verities are

- Jesus is both God and man,[22]
- Jesus's death on the cross possessed an atoning significance,[23]

16. For a more thorough discussion of the need to do justice to these two critical tasks, see Tyra, *Missional Orthodoxy*, 27, 65–95.
17. See 2 Cor. 11:13; 1 Tim. 1:3–4; 4:1, 7; 6:20; 2 Tim. 2:16; 2 Pet. 1:16; 2:1; 1 John 2:18, 22; Rev. 2:2.
18. See 2 Pet. 1:16–18; 1 John 1:1–3; cf. Acts 1:21–22.
19. See 1 Cor. 15:2, 9–11; Gal. 1:6–9; Titus 1:9; cf. Rom. 2:16; 16:25; 1 Cor. 2:4; 2 Cor. 1:18; Gal. 2:6; Eph. 3:7; Col. 1:16; 2 Tim. 1:11; 2:8.
20. Dean Flemming, *Contextualization in the New Testament: Patterns for Theology and Ministry* (Downers Grove, IL: IVP Academic, 2005), 303.
21. For additional support of this exegetical take, see Scot McKnight, *The King Jesus Gospel: The Original Good News Revisited* (Grand Rapids: Zondervan, 2011), 46–50, 61, 64–65, 68–69, 89–91.
22. See John 20:31; 1 John 5:5, 11–12; 2 John 7–9.
23. See 1 Cor. 15:1–3; 1 John 2:2; 4:10.

- Jesus rose bodily from the grave,[24] and
- Jesus is now Lord of all.[25]

This, I admit, is a bold proposal. It contends that there is such a thing as Christian dogma—doctrines so essential to the Christian faith that they should be considered orthodox, crucial, nonnegotiable. But before we write off the special significance I am attaching to these four christological doctrines as just another form of fundamentalism, four things should be kept in mind: first, nowhere in the New Testament do we find a description of the gospel that contradicts any of these four christological verities; second, a careful read of the epistolary literature will reveal that it is a shared commitment to these four christological verities that provides the continuity that exists in the ways the New Testament authors refer to the Jesus story in their various writings;[26] third, these four christological doctrines seem to be so absolutely integral to the Christ event that without them the story of Jesus loses its significance for Israel, the gentiles, and creation as a whole;[27] fourth, the New Testament really does seem to ascribe to these four christological doctrines a special, *soteriological* (salvific) significance that other biblical doctrines simply do not possess.

In sum, there really is such a thing as a *contending task* to which a missional faithfulness will need to do justice. To reiterate, the apostle Jude famously refers to this vital task when he writes, "Dear friends, although I was very eager to write to you about the salvation we share, I felt compelled to write and urge you to *contend* for the faith that was once for all entrusted to God's holy people" (Jude 3).

A Closer Look at the Contextualization Task

But the contending task, as important as it is, doesn't exist in isolation. There is a *contextualization* task that must be taken seriously as well. Once again, the trick is to do justice to both at the same time.

24. See Rom. 10:9–10; 1 Cor. 15:1–5.
25. See Rom. 10:9–10; cf. Rom. 14:9–12; 1 Cor. 12:3; Phil. 2:9–11; Heb. 3:1, 15. For a discussion of why the doctrine of Christ's atoning death should be considered an element of Christian dogma despite the fact that it is not a formal article in the Nicene Creed, see Mark DeVine, "Can the Church Emerge without or with Only the Nicene Creed?," in *Evangelicals and Nicene Faith: Reclaiming the Apostolic Witness*, ed. Timothy George, Beeson Divinity Studies (Grand Rapids: Baker Academic, 2011), 190–95.
26. Flemming, *Contextualization in the New Testament*, 297, 300.
27. See Darrell L. Guder, *The Continuing Conversion of the Church*, The Gospel and Our Culture Series (Grand Rapids: Eerdmans, 2000), 29–30, 44–48.

I must acknowledge that the discussion presented here will take us deeper into the rabbit hole, requiring of us a significant amount of missiological reflection. And yet I urge that the reader press ahead, since this is the path that leads to the missional faithfulness God desires and deserves.

First, let's define what we mean when we speak of the contextualization of the Christian gospel. At the risk of oversimplification, to contextualize the gospel is to communicate the Jesus story in a way that proves to be both *comprehensible* and *compelling* to the members of a particular people group. Obviously, a primary goal in Christian proclamation is to enable those with whom we are sharing the message of Christ to understand it. But mere comprehension, as important as this is, is not the only goal. A presentation of the gospel can be comprehensible without proving compelling. A fully adequate gospel contextualization will help people hear and receive the Christian message as *good news*—such good news that it must be embraced and acted upon at all costs (cf. Matt. 13:44–46). In other words, our aim should be a presentation of the Jesus story that is not only coherent but existentially relevant and impactful as well. For this to occur, the Christian message must address the existential questions and needs of the members of the target audience in a way that causes them to view it as wonderfully "good news" despite any challenges it presents to the way of life currently occurring within their cultural context.[28]

At the same, however, a compelling presentation of the Jesus story will not require that hearers entirely disavow their indigenous cultural heritage before they are able to understand, embrace, and live into the good news. A fully *contextualized* gospel presentation will enable those who receive the message and become Christ's followers to do so while retaining their current cultural identity. This is the idea behind this more nuanced definition of ministry contextualization provided by Michael Frost and Alan Hirsch:

> Contextualization, then, can be defined as the dynamic process whereby the constant message of the gospel interacts with specific, relative human situations. It involves an examination of the gospel in light of the respondent's worldview and then adapting the message, encoding it in such a way that it can become meaningful to the respondent. Contextualization attempts to communicate the gospel in word and deed and to establish churches in ways that make sense to people within their local cultural context. It is primarily concerned with presenting Christianity in such a way that it meets peoples' deepest needs and

28. See Robert J. Schreiter, *The New Catholicity: Theology between the Global and the Local* (Maryknoll, NY: Orbis Books, 1997), 1–2.

penetrates their worldviews, thus allowing them to follow Christ and remain in their own cultures.[29]

But since, as they say, the devil is in the details, a trio of important caveats is immediately called for. First, a compelling presentation of the gospel, while culturally sensitive, will not feel the need to completely ignore any genuine incompatibilities that exist between the revealed heart of God for his creation and the socio-ethical-religious conditions on the ground in this or that ministry context. Karl Barth was careful to remind missional theologians and practitioners that, even though the process of contextualization requires a sensitivity to and understanding of the felt needs among the members of the target audience, the gospel must not be accommodated to these felt needs. Indeed, genuine Christian mission will at times tell a "man to his face, that he misunderstands his own deep needs."[30]

Second, we must never forget that the end goal of Jesus's incarnational ministry was not merely to identify with sinful humanity but to redeem, heal, and re-create it. This means that a biblically informed and theologically astute attempt at ministry contextualization will be accompanied by a hope and expectation that the transformational dynamic Paul looked for in the lives of fully devoted Christ followers can and will affect not only the personal lives of those we share the gospel with but eventually their sociocultural environments (home, neighborhood, workplace, etc.) as well.

Third, and perhaps even more importantly, though we possess a certain flexibility in the way we explain how the Jesus story spells good news for different cultural settings, the *essential* meaning of the gospel is not up for grabs. I contend that, per Jude 3, it is never permissible to deny or even downplay the four christological verities in the attempt to make the Jesus story more palatable or acceptable to a target audience!

The Case for a Third Contextualization Option

I also contend that a missional faithfulness must therefore entail a biblically supported alternative to a *noncontextualization* of the gospel, on the one hand, and an *overcontextualization*, on the other. The third alternative I have in mind is referred to by some scholars as *recontextualization*. This approach calls for genuine ministry contextualization but doesn't involve

29. Frost and Hirsch, *Shaping of Things to Come*, 83.

30. Karl Barth, "Questions Which 'Christianity' Must Face," *Student World* 25, no. 1 (1932): 98, cited in John G. Flett, *The Witness of God: The Trinity, Missio Dei, Karl Barth, and the Nature of Christian Community* (Grand Rapids: Eerdmans, 2010), 85.

a wholesale *revisioning* (i.e., revising) of the gospel to make it palatable or acceptable to this or that people group. A recontextualization of the gospel is not a revisioning of the gospel but a *re-envisioning* of it. It involves taking a fresh, prayerful look at the Jesus story while at the same time keeping in mind the hopes, fears, imaginations, fascinations, modes of intellection, and social ethos of the people we are endeavoring to reach with the story. While the heart of the gospel—the four christological verities—never changes, the way we explain why and how the Jesus story spells good news for the people in this or that cultural milieu does. Thus, we are recontextualizing each time we share the gospel, endeavoring to present it in a way that is both understandable and existentially impactful to the people we are in conversation with.

The good news is that, if we let him, Jesus will mentor us in how we should communicate his story in this or that ministry moment. Indeed, our embrace of a christological and pneumatological realism means that, more often than we may realize, the risen Christ may speak and act through us into the lives of our pre- and post-Christian peers in a prophetic (Spirit-enabled) manner.[31] It is not going too far to say that a realist rather than nonrealist understanding and experience of Christ and his Spirit will take our engagement in missional ministry to a whole new level.[32]

The Connection between a Missional Faithfulness and Christ's Incarnation

Moving even deeper into the weeds, to do the concept of a missional faithfulness before God full justice, we must engage another critical topic: the vital importance of an *incarnational* ministry approach. More than one missional author has referred to Christ's incarnation as the best way to understand the biblical model for the contextualization of the Christian faith in a new location.[33]

Most treatments of this type focus on some of the last words Jesus spoke to his apostles: "As the Father has sent me, I am sending you" (John 20:21).

31. See Matt. 10:19–20; Mark 13:10–11; Luke 12:11–12; 21:12–15; Acts 1:8; Eph. 6:19.
32. For a more in-depth discussion of what I have in mind here, see Tyra, *Holy Spirit in Mission*, 129–58.
33. See, e.g., Ross Hastings, *Missional God, Missional Church: Hope for Re-evangelizing the West* (Downers Grove, IL: IVP Academic, 2012), 38, 82, 148–89; Guder, *Missional Church*, 11, 14; Roxburgh and Boren, *Introducing the Missional Church*, 32; Frost and Hirsch, *Shaping of Things to Come*, 35–41; Alan Hirsch, *The Forgotten Ways: Reactivating the Missional Church* (Grand Rapids: Brazos, 2006), 128–29, 131–47.

This dominical saying suggests that we would do well to give some careful consideration to the significance of Christ's incarnation for his own gospel contextualization ministry.

Defining Incarnational Ministry

According to one Christian missions expert, "The most effective witness the church makes will always be in the lives of those who in Christ's name bury themselves in the lives and struggles of another people, missionaries who serve the people, learn to speak their language, develop the capacity to feel their hurt and hunger, and who learn to love them personally and individually."[34] Thus, when used in a missional sense, the concept of incarnationalism, at the very least, encourages Christian missionaries to emulate the way Jesus made ministry an up-close-and-personal rather than impersonal endeavor. Rather than engage in ministry from a distance or in a drive-by manner, Jesus came near. Indeed, according to John 1:14, in order to redemptively communicate God's grace and truth to a world filled with divine image-bearing men and women estranged from him, Jesus not only tabernacled, or pitched his tent, among them but also assumed their fleshly condition (see Rom. 8:3; Phil. 2:6–8).

When referring to Christ's incarnation, the author of the Letter to the Hebrews emphasizes the manner in which it enables a sensitivity to and empathy for our human condition (Heb. 2:14–18; 4:15). Thus, it is not uncommon for missiologists to suggest that an incarnational approach to ministry calls for Christ's followers, like their Lord, to identify with and live among the people God has sent them to minister to. It is by our identifying with and living among our contemporaries—and doing so in Christ's name—that we become able, through Christ's Spirit, to adequately communicate the Father's heart to them. Therefore, to speak of an incarnational approach to ministry is neither theologically naive nor presumptive. It does, however, call for Christ's missional agents to *partner with him* in his ongoing ministry to the world rather than view their call to ministry as somehow separate from his. Inspired by Jesus's willingness to radically identify with humanity in general and empowered by his Spirit to do so, we may proclaim the gospel of Jesus to particular people groups in ways that resonate with them, that cause them to sense the reality of the risen Christ in and through us.

34. This quotation is from M. Theron Rankin, a former president of what is now the International Mission Board of the Southern Baptist Convention, cited in Alan Neely, "Incarnational Mission," in *Evangelical Dictionary of World Missions*, ed. A. Scott Moreau, Baker Reference Library (Grand Rapids: Baker Academic, 2000), 475.

Nuancing Incarnational Ministry

And yet incarnationalism in ministry is not simply about identifying with our cultural peers. Jesus assumed human flesh and embedded himself in a particular culture, but he did not "go native," becoming in every way like those to whom he proclaimed the good news. In addition to divine *grace*, he also embodied in his humanity divine *truth* (John 1:17–18).

We have already acknowledged that the hope of genuine *transformation* should earmark our engagement in gospel contextualization. This is because a focus on the incarnational approach to ministry modeled by Jesus indicates that the contextualization endeavor actually involves three critical dynamics: *identification, differentiation,* and *transformation.* The incarnate Christ did not take on human flesh simply to identify with human beings but to heal and transform their sinful humanity through his death and resurrection. As the apostle Peter puts it, "'He himself bore our sins' in his body on the cross, so that we might die to sins and live for righteousness; 'by his wounds you have been healed'" (1 Pet. 2:24).

The Relationship between Incarnation and Transformation in Christ's Ministry

In other words, the incarnation—the joining of the divine with the human in Christ—was crucial to his twin ministries of *revelation* and *redemption.*[35] On the one hand, for Jesus to fully *reveal* to the world who God is and what he is about, he had to be God himself rather than simply similar to him (see John 1:18; Heb. 1:3). On the other hand, for Jesus to *redeem*—to *reconcile* to God an estranged humanity by means of his sacrificial, substitutionary death on the cross—he had to be fully human himself (see 2 Cor. 5:21; Heb. 2:14–15). A saying made famous by an early church father puts it this way: "For that which He has not assumed He has not healed."[36]

It is precisely because the eternal Son of God assumed our human nature in his incarnation that he could heal it in his death and resurrection. Put differently, as the framers of the Niceno-Constantinopolitan Creed understood, the radically wonderful transformation we experience as Christ's followers is due to Jesus of Nazareth possessing both a fully human nature and a fully divine nature at the same time. With this thought in mind, we might rephrase the formula thusly: a real *transformation* of human beings required not only

35. See Roger E. Olson, *The Mosaic of Christian Belief: Twenty Centuries of Unity and Diversity* (Downers Grove, IL: IVP Academic, 2002), 236, 242.

36. Gregory Nazianzen, *The Sacred Writings of Gregory Nazianzen,* trans. Charles Gordon Brown and James Edward Swallow (Altenmünster, Germany: Jazzybee, 2017), 238.

Jesus's human nature by which he *identified* with humanity in a radically costly way, but also his divine nature by which he *differentiated himself*, revealing to humanity who God really is and then dying a sacrificial, substitutionary death that would prove salvific for every human being who would receive him as Lord (Rom. 3:25; 1 Cor. 15:1–3; 1 John 2:2; 4:10). There was something very powerful about the combination of *identification* and *differentiation* at work in the incarnate Christ; it made possible the phenomenon of genuine *transformation*.

A Closer Look at the Human and Divine in Missional Ministry

This discussion of the importance of the mystical union of Christ's divine and human natures for the efficacy of his ministry is pertinent also to the missional ministry engaged in by his followers. As with Jesus's own ministry, ours needs to possess both a human and a divine component.

First, as already indicated, an incarnational ministry approach requires that we fully *identify* with the people to whom we are sent, just as Jesus did (this is the human side of the ministry dynamic). We do this by taking very seriously the *conditions on the ground* in this and that ministry context. These conditions include not only the socio-ethical-religious realities that the people we are ministering to have been influenced by but also the resulting hopes, fears, and core beliefs that have hitherto determined how they have understood themselves and lived their lives. Put simply, our goal must be to genuinely understand those we have been called by God to minister to—to understand them from the inside out, to understand them better, perhaps, than they understand themselves. To do this we must not only live with them but listen to them as they tell us their stories, even when their stories contain references to the ways they have been hurt by Christians, the church, and God himself. We listen anyway, without becoming defensive. In the process, we evidence care and concern and earn the right to speak and act into their lives.

Second, an incarnational approach requires that we, like Jesus, embody in our message and our manner the dynamic of *differentiation* that is required for real, salvific, transformational change to occur (this is the divine side of the ministry dynamic). We boldly (yet humbly) announce that the message we are sharing is not of human origin. It is instead the gospel of God: the gospel that alone possesses the power to save (Rom. 1:16) and transform (see 2 Cor. 3:18).

Moreover, we are careful in our proclamation of the gospel to do more than encourage an allegiance to an idea about God or to a set of religious rules and rituals. Instead, we keep emphasizing the amazingly good news that it is possible through the work of the Holy Spirit for those who hear and embrace the Jesus story to enter into a genuine, real, existentially impactful relationship with the risen Jesus himself!

What's more, we humbly point to and evidence the life-story-shaping effect the gospel of God has already had, and is having, on us, his messengers. Having earned the right to speak into the lives of our friends, family members, neighbors, coworkers, and others, we share *our* stories. Never claiming to have arrived (Phil. 3:12), we nevertheless indicate the reasons for the hope we possess that even more experiences of transformation are in the offing (see Eph. 1:18; cf. 1 Pet. 3:15). In this way, we provide our friends, family members, neighbors, coworkers, and so forth with something very precious: a hope that is both existential and eschatological—that is, a hope for a better life here and now and a hope for a blessed and meaningful existence in the age to come.[37]

Incarnational Ministry: The Bottom Line

In sum, the goal of our "incarnational" attempts at ministry should be to see individuals and their sociocultural environments reconciled to God and then transformed in God-pleasing ways. That Jesus did this by embedding himself deeply within a particular historical-cultural context, while maintaining his integrity as the divine Son of God, should be instructive for us who are sent to do ministry in his name. Put simply, just as the incarnation of Christ was indispensable to God's plan to redeem his creation, so is an incarnational approach to the contextualization of the Jesus story indispensable for each person or people group God sends us to!

The Key to Our Incarnational Ministry: A Missional Spirituality!

The discussion above is likely to produce in us a version of Paul's exclamation: "Who is equal to such a task?" (2 Cor. 2:16). And rightly so, since the three critical dynamics at the heart of an incarnational ministry—*identification, differentiation, transformation*—do not simply happen. While they are Spirit enabled, some significant cooperation with the Holy Spirit on the part of Christ's followers is required (see 2 Cor. 3:5–6).

The good news is that we can do this! However, for this to happen, "we gotta commit!" Specifically, we must commit not only to the cultivation of

---

37. The New Testament contains several references to the reality and importance of the "age to come." See, e.g., Matt. 12:32; 28:19–20; Gal. 1:3–5; Eph. 1:18–21; 1 Tim. 6:17–19; Titus 2:11–14; Heb. 6:4–6.

a God-the-Father-pleasing lifestyle, nor only to the task of rendering to him a missional faithfulness, but also to the cultivation of a special kind of spirituality—one that enables the incarnational identification-differentiation-transformation ministry dynamic. If our aim is to please the God of the Bible, we simply must commit to the cultivation of a *missional spirituality*—a lifestyle spirituality that is intentionally and thoroughly missional in its orientation and performance. A God-the-Father-pleasing lifestyle spirituality will necessarily play out as a missional spirituality, one that has the effect of creating missional Christians and communities that emulate the identification-differentiation-transformation dynamic of Jesus's incarnational ministry.

The history of the Christian movement indicates that the cultivation of a missionally faithful lifestyle and spirituality is possible. But since it is in part 3 of this book that we will talk turkey about what is involved in honoring or actualizing all three of the crucial core commitments we have discussed here in part 2, I will hit the pause button at this point and simply inquire more generally: "So, how's your core?" How sturdy are the muscles that make up the midsection of your spirituality? How are you doing at present with respect to keeping in step with the Spirit, pursuing the empowering presence of Christ, and living your life in a missionally faithful, God-pleasing manner?

Regardless of how you are doing at present, I urge you not to despair. We have every reason to believe that the God we are so *eager to please* is himself *eager and pleased* to help us do just that. Thus, I offer this prayer from Paul: "May our Lord Jesus Christ himself and God our Father, who loved us and by his grace gave us eternal encouragement and good hope, encourage your hearts and strengthen you in every good deed and word" (2 Thess. 2:16–17). Also appropriate is this benediction from the Letter to the Hebrews: "Now may the God of peace, who through the blood of the eternal covenant brought back from the dead our Lord Jesus, that great Shepherd of the sheep, equip you with everything good for doing his will, and may he work in us what is pleasing to him, through Jesus Christ, to whom be glory for ever and ever. Amen" (Heb. 13:20–21).

With these words of hope and encouragement ringing in our ears, let's press on to the final phase of our journey down the rabbit hole. It is in part 3 of this book that the *convictions* and *commitments* at the foundation and core of a Pauline "I-Thou" lifestyle spirituality come together as we identify the *theologically real* lifestyle *customs* that such a spirituality entails. Indeed, we should probably buckle up. A whole bunch of things are about to get very, very real!

TOPICS FOR REVIEW

1. What are your thoughts about this chapter's suggestion that those who truncate God's mission by emphasizing *only* disciple making *or* social action *or* creation care need to take a step back and consider the possibility that, in truth, it includes a concern for all three endeavors?

2. What are your thoughts about this chapter's insistence that an engagement in the proclamation or sharing of the gospel (good news) concerning Jesus Christ toward the making of disciples should be considered primary and essentially foundational to pursuing God's mission?

3. As it relates to the proclamation of the gospel, how would you explain to someone the difference between the noncontextualization, overcontextualization, and recontextualization options?

4. How would you articulate the importance this chapter places on the dynamic of *identification* in incarnational ministry? *Differentiation*? *Transformation*?

5. How would you summarize for someone what this chapter considers to be the "bottom line" or "goal" of incarnational ministry?

6. The final section of this chapter alludes to the need for a lifestyle spirituality that is "intentionally and thoroughly missional in its orientation and performance," and that "enables the incarnational identification-differentiation-transformation ministry dynamic." In honesty, if such a spirituality were actually possible, how eager would you be to embody it? Why or why not?

PART THREE

The *Customs* (Fruit) of a Christian Lifestyle Spirituality

6

REALLY PRAYING WITHOUT CEASING

Who Knew?

> There is no mode of life in the world more pleasing and more full of delight
> than continual conversation with God.
>
> —Brother Lawrence, *The Practice of the Presence of God*

There seems to be an online tutorial for just about everything these days. Have you ever benefited from a do-it-yourself (DIY) video? I have—more than once.

Collectively, the next three chapters of this book are meant to provide some practical counsel on how to cultivate a Pauline "I-Thou" lifestyle spirituality. Having examined in part 1 the theological *convictions* that are necessary for such a spirituality and in part 2 the three lifestyle *commitments* that form the core of the spirituality, we turn our attention now to some day-to-day *customs* that, if employed, will enable us to honor those commitments and live out a Christ-emulating, Spirit-empowered, God-the-Father-pleasing lifestyle spirituality.

In this chapter, we will focus on some customs associated with the foundational commitment we have made to keep in step with the Spirit. The realist rather than nonrealist pneumatology we discussed in chapter 1 leads us to believe it must be possible for Christ's followers to do Galatians 5:24–25—that is, to develop the righteous habit of saying no to the flesh and yes to Christ's Spirit. But how does one do this day-to-day so that it plays out as a lifestyle? This is the key question that is addressed in this chapter. And since, as we will soon see, one spirituality practice seems to have been central to Paul's own spirituality—namely, prayer—some additional attention will be paid to it. These are the issues this chapter will explore as we begin to talk turkey about how to heed Paul's call to a lifestyle spirituality. Consider this to be the first of the DIY discussions that part 3 of this work provides.

Tips on Keeping in Step with the Spirit

Let's start with some "pro" tips on keeping in step with the Spirit. Of course, I'm speaking tongue in cheek when I refer to myself as a pro. The fact is, I'm on the same journey as everyone reading this book. At the same time, it's also true that I have been on the journey for a while, and the importance of keeping in step with the Spirit has been a prominent theme in my preaching, teaching, and writing for several years.[1] This discussion delves deeper, however, identifying several key actions that can be taken *daily* to improve our ability to say yes to the Holy Spirit's leadership in our lives. While I will do my best here not to provide any "tips" in an overly triumphalist manner, the reader should be aware that a genuine embrace of a trinitarian realism cannot help but infuse a biblically informed discussion of this topic with huge amounts of spiritual confidence and hope. So, with that being said, let's get the tutorial started.

Greeting, Acknowledging, and Realizing the Spirit

According to the Scriptures, merely acknowledging God is a big deal.[2] One passage seems to stand out in bold relief. The prophet Hosea urges ancient Israel thusly: "Let us *acknowledge* the Lord; let us press on to *acknowledge* him. As surely as the sun rises, he will appear; *he will come to us* like the winter rains, like the spring rains that water the earth" (Hosea 6:3). For sure,

---

1. See, e.g., Gary Tyra, *The Holy Spirit in Mission: Prophetic Speech and Action in Christian Witness* (Downers Grove, IL: IVP Academic, 2011), 32; Tyra, *Pursuing Moral Faithfulness: Ethics and Christian Discipleship* (Downers Grove, IL: IVP Academic, 2015), 275; Tyra, *Getting Real: Pneumatological Realism and the Spiritual, Moral, and Ministry Formation of Contemporary Christians* (Eugene, OR: Cascade Books, 2018), 3, 6, 131; and Tyra, *The Dark Side of Discipleship: Why and How the New Testament Encourages Christians to Deal with the Devil* (Eugene, OR: Cascade Books, 2020), 89, 122, 166, 193, 195.

2. See, e.g., Deut. 4:39–40; 1 Chron. 28:9; Pss. 79:6; 87:4; Isa. 19:21; Jer. 9:3, 6; Hosea 2:20; 5:4; 6:3; 8:2; 13:4; Matt. 10:32; Luke 12:8; Rom. 1:18–23; 14:11; Heb. 3:1; 1 John 4:3.

the historical context of this passage has to do with circumstances other than the devotional beginning of one's day. That said, it cannot be denied that the prophet was convinced that a connection exists between the act of acknowledging God and his coming to us—that is, the experience of his empowering presence.[3] I have found that this principle seems to hold true in my spirituality. As basic as it may seem, a requirement for a realist rather than nonrealist walk with God requires a daily acknowledgment of his reality, glory, and faithfulness toward those who belong to him (see Heb. 11:6).

To be sure, the act of acknowledging or "realizing" God should be engaged in throughout one's day rather than only at the beginning of it (see Ps. 89:15–16).[4] (In chap. 7, we will discuss what an ongoing experience of Christ's empowering presence would seem to entail.) At the same time, I have found that an initial act of *greeting* (acknowledging) God each day is especially important.

To be clear, I am not suggesting that this greeting either conjures God's presence or suggests that he has now become proximate in a way he wasn't before. The apostle Paul affirms that all human beings live and move and have their being "in him" (Acts 17:28). Psychiatrist and spiritual-life author Gerald May reminds us that this is why theologians such as Augustine and mystics such as Teresa of Ávila and John of the Cross have maintained that "God is closer to us than we are to our very selves."[5] May says, "The problem for most of us is that we don't *realize* how united we are with God. . . . Even if we believe devoutly that God is present with us, our usual experience is that we are 'here' and God is 'there,' loving and gracious perhaps, but irrevocably separate."[6] May goes on to express that "The spiritual life for Teresa and John has nothing to do with actually getting closer to God. It is instead a journey of *consciousness*. Union with God is neither acquired or achieved; it is *realized*, and in that sense it is something that can be yearned for, sought after, and—with God's grace—found."[7]

Thus, I am in the habit of greeting or acknowledging the Lord most mornings the way I would any other "thou" in my life. Trite as it may seem, one of my spirituality practices is to reckon with the reality of our trinitarian God (Father, Son, and Holy Spirit) by prayerfully uttering the phrase "Good

---

3. Duane A. Garrett, *Hosea, Joel*, New American Commentary 19A (Nashville: Broadman & Holman, 1997), 159.

4. See also Pss. 25:5; 35:28; 44:8; 71:8, 15, 24; 86:3.

5. See Gerald G. May, *The Dark Night of the Soul: A Psychiatrist Explores the Connection between Darkness and Spiritual Growth* (New York: HarperSanFrancisco, 2004), 43.

6. May, *Dark Night of the Soul*, 44 (emphasis original).

7. May, *Dark Night of the Soul*, 46–47 (emphasis original).

morning, Lord" as early in the day as possible. All I can say is that doing so helps me begin the process of becoming centered, existentially grounded, and more alert to him than I would have been otherwise. If this is how I greet other important persons in my life, why wouldn't I greet God this way as well? A theological realism veritably demands that I do so.

Surrendering to the Spirit

It is one thing to greet the Spirit; it is another to genuinely surrender the control of one's being to him, to yield oneself to his leadership, influence, and direction. We have already taken note of how the apostle Paul's exhortation that his readers "be filled with the Spirit" (Eph. 5:18) is best translated in a way that connotes ongoing action (cf. Acts 4:8, 31; 13:9). Apparently, Paul was encouraging the church members in Ephesus to be continually "filled with the Spirit." As we have already discovered, because the Greek verb Paul uses in Ephesians 5:18 when instructing his readers to "be filled" with the Spirit is present imperative in its tense and mood, "the practical implication is that the Christian is to leave his life open to be filled constantly and repeatedly by the divine Spirit."[8]

Something else we have already noted is Paul's awareness that the work of the Spirit in our lives, far from being automatic, can be *resisted* (Acts 7:51), *grieved* (Eph. 4:30), *rejected* (1 Thess. 4:8), and *quenched* (1 Thess. 5:19). This too suggests the need for an ongoing *surrender* to the leadership of the Spirit in our lives. Thus, my daily custom is also to utter a foundational prayer of *resurrender*, inviting the Holy Spirit to once again fill me, control me, and lead me (see Ps. 143:10).

More precisely, I have Jesus as well as the Holy Spirit in mind when I pray in this manner each day. This invitational invocation essentially goes something like this: "Come, Spirit of God, take control of me. Let Jesus be big in me. May everyone I interact with today sense him in and through me." While I do not have a problem addressing the Holy Spirit in prayer, I am also aware that it is Christ's Spirit I am interacting with and that the Spirit's greatest desire is to glorify, manifest, promote Jesus (see John 16:12–14). The bottom line is that whenever I interact with the Holy Spirit, I have the risen Christ also in view, and I am ever mindful of the connection between the first two commitments at the core of a lifestyle spirituality: (1) our keeping in step with the Spirit

8. Francis Foulkes, *Ephesians*, Tyndale New Testament Commentaries (Downers Grove, IL: InterVarsity, 1983), 152. See also James D. G. Dunn, *Jesus and the Spirit: A Study of the Religious and Charismatic Experience of Jesus and the First Christians as Reflected in the New Testament* (Grand Rapids: Eerdmans, 1997), 193.

and (2) thereby our being empowered to experience a moment-by-moment mentoring relationship with the risen Jesus.

Finally, please don't construe my references to *daily* customs to mean that I perform these prayers only once every twenty-four hours. In truth, the importance to my own spirituality of this "prayer of surrender" just referred to is evidenced by how often I offer it each day, which is multiple times: whenever I sense the need for the Spirit's empowerment in this or that situation.

I interacted recently with a young minister who, having taken a class with me, was eager to gain some insight into my spirituality. Our conversation indicated that he had fallen prey to a debilitating false antithesis: the notion that Christian disciples must choose to be primarily about the Scriptures or the Spirit. I spoke to him of the possibility of being about both. Though this is such a simple suggestion, it seemed revelatory—even liberating—to him.

We don't have to choose between being people of the Word or people of the Spirit. We can and must be both! But this requires more than a commitment to the authority of the Scriptures; we must also surrender ourselves repeatedly to the leadership of the Spirit who inspired those Scriptures (2 Tim. 3:16). This spiritual equipoise I've tried to maintain over the years has been advocated by many brilliant theologians, including the eminent Karl Barth (1886–1968), who spoke eloquently of its payoff—the spiritual and ministry "freedom" that is only experienced when one is surrendered to both the Word and Spirit of Christ. Barth wrote:

> To receive the Spirit, to have the Spirit, to live in the Spirit *means being set free and being permitted to live in freedom. . . .* To have inner ears for the Word of Christ, to become thankful for His work and at the same time responsible for the message about Him and, lastly, to take confidence in men for Christ's sake—*that is the freedom which we obtain, when Christ breathes on us, when He sends us His Holy Spirit.* If He no longer lives in a historical or heavenly, a theological or ecclesiastical remoteness from me, *if He approaches me and takes possession of me,* the result will be that I hear, that I am thankful and responsible and that finally I may hope for myself and for all others; in other words, that *I may live in a Christian way.* It is a tremendously big thing and by no means a matter of course, to obtain this *freedom.* We must therefore every day and every hour pray *Veni Creator Spiritus* [Come, Creator Spirit] in listening to the word of Christ and in thankfulness. That is a closed circle. We do not "have" this freedom; it is again and again given to us by God.[9]

9. Karl Barth, *Dogmatics in Outline* (New York: Harper & Row, 1959), 138–39 (emphasis added).

I could tell this young minister was appreciatively tracking with me at this point in our conversation. Therefore, after speaking to him of my *ongoing* habit of resurrendering myself to the influence, leadership, and assistance of Christ's Spirit, I proceeded to unpack for him a third "keeping-in-step" custom.

Praying in the Spirit

The special importance to Paul's lifestyle spirituality of one prayer practice in particular was referred to in chapter 3. As promised, we will explore here the nature of that prayer custom and how to cultivate it in our own lives.

For the sake of argument, let's concede that the apostle Paul's several references to ongoing or continual prayer (e.g., 1 Thess. 5:17; Phil. 4:6) might have contained some hyperbole for effect. But rather than conclude that these exhortations are not to be taken seriously, we should consider the possibility that there really is a way for prayer to become an especially prominent and impactful feature of our day-to-day lives. I have in mind here the spirituality practice known as "praying in the Spirit."

To review, the phenomenon of Spirit-enabled prayer is referred to several times in the New Testament, principally by the apostle Paul but also in the Epistle of Jude. In addition to a couple of passages in which Paul indicates that it is the Spirit who assures Christ's followers of their familial status before God by inspiring them to pray in an "I-Thou" manner (Rom. 8:15; Gal. 4:6), the apostle also provides the readers of his Letter to the Romans with these profound words of encouragement: "In the same way, the Spirit helps us in our weakness. We do not know what we ought to pray for, but the Spirit himself intercedes for us through wordless groans" (Rom. 8:26).

Moreover, Paul refers to this practice again at the conclusion of his "armor of God" discussion located in Ephesians 6:10–20. In that "classic spiritual warfare passage,"[10] Paul exhorts his readers thusly: "And pray *in the Spirit on all occasions* with all kinds of prayers and requests. With this in mind, be alert and *always keep on praying* for all the Lord's people. Pray also for me, that whenever I speak, words may be given me so that I will fearlessly make known the mystery of the gospel, for which I am an ambassador in chains. Pray that I may declare it fearlessly, as I should" (Eph. 6:18–20). The significance Paul attaches to the Holy Spirit in his armor of God discussion

---

10. Clinton E. Arnold, *3 Crucial Questions about Spiritual Warfare* (Grand Rapids: Baker Academic, 1997), 37, 120. See also David Powlison, "The Classical Model," in *Understanding Spiritual Warfare: Four Views*, ed. James K. Beilby and Paul Rhodes Eddy (Grand Rapids: Baker Academic, 2012), 92.

as a whole,[11] when combined with the way he concludes this discussion by exhorting his readers to *pray in the Spirit* "on all occasions" and "always," essentially mandates that we seek to understand the role such praying may play in the cultivation of a lifestyle spirituality. But, of course, this presumes an awareness of what praying in the Spirit involves.

Some have suggested that all Paul has in mind when he refers to praying "in the Spirit" is unscripted, extemporaneous prayer or praying in an especially fervent manner.[12] But these perspectives do not take into account the way Paul practiced this type of prayer himself, which appears to have been decidedly charismatic and prophetic in nature.[13] Not a few reputable New Testament scholars are willing to acknowledge that when Paul refers to praying in the Spirit he has in mind the phenomenon of *glossolalic* prayer—namely, praying in tongues (see 1 Cor. 14:2, 14–19).[14] For example, the way Paul speaks in Romans 8:26 of how the Spirit "intercedes for us through wordless groans"— suggesting as it does a kind of praying that is directly and immediately enabled by the Spirit[15]—leads New Testament scholar James Dunn to concede, "There is a praying which is determined wholly by the Spirit, where the words and sentiments come to the pray-er's lips as given from God—inspired utterance. That is the implication in 1 Cor. 11.4f., 13, where praying and prophesying are probably both to be thought of as charismatic speech."[16]

Moreover, commenting on the reference to praying in the Spirit in Jude 20, evangelical biblical scholar Bruce Barton writes, "The Holy Spirit prays on behalf of believers (Romans 8:26–27; Galatians 4:6; Ephesians 6:18), opens their minds to Jesus (John 14:26), and teaches believers more about their Lord (John 15:26). This most likely includes, but is not limited to, prayer in tongues."[17] We must therefore at least consider the possibility that what Paul had in mind in

11. For a thorough discussion of the importance of the Spirit for Paul's armor of God discussion, see Tyra, *Dark Side of Discipleship*, 163–96.

12. See, e.g., Gregory Brown, *The Armor of God: Standing Firm in Spiritual Warfare*, 2nd ed. (n.p.: BTG, 2017), 91–105. See also Brian Borgman and Rob Ventura, *Spiritual Warfare: A Biblical and Balanced Perspective* (Grand Rapids: Reformation Heritage Books, 2014), 90–92; Joel R. Beeke, *Fighting Satan: Knowing His Weaknesses, Strategies, and Defeat* (Grand Rapids: Reformation Heritage Books, 2015), 56–58.

13. See Dunn, *Jesus and the Spirit*, 239.

14. See, e.g., Dunn, *Jesus and the Spirit*, 245; Gordon D. Fee, *God's Empowering Presence: The Holy Spirit in the Letters of Paul* (Peabody, MA: Hendrickson, 1994), 731; F. F. Bruce, *Romans*, Tyndale New Testament Commentaries (Downers Grove, IL: InterVarsity, 1985), 165; C. K. Barrett, *The Epistle to the Romans*, Harper's New Testament Commentaries (New York: Harper & Row, 1957), 164, 168.

15. Dunn, *Jesus and the Spirit*, 241.

16. Dunn, *Jesus and the Spirit*, 239.

17. Bruce B. Barton, *1 Peter, 2 Peter, Jude*, Life Application Bible Commentary (Wheaton: Tyndale House, 1995), 258–59.

his multiple references to praying in the Spirit was a pneumatologically real type of praying that involves not only our being sensitive to the Spirit but the Spirit praying through us in a prophetic manner.[18]

At the same time, it is also possible to argue that the Spirit can pray through us by means of literal "wordless groans."[19] In 1 Corinthians 14:2 and 14 and Romans 8:26, the apostle seems to be describing a kind of praying that neither originates in nor is limited by human understanding. Thus, a realist reading of these Pauline passages would suggest the possibility that a genuine partnering in prayer with the Spirit can occur whether it is by means of *glossolalia* or literal *wordless groans*. In both prayer methods, the Spirit of Christ is praying *through* the disciple.[20] Perhaps, therefore, there is reason to believe that both are pathways to a prophetic, empowering interaction with God![21]

Going further, it is this pneumatologically real understanding of praying in the Spirit that seems to best explain why Paul can suggest in Ephesians 6:18 that it can be practiced in an "on all occasions," "always" manner. For sure, prayer that is a purely human endeavor will require a level of concentration (cognitive focus) that will make the practice of "continual" prayer a literal impossibility. But according to some neurolinguistic research that will be referred to later in this chapter, there is also a type of prayer that is more visceral in nature, that does not originate in one's intellect, and that therefore doesn't require huge amounts of human concentration. This kind of praying can occur throughout one's waking moments, between and even during the busiest seasons of the day.[22]

I have found that praying in this way engenders a sort of *visceral, hopeful agonizing* before the Lord as we enter into a fresh season of "waiting" on him with listening ears and a receptive heart (see, e.g., Pss. 77:1–4; 123:1–2).[23] Whether this type of prayer takes the form of glossolalia or a "sighing too deep for words" or both, it will ultimately manifest itself as a prayerful *mood* that lingers even as we engage in necessary activities. In other words, it is possible to develop the habit of turning to God in the way I have just described

18. For more on the role the Spirit plays in the prophetic dynamic, see Tyra, *Holy Spirit in Mission*, 40–74; Tyra, *Pursuing Moral Faithfulness*, 166–67.

19. See, e.g., Dunn, *Jesus and the Spirit*, 241. See also Arthur Wallis, *Pray in the Spirit* (Fort Washington, PA: CLC, 1970), 95–96.

20. See Dunn, *Jesus and the Spirit*, 241.

21. Dunn, *Jesus and the Spirit*, 241. See also Tyra, *Dark Side of Discipleship*, 192.

22. I will have more to say later in this chapter about the notion that "praying in the Spirit" is essentially a right-brain rather than left-brain activity and the implications of this for a Christian lifestyle spirituality.

23. See also Num. 9:8; Pss. 5:3; 27:14; 33:20; 38:15; 40:1; 130:5–6; Isa. 30:18; 40:30–31; Lam. 3:24–26; Mic. 7:7.

at various times during the day (see Ps. 55:17). The result can be a prayerful *posture* or *state of being* that is virtually ongoing—a lingering season of hope ful waiting on God that is sustained by occasional yet consonant expressions of *whispered glossolalia* or *wordless groaning*.

The bottom line, it seems to me, is that it is one thing to be aware that a practice called "praying in the Spirit" is referred to in the New Testament, but it is another to reckon with its charismatic, prophetic nature and then open ourselves to it. In his Letter to the Romans, the apostle Paul links this type of praying to the Christian's ability to maintain a sense of hope in the face of present suffering (see Rom. 8:18–39). In his Letter to the Ephesians, Paul connects praying in the Spirit with overcoming the evil one (Eph. 6:10–20). Not unimportant discipleship dynamics, these! Thus, I heartily encourage a realist rather than nonrealist approach to this spirituality practice. Indeed, I contend that an ongoing partnering with the Spirit in prayer is critical to both keeping in step with the Spirit and embodying a Christian lifestyle spirituality.

Listening to the Spirit

In his book *Hearing God*, Dallas Willard boldly announces:

> Today I continue to believe that people are meant to live in an ongoing conversation with God, speaking and being spoken to. Rightly understood I believe that this can be abundantly verified in experience. God's visits to Adam and Eve in the Garden, Enoch's walks with God and the face-to-face conversations between Moses and Jehovah are all commonly regarded as highly exceptional moments in the religious history of humankind. Aside from their obviously unique historical role, however, they are not meant to be exceptional at all. Rather they are examples of the normal human life God intended for us: God's indwelling his people through personal presence and fellowship. Given who we are by basic nature, we live—really live—only through God's regular speaking in our souls and thus "by every word that comes from out of the mouth of God."[24]

The biblical examples of God's speaking directly to his people referred to in this quote are all from the Old Testament; however, the New Testament likewise refers to God's speaking to Jesus and his followers (e.g., Matt. 3:16–17; 17:5; John 12:28; Acts 10:9–16), often by means of his Holy Spirit (e.g., Acts 8:29; 10:19; 11:12; 13:2). Moreover, Jesus promises his followers that, after

---

24. Dallas Willard, *Hearing God: Developing a Conversational Relationship with God* (Downers Grove, IL: InterVarsity, 1999), 18.

his ascension to the right hand of the Father, the Spirit will speak to them on his behalf (John 14:26). Thus, it shouldn't surprise us to find that Paul would later begin an important section of one of his letters with this assertion: "The Spirit clearly says . . ." (1 Tim. 4:1). This is why I contend, fully aware of the debate regarding the degree to which contemporary Christians should expect to experience the Spirit's speaking to them in direct, personal ways, that a robust, realist pneumatology encourages us to develop the spirituality practice of "listening to the Spirit."

This dynamic may occur in various ways as we interpret what we "overhear" the Spirit praying or singing through us (1 Cor. 14:13–17) or as we "hear" the Spirit speaking directly to us through the Scriptures, other disciples, his still small voice, or intuitive promptings (see, e.g., Acts 10:19; 13:2). Regardless of how this is done, the Holy Spirit will, according to Paul, communicate with Christ's followers, enabling them to "understand" some important theological realities and "prompting" them about their ethical decision-making and engagement in mission (see 1 Cor. 2:6–16; Col. 1:9–10). Indeed, it is not going too far to say that rendering to God the threefold faithfulness he is looking for requires that we cultivate a sensitivity to the spiritual, moral, and ministry promptings provided us by the Spirit of Christ.

Sometimes, however, I have had church members or students push back, protesting that they have never experienced the Spirit either "speaking to" or "prompting" them. After suggesting to them the possibility that this prophetic dynamic may have been occurring in their lives but in such a subtle manner that it went unnoticed, I go on to point out how passages such as Proverbs 2:1–6 seem to indicate that two devotional practices need to be in play *at the same time* and *in a theologically real manner* for God's people to effectively receive guidance from him. I suggest that these two crucial spirituality practices involve a fervent crying out to God in prayer (see Prov. 2:3) and a rigorous study of the Scriptures (as if one were searching for buried treasure; see Prov. 2:4). My pastoral experience has been that it is when God's people engage in *both* of these devotional practices at the same time and in theologically real ways that we acquire the "ears" we need to "hear" what Jesus, through the Spirit, is saying to us.

Keeping in mind the charismatic, prophetic nature of Paul's own interactions with the Spirit (1 Cor. 14:1–19; cf. vv. 26–32) and the way he reminds the Galatians of the evidential value of their previous *experiences* with the Spirit (see Gal. 3:1–5), it is hard for me to imagine that his exhortation in Galatians 5:25 to keep in step with the Spirit doesn't presume the need to, in a pneumatologically real manner, be careful to "listen" in an ongoing way to what the Spirit is saying.

Discerning, Obeying, and Trusting the Spirit

Finally, keeping in step with the Spirit is empty of meaning if it doesn't ultimately call for us to *obey* the Spirit's promptings. The idea here is that the Spirit may call us as Christ's followers to do something.

But this call to obey creates a conundrum. Our sense that the Spirit is speaking to us, calling us to believe, say, or do something specific on behalf of the risen and ascended Christ, doesn't guarantee that we have correctly understood what the Spirit is calling for or that the prompting is genuinely from him. Thus, essentially coinciding with the call to *obey* the Spirit is the call to engage in the process of *discernment*.

Discerning the Spirit means doing our due diligence to be as confident as possible that we are genuinely hearing from the Spirit and correctly interpreting his leading. Any sort of prompting by the Spirit, especially if it derives from a sense of God's Spirit speaking directly to our hearts, must be validated against the Scriptures as a whole and against one's community of faith (including the church's rich history of biblical interpretation). It is in this way that we guard against the dynamic of psychological projection—our projecting onto the Spirit promptings that actually originated within our subconscious selves.[25] Even then we need to be careful. My experience has been that while Christ's Spirit can communicate with us by means of a potent inner prompting, such a prompting will always be accompanied by a sense of inner peace rather than fear, dread, anxiety, or panic. We never read of Jesus being driven by these negative impulses.[26] Moreover, a genuine prompting of the Spirit to believe, say, or do something specific at the behest of the risen Jesus will *never*

- disparage or diminish the importance of Jesus (1 Cor. 12:3; 1 John 4:2),
- encourage us to disregard the clear teaching of the Scriptures he inspired (2 Tim. 3:16), or
- call for us to behave in a way that is at odds with the Christ virtues he is committed to producing in us (see Gal. 5:22–25).

I am convinced that these biblically supported criteria can enable us to, with some confidence, qualify (judge as genuinely Christ-emulating and Christ-honoring) any promptings we believe may derive from Christ's Spirit.

Still, the reality is that because discerning the Spirit is a process that always allows for some ambiguity, it can be tempting for some to simply rule

---

25. See Michael F. Bird, *Evangelical Theology: A Biblical and Systematic Introduction* (Grand Rapids: Zondervan, 2013), 73.

26. For more on this, see Tyra, *Holy Spirit in Mission*, 168.

out the possibility that the Spirit can speak directly to church members in a prophetic manner. But the apostle Paul, who knew very well how messy the discernment dynamic sometimes is, does not allow for this option. His instructions are clear: "Do not quench the Spirit. Do not treat prophecies with contempt but *test them all*; hold on to what is good, reject every kind of evil" (1 Thess. 5:19–22).

Mark it down: when it comes to listening to the Spirit, nuance is necessary (cf. 1 John 4:1). What is not permissible, according to Paul, is to embrace a nonrealist pneumatology simply because a realist one sometimes creates ambiguity. Ambiguity, though uncomfortable, is crucial to a theologically real walk with Christ, not only because all real relationships entail some ambiguity but also because it is the ambiguity that God sometimes allows us to experience that drives us to our knees in prayer, seeking a fresh experience of God's presence, power, and direction in our lives. There is such a thing as purposeful ambiguity.[27] This is why it is necessary for Christian disciples to learn what it means to live by faith rather than by sight (2 Cor. 5:7).

Going further, just as the dynamic of discernment precedes our obeying the Spirit's promptings, the dynamic of *trusting* the Spirit follows it. There are times when we can second-guess ourselves: Did we really hear from the Spirit? If so, did we get it right? Can we now trust God to take our act of obedience and make it work for good? Once again, ambiguity happens!

The book of Acts is filled with passages that depict the Spirit prompting disciples to speak and act into the lives of others on behalf of the risen Christ (see, e.g., Acts 8:29; 9:11, 17; 10:19; 13:2–3; 16:6–10). In none of these passages do we find the Spirit providing an unambiguous assurance that the disciple's obedience would obtain a certain result. The disciples obeyed these promptings by faith, leaving the ultimate consequences in God's hands. One passage is especially instructive. Near the end of his missionary ministry, the apostle Paul feels called to return to Jerusalem with a relief offering provided by the gentile churches. Nevertheless, on his way to Jerusalem, he keeps hearing the Holy Spirit warn him that his future will involve prison and hardships. He proceeds anyway, explaining that he is "compelled by the Holy Spirit" to do so (Acts 20:22–23). Paul trusts, obeys, and then trusts some more!

The fact that all these New Testament examples of promptings by the Holy Spirit are ministry related should not surprise us, given the missionary, "sending" nature of our triune God. More will be said in chapter 8 about how Christ's followers can fully cooperate with the Holy Spirit's penchant for using God's people to fulfill God's missional purposes in the world. The

---

27. For an extended discussion of this notion, see Tyra, *Pursuing Moral Faithfulness*, 258–68.

point to be made here is that Paul's example of being "compelled by the Spirit" to do something for Christ—and then responding by "going" though "not knowing" what would happen (Acts 20:22)—is one all Christ's followers are called to emulate. In sum, this final custom related to keeping in step with the Spirit is three pronged: it involves *discerning* the Spirit's prompting, then *obeying* the Spirit's instructions, and then *trusting* that God can and will cause our obedient actions to ultimately work toward the fulfillment of his purposes in the world (2 Cor. 5:7).

Praying in the Spirit: Some Supplementary Support

We have seen that keeping in step with the Spirit is essential to a lifestyle spirituality. As promised, I will, in the final section of this chapter, cite some supplementary support for my contention that unceasing prayer in general and praying in the Spirit in particular are central to keeping in step with the Spirit. While this concluding discussion does not purport to *prove* anything, it does aim at *providing* some additional reasons why we might choose to engage in the practice of praying in the Spirit as part of an existentially impactful lifestyle spirituality.

Many years ago, I ran across a newspaper article that suggested a connection between repeating a mantra (or any meaningless phrase) and the actualization of the right hemisphere of the brain. The impression I gained from reading this article was that intentionally doing something the left side of the brain considers nonsensical or simply boring allows the right side of the brain to rise to the fore or, as it were, "come out to play." This led me to wonder whether praying in tongues or via wordless groans might have the same effect. I began to pay attention to this possibility.

Though I cannot rule out that some confirmation bias may have been at work, the inkling I gained over time was that my hunch possessed merit. Thus, for a couple of decades now, I have reported to parishioners and students my sense that a discernible correlation seems to exist between my praying in the Spirit and the experience of several lifestyle spirituality benefits: an increased sense of peace, trust, hope, endurance, and spiritual sensitivity; an unusual degree of creativity; and the likelihood that something prophetic might occur during the preaching, teaching, counseling, or writing activity for which I was often preparing. It was largely due to that newspaper article I read many years ago, alongside passages such as Romans 8:26; 1 Corinthians 14:2, 16–18; Ephesians 6:18; and Jude 20, that praying in the Spirit came to play a significant role in my own spirituality.

But as the title of this subsection suggests, some scientific support for the discernible correlation I have just described eventually became available as a result of the emergence of an academic discipline known as *neurotheology*. This field of study focuses on what is happening in the brain during a religious experience.[28] It turns out that the article I read years ago about the effect on the right side of the brain by merely chanting a prayer or repeating a mantra was not entirely accurate, but my hunch about praying in the Spirit was. Some recent studies of this type suggest that praying in the Spirit might genuinely involve a Spirit-enabled interaction with God that, while initiated by Christian disciples, does not require huge amounts of concentration but does indeed stimulate the right hemisphere of the brain. Though one's Christian faith and practice should not hinge on the findings of empirical science, these recently discovered neurolinguistic realities certainly suggest that the impact that praying in the Spirit has on one's brain might contribute greatly to the cultivation of a Spirit-empowered lifestyle spirituality.

Andrew Newberg's Landmark Brain Imaging Studies

Until recently, scientists believed that the only part of the human brain involved in religious activity was the temporal lobe. "Recent imaging studies, however, have shown that many parts of the brain are activated during a religious experience."[29] Chief among these brain imaging studies were those performed in 2001 and 2006 by Andrew Newberg, a medical doctor at the University of Pennsylvania.[30] In both of these projects, Newberg used a technology known as SPECT (single photon emission computed tomography) to take pictures of the brain while members of various religions engaged in religious activity. "SPECT provides a picture of blood flow in the brain at a given moment, so more blood flow indicates more activity."[31]

During the first phase of the study, Newberg analyzed the brain activity of a group of Buddhist monks engaged in deep meditation and a group of Roman Catholic nuns engaged in a contemplative practice known as "cen-

---

28. Molly Edmonds, "Is the Brain Hardwired for Religion?," HowStuffWorks, accessed August 11, 2021, https://science.howstuffworks.com/life/inside-the-mind/human-brain/brain-religion.htm.

29. Edmonds, "Is the Brain Hardwired for Religion?"

30. See Andrew B. Newberg et al., "The Measurement of Regional Cerebral Blood Flow during Glossolalia: A Preliminary SPECT Study," *Psychiatry Research: Neuroimaging* 148 (November 2006): 67–71, https://doi.org/10.1016/j.pscychresns.2006.07.001.

31. Edmonds, "Is the Brain Hardwired for Religion?"

tering prayer."[32] In the second phase of the study, the religious practitioners under observation were several Pentecostal Christians. The activity of their brains was first analyzed while they sang Christian hymns and then again while they engaged in glossolalic prayer. Both study phases are reported in the book *Born to Believe*, coauthored by Newberg and Mark Robert Waldman, a neuroscience researcher who, at the time, was an associate fellow at the Center for Spirituality and the Mind at the University of Pennsylvania.

During the meditation of the monks and the contemplation of the nuns, Newberg found increased activity in the frontal lobe, which indicated that the monks and nuns were concentrating on the activity.[33] Newberg explains: "The frontal lobes monitor our ability to stay attentive and alert, helping us to focus on a task."[34] But the SPECT imaging also indicated "an immense decrease of activity in the parietal lobe" of the monks and nuns, indicating that both groups had lost a sense of their spatial presence in the world—that is, their *mindfulness* of who they were and where they were was diminished. They had entered an altered state of consciousness.[35] After describing how damage to the parietal lobes interferes with or distorts one's self-awareness, Newberg and Waldman go on to say that "if you could consciously decrease activity to your parietal lobes, you would probably feel a brief suspension of self-awareness. You might also experience a loss of your sense of space and time. We discovered that both the nuns and Buddhists did just that—they were able to deliberately reduce activity in their parietal lobes while meditating. Thus, it should come as no surprise that these individuals describe themselves as entering a state of timelessness and spacelessness, states commonly associated with spiritual, mystical, and transcendent experiences."[36]

Interestingly, similar measurements of brain activity were observed during the worshipful singing of the Pentecostal Christians. They too essentially lost track of time and space and entered a mild and temporary dissociative state.[37] However, the images indicating the brain activity of the Pentecostals while they were praying in the Spirit looked significantly different.[38] Those engaged

32. Andrew Newberg and Mark Robert Waldman, *Born to Believe: God, Science, and the Origin of Ordinary and Extraordinary Beliefs* (New York: Free Press, 2006), 170.

33. Edmonds, "Is the Brain Hardwired for Religion?"

34. Newberg and Waldman, *Born to Believe*, 175.

35. Edmonds, "Is the Brain Hardwired for Religion?"

36. Newberg and Waldman, *Born to Believe*, 176.

37. Edmonds, "Is the Brain Hardwired for Religion?" See also Newberg et al., "Regional Cerebral Blood Flow during Glossolalia," 69.

38. Newberg et al., "Regional Cerebral Blood Flow during Glossolalia," 70. See also Newberg and Waldman, *Born to Believe*, 200.

in glossolalic prayer "actually experienced a decrease in frontal lobe activity"[39] and an increase of activity in the parietal lobes. The decreased activity in the frontal lobe indicated that the subjects were participating in an activity that was not under their direct control, and it was not something they felt the need to concentrate on.[40] Though they were speaking (in tongues) and doing so at will, the language center of the brain was not activated.[41]

Thus, say Newberg and Waldman, the brain images were precisely what we would expect of a group of Christians experiencing the dynamic of the Spirit praying through them. The part of the brain that normally made them feel responsible had been essentially "shut down."[42] And yet, rather than entering a dissociative state, the parietal lobes remained "online"—that is, the pray-ers maintained a personal and spatial mindfulness.[43] This too makes sense, they say, because while speaking in tongues involves relinquishing control, it does not entail an experience of dissociation (a trancelike state). Instead, it connotes a "very intense experience of how the self relates to God."[44] The ones praying never entered a trancelike state, but they did experience what they perceived to be an overwhelming yet comforting sense of God's presence. Newberg and Waldman assert that "These findings could be interpreted as the subject's sense of self being taken over by something else. We, scientifically, assume it's being taken over by another part of the brain, but we couldn't see, in this imaging study, where this took place. We believe this is the first scientific imaging study evaluating changes in cerebral activity—looking at what actually happens to the brain—when someone is speaking in tongues."[45] In other words, they are saying that praying in the Spirit either evidences one's belief in and sense of connection with God or strengthens this sense of intimacy—or both (see Jude 20–21).[46]

A related aspect of Newberg's studies that seems appropriate to comment on here has to do with the "asymmetrical activity between the two sides of the thalamus" that he observed in the brains of the monks, the nuns, and the Pentecostal pray-ers. Since this condition is not usual, he says, it might suggest

39. Edmonds, "Is the Brain Hardwired for Religion?"
40. See Newberg and Waldman, *Born to Believe*, 201.
41. Edmonds, "Is the Brain Hardwired for Religion?"
42. Constance Holden, "Tongues on the Mind," *Science*, November 2, 2006, https://www.sciencemag.org/news/2006/11/tongues-mind.
43. See Newberg and Waldman, *Born to Believe*, 205, 207.
44. Holden, "Tongues on the Mind."
45. Quoted in University of Pennsylvania School of Medicine, "Language Center of the Brain Is Not under the Control of Subjects Who 'Speak in Tongues,'" *ScienceDaily*, October 31, 2006, www.sciencedaily.com/releases/2006/10/061030183100.htm.
46. See Newberg and Waldman, *Born to Believe*, 178.

that "the people we have been scanning are born with a unique capacity to have spiritual revelations, *or that they have altered their neural functioning in permanent ways as a result of years of intensive practice.*"[47] Could it be that God created the human brain in such a way that meditation, contemplation, and, to an even greater degree, praying in the Spirit can, over time, increase within the disciple a heightened sensitivity to the presence, voice, and touch of God? I contend that the fact that the brains of meditating monks might interpret this phenomenon as becoming one with the universe does not mean that the dynamic was not originally designed by God to help his people experience a special degree of intimacy with him.

As for peer review, psychologist Michael Persinger of Laurentian University in Ontario, Canada, who has done brain wave research with glossolalia, referred to Newberg's research as an "excellent study." He went on to offer, "Each of Dr. Newberg's results have specific implications. For example, increased parietal activity would go with a sense of one's self being 'touched by the spirit.'"[48]

While Newberg's studies do not prove anything, they do seem to support my contention that praying in the Spirit may be viewed as highly productive of a lifestyle spirituality. The activity does not require huge amounts of mental concentration (thus allowing an ongoing engagement), but at the same time the activity effects a powerful, life-story-shaping sense of surrender to and communion with God.[49] And once again, my contention is that this is true whether our praying in the Spirit is glossolalic in nature or takes the form of wordless groans, both of which involve prayer that bypasses human understanding.

Other Scientific Studies of the Effect of Glossolalia on the Brain

Some additional neurotheological studies conducted in recent years also point to the contribution that praying in the Spirit can make to the cultivation

---

47. Newberg and Waldman, *Born to Believe*, 214 (emphasis added).
48. Holden, "Tongues on the Mind."
49. Emphasizing the manner in which glossolalic prayer is nonsensical to the practitioner, Christopher Stephenson argues that such praying can be engaged in deliberately as a spirituality practice designed to cultivate a greater degree of "submission to the divine through the suspension of comfort and familiarity that comes with intelligible words." In other words, Christian disciples can engage in glossolalic prayer in an intentional, self-emptying manner "that promotes in the speaker a greater docility to the Spirit in all moments of life." Christopher A. Stephenson, "Un-speaking in Tongues: Glossolalia as Ascetical Prayer," *Journal of Spiritual Formation and Soul Care* 13, no. 1 (May 2020): 96–97, https://doi.org/10.1177/1939790919893278.

of a lifestyle spirituality.[50] For example, a 2011 article published in the journal *Religion, Brain and Behavior* reported on some research conducted by biological anthropologist Christopher Lynn and his coworkers at the State University of New York at Albany. According to Lynn and his team, "The study assessed Apostolic Pentecostals in New York's Hudson Valley from September 2006 to June 2009 and investigated whether successive experiences with culturally-moderated arousal, via glossolalia, would result in lower arousal and stress during non-worship times. It was hypothesized that glossolalia experience stimulates arousal and, over time, entrains stress response, reducing arousal and stress reactions to normal daily stressors."[51]

The research methodology involved the measurement of two biomarkers of stress and arousal (cortisol and amylase) in the saliva of the research subjects, taking into consideration the church status of the subjects and the effect this had on the degree to which the subjects engaged in glossolalic praying during worship settings. The measurements were taken on a Sunday and then the following day. Says Lynn, "I was comparing both biomarkers on Sunday and Monday because I wanted to see if people with more glossolalia experience would have less reactive nervous systems, as though their experience had caused them to be less anxious people in the face of stress, as meditation is reputed to do."[52] Lynn explains the results of the study as follows:

> This study tested the predictions that (1) biomarkers of stress and arousal on a service day would be the same for all Apostolic Pentecostals, and (2) there would be subsequent indications of reduced stress in those biomarkers on a non-service day among Pentecostals with greater glossolalia experience. The results affirm both predictions, though biomarkers are uniformly higher among the high-glossolalists on Sunday. Both groups displayed overlapping distributions, suggesting there were active and inactive individuals in both groups. On Monday, high-glossolalists showed stress and arousal reductions not evident in low-glossolalists.[53]

Clearly, any spirituality practice that can serve to engender in the disciple a greater ability to deal with stress would be considered immensely helpful

50. While Newberg's study also alluded to some additional effects in the emotions of the glossolalists, it suggested that further research was warranted. Some, if not all, of these subsequent studies should be viewed in this light.

51. Christopher Dana Lynn et al., "Glossolalia Is Associated with Differences in Biomarkers of Stress and Arousal among Apostolic Pentecostals," *Religion, Brain and Behavior* 1, no. 3 (2011): 174, https://doi.org/10.1080/2153599X.2011.639659.

52. Quoted in Dirk Hobson, "Speaking in Tongues: Glossolalia and Stress Reduction," Dana Foundation, October 23, 2013, https://dana.org/article/speaking-in-tongues-glossolalia-and-stress-reduction/.

53. Lynn et al., "Glossolalia Is Associated with Differences in Biomarkers," 183–84.

in everyday life and emblematic of what we hope would be produced by a Spirit-enabled, theologically real lifestyle spirituality.

Pressing further, Dieter Christian Mueller, the author of a 1989 PhD dissertation titled "Glossolalia and the Right Hemisphere of the Brain," proffered the following query or thesis: "Is it conceivable that glossolalia might be right hemispheric speech? Speech unadulterated by the cognitive vocabulary of a culturally enforced dominant left hemisphere?"[54] After conducting some clinical research that involved measuring the "conjugate lateral eye movement" of the research subjects, Mueller eventually answered his own question: "Glossolalia could be seen to be, essentially, pure, affective, non-cognitive, right hemisphere speech."[55] This too would seem to corroborate what I indicated previously about the benefit of a spirituality practice that seems to increase activity in the right hemisphere of the brain.

Mueller goes on to explain that "the left hemisphere contributes its prime aptitudes in sequential, logical deductive, rational, cognitive linguistic thought processes. The right hemisphere provides its special attitudes in the realm of intuition, holistic perception, art and music appreciation, spirituality, randomness, self-fulfillment and release from logical, rational strictures."[56] In other words, there may be a connection between praying in the Spirit and the creativity and spiritual sensitivity Mueller associates with the right side of the brain. I would offer, however, that rather than concluding that all glossolalists are by nature "right-hemisphere dominant,"[57] it makes more sense to postulate that one of the neurological *effects* of praying in the Spirit is the stimulation of the right side of the brain, and that this physiological reality produces two spiritually significant, interrelated benefits. First, this stimulation makes it possible for the one praying in the Spirit not only to experience an enhanced degree of creativity with respect to the task at hand but also to possess a greater degree of sensitivity to the presence of God. Second, this increased sensitivity to God has the effect of thus encouraging prophetic activity in the sense of hearing God's voice, receiving ministry assignments from him, and then speaking and acting into the lives of others on his behalf.[58]

A companion study of sorts was later conducted by Mueller and Ron Philipchalk. Though the brain-measuring methodology in this study changed, the

54. Dieter Christian Mueller, "Glossolalia and the Right Hemisphere of the Brain" (PhD diss., University of British Columbia, August 1989), 319–20, https://open.library.ubc.ca/media/stream/pdf/831/1.0076968/2.

55. Mueller, "Glossolalia and the Right Hemisphere of the Brain," 322.

56. Mueller, "Glossolalia and the Right Hemisphere of the Brain," 479.

57. Mueller, "Glossolalia and the Right Hemisphere of the Brain," iii.

58. For more on the "prophetic capacity" I associate with the infilling of the Holy Spirit, see Tyra, *Holy Spirit in Mission*, 39–108, esp. 68, 98.

results did not. The researchers behind this project provide this overview: "A sophisticated infrared camera measured temperature changes presumed to be related to activation of either the right or left brain hemispheres. Measurements were taken before and after participants spoke in tongues and before and after they read aloud. Results indicated increasing activation of the right hemisphere relative to the left after speaking in tongues and the opposite relation after reading aloud."[59]

The upshot is that all these neurotheological studies seem to be suggesting the same thing: there are reasons to believe that praying in the Spirit can and perhaps should be considered a vital practice in the cultivation of a pneumatologically real lifestyle spirituality.

In his book *Prayer: Finding the Heart's True Home*, Richard Foster, a former university professor and author of many works on Christian spirituality, includes a chapter-length discussion of the practice of "unceasing prayer." He begins that discussion with a testimonial that implies the importance of unceasing prayer to a theologically real Christian spirituality: "I want to tell you of a wonderful way of living always in God's presence. I cannot witness that I have entered fully into this life of perpetual communion with the Father, but I have caught enough glimpses that I know it to be the best, the finest, the fullest way of living."[60] Foster goes on to underscore the importance of unceasing prayer for a theologically real Christian spirituality with this compelling compendium of quotations:

> Ordinary folk throughout the ages tell us it is possible. Brother Lawrence shares simply, "There is no mode of life in the world more pleasing and more full of delight than continual conversation with God." Saint John of the Ladder advises, "Let the memory of Jesus combine with your breath." Juliana of Norwich says frankly, "Prayer unites the soul to God." Kallistos, a Byzantine spiritual writer, teaches, "Unceasing prayer consists in an unceasing invocation of the name of God." It was said of Saint Francis that he "seemed not so much a man praying as prayer itself made man." And Frank Laubach reports, "Oh, this thing of keeping in constant touch with God, of making him the object of my thought and the companion of my conversations, is the most amazing thing I ever ran across."[61]

---

59. Ron Philipchalk and Dieter Christian Mueller, "Glossolalia and Temperature Change in the Right and Left Cerebral Hemispheres," *International Journal for the Psychology of Religion* 10, no. 3 (2000): 181–85, https://doi.org/10.1207/S15327582IJPR1003_04.

60. Richard Foster, *Prayer: Finding the Heart's True Home* (San Francisco: HarperSanFrancisco, 1992), 119.

61. Foster, *Prayer*, 119. Foster notes that the quotations, in order, are from the following sources: Brother Lawrence, *The Practice of the Presence of God* (Philadelphia: Judson, n.d.), 60; *Writings from the Philokalia on Prayer of the Heart*, trans. E. Kadloubovsky and G. E. H. Palmer

The aim of this chapter overall has been to provide some practical suggestions about how to keep in step with the Spirit and to underscore the importance of unceasing prayer in our doing so. It was also my intention to accomplish this goal in a way that was not overly triumphalist. I am not sure how well I succeeded at the latter goal, but I hope I made good on the former.

In the next chapter, we will focus on yet another core commitment: the cultivation of an ongoing mentoring relationship with the risen Christ. We are now about two-thirds of the way along in our journey. Let's not allow our momentum to abate at this point. The sooner we hit the "play" button on the next DIY tutorial, the better!

TOPICS FOR REVIEW

1. What were your thoughts when you read the discussion that focused on the need to greet, acknowledge, and "realize" our trinitarian God each day? Did this suggestion strike you at first as being simple-hearted or simple-minded? Do you still feel that way, or have you changed your mind?

2. This chapter suggests that to be continually filled with the Spirit (Eph. 5:18) is to be continually surrendering to the Spirit's leadership in our lives. Do you see the value of some sort of spirituality practice that has us doing this in a meaningful, theologically real way repeatedly every day? Have you developed such a practice yet? If so, how is it going?

3. Do you agree that the apostle Paul probably believed it was possible for Christ's followers to experience the phenomenon of the Spirit praying through them? How do you feel about the notion that this can occur either through glossolalia or wordless groans? Did this chapter's discussion of praying in the Spirit encourage you in the practice? Why or why not?

4. Have you ever sensed God speaking to you through the Spirit? What's your take on the notion that Christ's followers can increase their sensitivity to God's spiritual direction by engaging in *theologically real* versions of prayer and Scripture study *at the same time*?

(London: Faber & Faber, 1975), 85; Julian of Norwich, *Showings*, trans. Edmund Colledge and James Walsh (New York: Paulist Press, 1978), 253; *On the Prayer of Jesus: From the Ascetic Essays of Bishop Ignatius Brianchaninov*, trans. Father Lazarus (London: John M. Watkins, 1965), 60; Gloria Hutchinson, *Six Ways to Pray from Six Great Saints* (Cincinnati: St. Anthony Messenger, 1982), 10; Frank C. Laubach, *Letters by a Modern Mystic* (Syracuse: New Readers, 1979), 23.

5. How needful and helpful did you judge the discussion under the heading "Discerning, Obeying, and Trusting the Spirit"? What might you add to this discussion? Are there parts that you disagree with?

6. To what degree did you find interesting and helpful the supplementary (neurotheological) support for praying in the Spirit that this chapter provided? Why? What is your personal takeaway from this discussion?

7

TAKING ABIDING IN CHRIST
TO THE NEXT LEVEL

It is unlikely that we will deepen our relationship with God in a casual or haphazard manner. There will be a need for some intentional commitment and some reorganization in our own lives. But there is nothing that will enrich our lives more than a deeper and clearer perception of God's presence in the routine of daily living.

—William O. Paulsell, "Ways of Prayer"

One of my favorite quotations concerning the mentoring dynamic was authored not by an academic, a business professional, or a leadership expert but by an actor. Denzel Washington writes, "Show me a successful individual and I'll show you someone who had real positive influences in his or her life. I don't care what you do for a living—if you do it well, I'm sure there was someone cheering you on or showing the way. A mentor."[1] Washington seems to be suggesting that the two main things mentors do for us is cheer us on and show us the way. It should be obvious by now that I view the apostle Paul as a trusted spiritual-life mentor whose personal example and writings

1. Denzel Washington, "The Mentors He'll Never Forget," *Guideposts*, January 1, 2007, https://www.guideposts.org/better-living/positive-living/the-mentors-hell-never-forget.

do indeed serve to inspire and inform. But he has passed on to his reward and is not available to anyone for current, personal spiritual direction. Where does this leave us? Where do those of us who desire to heed the apostle's call to a lifestyle spirituality go for some personal, theologically real, in-the-moment spiritual direction?

Our focus in this discussion is on the second core commitment of a realist, trinitarian "I-Thou" lifestyle spirituality. Taking seriously Paul's call to keep in step with the Spirit (the first core commitment) makes possible a Spirit-enabled engagement in the pursuit of the empowering presence of Christ (the second core commitment). Honoring these two commitments enables us to experience a personal, interactive, ongoing mentoring relationship with the risen Jesus himself (see John 14:16–18, 23). Think about it: how immensely valuable to have Jesus himself cheering us on and showing us the way as we endeavor to render to God the spiritual, moral, and missional faithfulness he desires and deserves. This is what I have in mind when I refer to the possibility of taking the dynamic of *abiding in Christ* (John 15:1–8) to the next level.

More specifically, the focus in this chapter will be on what some fellow "rabbit-hole explorers," past and present, have had to say about the nuts and bolts of pursuing Christ's empowering presence. I have in mind such spiritual-life experts as Brother Lawrence, Francis de Sales, Frank Laubach, Jan Johnson, William Paulsell, and Dallas Willard. But rather than take the biographical approach that was utilized in chapter 4, I am going to synthesize the cardinal spiritual-life customs suggested by these "masters" into a discussion of what a day in the life of someone engaged in the "hot pursuit" might look like in our own era. Indeed, for what it is worth, I will at times also allude to my own practices. While there is not one right way to engage in the pursuit, the spiritual-life practices presented in the next few pages have greatly impacted my own spirituality. I sincerely hope they prove helpful to the readers of this book as well.[2]

Pursuing Christ in the Morning

Let's begin this discussion of a typical day in the life of someone committed to the cultivation of a lifestyle spirituality with an overview of how those engaged in the pursuit might begin their day.

2. The presentation of these strategies has been adapted from a similar discussion located in Gary Tyra, *Christ's Empowering Presence: The Pursuit of God through the Ages* (Downers Grove, IL: IVP Books, 2011), 149–71.

Prayer upon Awakening

In the previous chapter, I referred to the importance of greeting the Spirit each morning by acknowledging the reality and faithfulness of our triune God. Dallas Willard encouraged his students to do this as early as possible. One of the first things we might do each day, says Willard, perhaps even before we get out of bed, is commit the day before us to the Lord's care so that we might enter it boldly, counting on Christ's very real assistance. Willard writes,

> Jesus' resurrected presence with us, along with his teaching, assures us of God's care for all who let him be God and let him care for them. "Do not be afraid, little flock, for your Father has chosen gladly to give you the kingdom" (Luke 12:32). It is love of God, admiration and confidence in his greatness and goodness, and regular experience of his care that frees us from the burden of "looking out for ourselves."
>
> What remarkable changes this introduces into our day-to-day life! Personally, at the beginning of my day—often before arising—I commit my day to the Lord's care. Usually I do this while meditatively praying through the Lord's Prayer, and possibly the twenty-third Psalm as well. Then I meet everything that happens as sent or at least permitted by God. I meet it resting in the hand of his care. This helps me to "do all things without grumbling or disputing" (Phil. 2:14), because I have already "placed God in charge" and am trusting him to manage them for my good. I no longer have to manage the weather, airplanes, and other people.[3]

A Morning Quiet Time

Going further, another key to engaging successfully in the pursuit is to spend at least a few minutes each morning getting centered in Christ. Trite as this may seem to some, I am referring here to the practice of a daily devotional routine.

Time Spent in the Scriptures

I realize that not everyone is a "morning person." Still, I encourage my students to take at least a minute or two to fill their minds with the truth of Scripture as they begin their day. Of course, my confident expectation is that if I can successfully encourage my students to cultivate the habit of opening God's Word and drinking from it in a theologically real manner for only a minute or two first thing in the morning, these few minutes will eventually

3. Dallas Willard, *Renovation of the Heart: Putting on the Character of Christ* (Colorado Springs: NavPress, 2002), 70.

turn into a more significant amount of time. Such is the power of really interacting with the risen Christ!

My own practice is to prayerfully contemplate five chapters from the Psalms, the chapter from the book of Proverbs that corresponds with the day of the month, another chapter from the Old Testament, and a chapter from the New Testament. Reading through the Bible in this comprehensive yet consecutive manner provides me with the context in which each scriptural passage is located. The goal here is not simply to read through the Bible each calendar year but to indwell it, to keep reminding myself who God is and what he is about so that I might grow in my ability to understand and cooperate with what he is up to in the world. That said, in the past twenty years I have probably engaged in a prayerful, thoughtful contemplation of the entirety of the Scriptures no less than a dozen times. But it is one thing to read the Bible through; it is another to keep reading it through, to indwell the story it tells!

Moreover, Willard emphasizes the importance of also memorizing and meditating often on key portions of Scripture:

> There are certain tried-and-true disciplines we can use to aid in the transformation of our thought life toward the mind of Christ. . . .
>
> The most obvious thing we can do is to draw certain key portions of Scripture into our minds and make them a part of the permanent fixtures of our thought. This is the primary discipline for the thought life. We need to know them like the back of our hand, and a good way to do that is to memorize them and then constantly turn them over in our minds as we go through the events and circumstances of our life (Josh. 1:8; Ps. 1).[4]

What portions of Scripture does Willard have in mind? I can personally attest to the fact that Willard exhorted all his doctoral students to memorize Colossians 3:1–17. However, a careful reading of Willard's book *Renovation of the Heart* suggests some other passages we might decide to meditate upon often: Romans 12:1–21; 1 Corinthians 13:1–13; 2 Corinthians 3:12–7:1; Galatians 5:22–6:10; Ephesians 4:20–6:20; Philippians 2:3–16; 4:4–9; 1 Peter 2:1–3:16; 2 Peter 1:2–11; and 1 John 4:7–21.[5]

I have come to think of my time in the Scriptures each morning as a way for me as a contemporary disciple to experience three formative dynamics: at times I find myself, figuratively speaking, sitting among the crowds, hearing Jesus enunciate some hugely important, fundamental spiritual realities (see Matt. 5:1–2); at other times I seem to be among the Twelve receiving some

---

4. Willard, *Renovation of the Heart*, 112–13.
5. Willard, *Renovation of the Heart*, 221.

vital kingdom-specific clarifications (see Matt. 17:1–13; Mark 4:33–34); and every once in a while, it becomes, through the Spirit, much more personal—I sense Jesus speaking directly to me in a timely, prophetic, honest yet encouraging way, as he sometimes did (and does) to his intimate associates (see John 16:16–24). The point is that I am convinced that regardless of whether one's time spent in the Scriptures occurs in the morning, in the afternoon, or in the evening, an ongoing, theologically real version of this spirituality custom is simply crucial to our walk with Christ.

Time Spent in Spiritual Reading

As important as spending some time each day studying the Scriptures was for Dallas Willard, he also encouraged his students to "master the masters"—to engage in the kind of reading that would enable them to become familiar with the methods used by both contemporary and historical models of Christian spirituality. Willard has in mind an ongoing engagement in a practice I refer to as "spiritual reading" when he writes,

> We must pray that God will lead us to others who can walk with us with Christ—whoever and wherever they may be. And then in patience stay with them.
>
> This will naturally lead us to include . . . older practitioners of The Way [i.e., the masters]. We need to understand those who have learned how to live with a transformed mind and study carefully what they did—not necessarily in order to do exactly what they did, for they are not lawgivers, nor are they always right, much less perfect. But we cannot easily or wisely dispense with what they have learned and what can be learned from them. . . . How did they come to be able to live with "the Lord always before them"? We learn from them how to do that by making them our close companions on the way.[6]

In other words, it is also a good idea to always be working our way through a book that has the effect of encouraging us in our journey toward a lifestyle spirituality. To be more specific, given the importance of the threefold faithfulness to a Christian life well lived, we should continually be "nursing" from a book that is both informational and inspirational with respect to our cultivation of a spiritual, moral, or missional faithfulness before God.

Contemporary spiritual theologian William Paulsell provides some additional encouragement here: "Reading of the great spiritual classics and writings of contemporary spiritual writers is an important stimulus to growth. It

---

6. Willard, *Renovation of the Heart*, 114.

is useful to have a book around to be reading, even if only a few pages a day can be read. The best devotional literature is that written by people who have been through deep struggles of faith. Those that make faith sound easy are of little use in the crises of life."[7] Paulsell is right: the best teachers are those Henri Nouwen famously refers to as "wounded healers"—faithful guides who, because they have been through the dark valley themselves, know best how to encourage those who will traverse this scary and treacherous spiritual terrain in turn.[8]

Time Spent in Prayer

When it comes to the crucial spirituality practice of time spent in prayer, some suggestions proffered by the medieval Roman Catholic bishop and spiritual director Francis de Sales can be helpful. He obviously had something akin to the hot pursuit in mind when he encouraged his acolytes to contemplate or meditate often on the life and passion of Christ and to be careful to do so in a theologically real manner. He refers to the first of these two prayer-related suggestions when he writes, "I especially counsel you to practice mental prayer, the prayer of the heart, and particularly that which centers on the life and passion of our Lord. By often turning your eyes on him in meditation, your whole soul will be filled with him. You will learn his ways and form your actions after the pattern of his."[9] His emphasis on a theological realism is apparent in the way he exhorts his mentees to begin and end each prayer really intending to connect with God rather than simply perform a necessary ritual. He did this in a couple of places. First, he wrote, "Begin all your prayers, whether mental or vocal, in the presence of God." Keep to this rule without any exception and you will quickly see how helpful it will be."[10] And then he fairly implores his mentees thusly, "Therefore, when you prepare to pray you must say with your whole heart and in your heart, 'O my heart, my heart, God is truly here!'"[11]

As for what a formal morning prayer time might look like, Paulsell is, once again, helpful: "Minimally, our daily prayer should include praise and thanksgiving, confession or examination of conscience, and intercession. We should pray for our own calling, our local congregation, our co-workers, our

7. William O. Paulsell, "Ways of Prayer: Designing a Personal Rule," *Weavings* 2, no. 5 (September/October 1987): 44.

8. Henri J. M. Nouwen, *The Wounded Healer: Ministry in Contemporary Society* (New York: Doubleday, 1979).

9. Francis de Sales, *Introduction to the Devout Life* (New York: Doubleday, 1966), 81.

10. Francis de Sales, *Introduction to the Devout Life*, 82.

11. Francis de Sales, *Introduction to the Devout Life*, 84–85.

friends, our families, and all with whom we are in regular contact. There are many who will ask us to pray for them if they sense that we are serious about prayer. There are also those larger concerns of peace and justice that should be part of our prayer."[12]

Going further, though the classic postures of prayer are on one's knees or standing with hands lifted toward heaven, Paul's call for prayer to be engaged in "continually" and "always" would seem to indicate that he did not feel we are limited to a certain posture while praying. For what it's worth, a significant portion of my own morning prayer time occurs during a daily walk. In 1 Timothy 4:8, the apostle Paul makes a distinction between physical and spiritual exercise. While he definitely promotes the latter, he does not completely disparage the former. The good news is that a lifestyle spirituality has room in it for both!

Before I participated in the doctoral seminar I referred to in chapter 4, I had been in the practice of engaging daily in a long walk. Originally, the main purpose of these walks was to burn some calories. But during the two weeks I spent with Willard at a Catholic retreat center studying Christian spirituality, this daily physical exercise regimen became a cardinal spirituality practice as well. Anyone who is familiar with Willard's take on spirituality knows that he placed a huge emphasis on the spiritual discipline known as solitude—deliberately separating ourselves from the company of others so that we may be alone with God. Every day during that intensive doctor of ministry seminar, I carved out time for a one-hour walkabout during which I explored the hills above the quaint community of Sierra Madre, California, all the while communing with God.

The value of these daily excursions for my own spirituality cannot be overstated. It was at this time that I became aware of the difference between praying toward the idea of God and actually conversing with him. I also realized that there was something about praying while walking that just seemed right, at least for me. Just as Jesus's first disciples must have conversed with him as they walked hither and yon (see, e.g., Mark 8:27–30), I am, with the help of the Holy Spirit, able to do so as well.

Thus, ever since the summer of 2002, one of my own morning spirituality customs has been a two-mile "prayer walk," during which I walk some trails near my home in Yorba Linda, California. This special activity not only has been of immense value for my physical wellness but also has afforded me the opportunity to reckon with God's reality, to experience Christ's empowering presence, and to pray in the Spirit for family, friends, colleagues, students, and

12. Paulsell, "Ways of Prayer," 44.

so forth. It is also a time for me, each morning, to surrender to the leadership of the Spirit and invite him to reveal to me and through me the risen Jesus. So significant is this simple practice for my spirituality and ministry that there are not very many days when this precious and powerful opportunity to tryst with Christ through the Spirit does not occur.

Now in the interest of full disclosure, owing to the COVID-19 pandemic, for the past year and a half (as of the time of this writing) my morning prayer walk has often included my wife, Patti, as a walking and praying partner. Of course, we converse about the things and people we both care deeply about, but this has not meant that our morning prayers have been curtailed. We have learned to converse with one another while at the same time being sensitive to the presence of Christ and the lifestyle and ministry promptings his Spirit sometimes provides as we commune with our triune God together.

The upshot is that, for nearly two decades now, this daily prayer practice has played a significant role in my spiritual-life journey, providing many devotional, moral, and ministry benefits. The bottom line is that whether we pray on our knees or while walking or engaging in some other form of exercise, the key is to engage in some theologically real, conversational prayer—not to the idea of Christ but to the risen Jesus himself!

Pursuing Christ throughout the Day

All the spirituality authors we are interacting with in this chapter are advocates for an "all day, every day" Christian spirituality. Their constant refrain is that we must not confine our pursuit of Christ to some morning devotional routines. Accordingly, Francis de Sales exhorts us to move as seamlessly as possible from prayer to our everyday activities. He had this to say to the readers of his book, *Introduction to the Devout Life*:

> You must even accustom yourself to know how to pass from prayer to all the various duties your vocation and state of life rightfully and lawfully require of you, even though they may appear far different from the affections you received in prayer. I mean that the lawyer must be able to pass from prayer to pleading cases, the merchant to commerce, and the married woman to her duties as wife and her household tasks with so much ease and tranquility that their minds are not disturbed. Since both prayer and your other duties are in conformity with God's will, you must pass from one to the other with a devout and humble mind.[13]

13. Francis de Sales, *Introduction to the Devout Life*, 91.

The Daily Commute

The good bishop seems to be encouraging a smooth rather than abrupt transition between our devotional activities for the day and the work we must eventually attend to. For me, this transition occurs during my daily commute. Yes, it is possible to be engaged in the pursuit even while driving the California freeways! Obviously, our eyes must be opened wide, but it is still possible to converse with Christ as we drive—praising him, worshiping him, and inviting him to be big in our lives as we move into the next segment of the day. It is also a prime time for me to deal with my "addiction to hurry" by engaging in what some refer to as the practice of "slowing": deliberately, prayerfully calling on Christ for a greater degree of patience and trust.[14] There really is a difference between being busy and being in a hurry. How ironic that something as banal as one's daily commute can be infused with a rich interaction with the risen Jesus! It is hard for me to overstate how impactful and therefore important my daily commute is to my attempt at cultivating a lifestyle spirituality.

Pursuing Christ While Busy at Work

At the same time, some readers might aver that the trickier chore for them is staying focused on the spiritual dimension of their existence once they are at work, engaged in necessary tasks and surrounded by other people who fairly demand their attention. Church history tells us that the ancient Christian hermits who fled from the cities to the Egyptian desert in the fourth century did so because they were convinced that cultivating a God-honoring spirituality required a complete escape from the distractions caused by secular vocations and interactions with others. According to one Christian spirituality historian, "These people believed wholeheartedly as they read the Gospel that the only way to respond authentically to Christ was to get away from the din of the world and to go out to the desert to find Him there. One had to flee the city of sin in order to find God, the pure God who was wholly other, wholly apart, and wholly transcendent to this city of sinful men."[15] But many spiritual masters later in the history of the Christian movement went on to argue just the opposite: we can pursue Christ even while engaged in supposedly "secular" endeavors; it is possible for our life with others to

14. For an excellent discussion of the "hurry sickness" and how we might develop a spirituality that mitigates it, see John Ortberg, *The Life You've Always Wanted: Spiritual Disciplines for Ordinary People* (Grand Rapids: Zondervan, 1997), 81–96.

15. George Lane, *Christian Spirituality: An Historical Sketch* (Chicago: Loyola, 1984), 3.

improve rather than impede our ability to experience Christ's presence on a moment-by-moment basis.

Praying While Taking Care of Business

Francis de Sales was adamant about the possibility of remaining connected to Christ even while engaged in workday matters. The trick, he said, was to learn how to keep one eye (and ear) open to the Lord even as we engage in activities that would seem to require all our attention:

> In ordinary affairs and occupations that do not require strict, earnest attention, you should look at God rather than at them. When they are of such importance as to require your whole attention to do them well, then too you should look from time to time at God, like mariners who to arrive at the port they are bound for look at the sky above them rather than down on the sea on which they sail. Thus God will work with you, in you, and for you, and after your labor consolation will follow.[16]

Perhaps the most well-known advocate for not letting work activities interfere with our spirituality is the spiritual master most of my students are especially taken with: Brother Lawrence. Born into the world as Nicholas Herman, this famous practitioner of the pursuit eventually entered the Order of the Discalced (or "shoeless") Carmelites, a monastery in Paris, as Brother Lawrence of the Resurrection.[17] Within the monastery, Brother Lawrence was assigned to the kitchen, where he labored for fifteen years. It was in this busy, noisy kitchen that this good brother learned he could continually commune with God, not only worshiping him while working but ultimately performing his work for him as an act of worship!

Brother Lawrence once expressed the guiding principle of his lifestyle spirituality in the form of a rhetorical question: "Since you cannot but know that God is with you in all you undertake, that He is at the very depth and centre of your soul, why should you not thus pause an instant from time to time in your outward business . . . to worship Him within your soul, to praise Him, to entreat His aid, to offer Him the service of your heart, and give Him thanks for all His loving-kindnesses and tender-mercies?"[18] In another place, Brother

---

16. Francis de Sales, *Introduction to the Devout Life*, 153.

17. "Brother Lawrence: Practitioner of God's Presence," *Christianity Today*, accessed February 4, 2010, http://www.christianitytoday.com/ch/131christians/innertravelers/brotherlawrence.html.

18. Brother Lawrence, *The Practice of the Presence of God* (New Kensington, PA: Whitaker House, 1982), 71–72.

Lawrence became more specific, indicating how this guiding principle played out in the kitchen:

> At the beginning of my duties, I would say to the Lord with confidence, "My God, since You are with me and since, by Your will, I must occupy myself with external things, please grant me the grace to remain with You, in Your presence. Work with me, so that my work might be the very best. Receive as an offering of love both my work and all my affections." During my work, I would always continue to speak to the Lord as though He were right with me, offering Him my services and thanking Him for His assistance. Also, at the end of my work, I used to examine it carefully. If I found good in it, I thanked God. If I noticed faults, I asked His forgiveness without being discouraged, and then went on with my work, still dwelling in Him.
>
> Thus, continuing in the practice of conversing with God throughout each day and quickly seeking His forgiveness when I fell or strayed, His presence has become as easy and natural to me now as it once was difficult to attain.[19]

Both Francis de Sales and Brother Lawrence seem to be saying the same thing: the practice of Christian spirituality need not be limited to day-beginning devotional times. We can and should learn to bring Jesus with us into our workday, communing with him even as we take care of business.

Praying While Interacting with Others

It was not just mundane work the first Christian monks sought to distance themselves from when they fled to the Egyptian desert in the fourth century. They also perceived their peers to be a problem. Thus, the first Christian monks were "hermits" whose spirituality mandated a life of rigorous solitude. This way of life came to be known as *eremitic* monasticism. Eventually, however, a form of monasticism arose that emphasized the importance of monks living in community as they pursued lives of holiness before God. This is known as *cenobitic* monasticism. While there are lessons to be learned from the *desert fathers* who lived as hermits,[20] our focus here will be on those spiritual masters who discovered this very important reality: it is possible to remain in an attitude of prayer throughout one's day, even when surrounded by others.

Our friend Francis de Sales is one such exemplar. Notice how he combined the themes of solitude with community: "Always remember . . . to retire at various times into the solitude of your own heart even while outwardly

---

19. Lawrence, *Practice of the Presence*, 82–83.
20. For more on this, see Tyra, *Christ's Empowering Presence*, 35–37.

engaged in discussion or transactions with others. This mental solitude cannot be violated by the many people who surround you since they are not standing around your heart but only around your body. Your heart remains alone in the presence of God."[21]

Francis is not the only one to suggest that the presence of others need not interrupt our communion with Christ. Contemporary spiritual life author Jan Johnson likewise encourages us to develop the habit of turning our hearts toward God each time we converse with others. Citing the contemporary mystic Frank Laubach, she writes,

> As God becomes our life companion, it seems normal to invite Him to participate in our conversations with others. Frank Laubach described these experiences as "continuous silent conversations of heart to heart with God while looking into other eyes and listening to other voices." You might think this sounds like a confusing dual conversation, but it isn't. . . .
>
> As people's motives and feelings unfold, we may see that God is working within them in ways that surprise us. . . . We ask God, *How can I be present for them? Is there something they need that I have to offer? How can I cooperate with You, God, in helping them pursue Your purposes for their life?*[22]

Ultimately, these quotes by Francis de Sales, Frank Laubach, and Jan Johnson underscore the fact that one does not have to be a hermit to enjoy a pervasive sense of Christ's presence. Indeed, our conversations with others can actually become the means by which we experience an increased number of intimate interactions with the risen Lord each day!

In the previous chapter, I made much of the practice of praying in the Spirit, arguing that because this form of prayer can occur throughout one's day, it should be considered central to the cultivation of a Christian lifestyle spirituality. I have personally found tremendous benefit in staying in contact with God throughout the day by means of multiple brief but pungent seasons of glossalic praying engaged in under my breath. I have also experienced genuine blessing by pausing from time to time, throughout my day, to utter this short but powerful prayer: "Okay, God, what are you up to now, and how can I cooperate with you in it?" Indeed, this prayer seems to be perennially appropriate, not just when we feel good about having finished a task and are wondering what is next but also when our busy agenda has been interrupted by some unexpected event or person requiring our immediate attention. Rather

---

21. Francis de Sales, *Introduction to the Devout Life*, 97.
22. Jan Johnson, *Enjoying the Presence of God: Discovering Intimacy with God in the Daily Rhythms of Life* (Colorado Springs: NavPress, 1996), 30 (emphasis original).

than giving in to the inclination of the flesh to be exasperated by any unexpected interruptions, we can learn to interpret them as God-ordained ministry opportunities—to once again connect with Christ and experience, through the Spirit, his empowering presence.

Pursuing Christ at Day's End

Just as we are careful to begin each day talking to God about it in advance, we should probably also conclude each day talking to him about it in retrospect. Not only is it my habit to do this during my evening commute home, it is my sense that communing with God for even just a few moments before we drift off to sleep each evening significantly increases the likelihood that we will wake up in the morning ready and eager to begin the pursuit once again.

But what might a day-ending engagement in the pursuit entail? Once again, the spiritual masters can be of service.

As we have seen, Brother Lawrence was careful not only to *commit* his work to the Lord beforehand and to *communicate* with him during it but also to *evaluate* it afterward. I am wondering why the godly monk's example regarding how to approach our work each day should not be considered paradigmatic for how we approach each day's engagement in the pursuit. In other words, if, as I have suggested in this chapter, we are to be careful to spend some time at the beginning of each day *committing* the day to the risen Christ and then to endeavor throughout the day to *commune* (interact) with Christ, should we not also at the end of each day spend some time evaluating the degree to which we succeeded or failed at keeping in step with the Spirit and benefiting thereby from Christ's mentoring, encouraging, enabling presence?

I am also pretty sure Frank Laubach would have agreed with this "before, during, and after" way of thinking about each day's engagement in the pursuit. He playfully referred to this lifestyle-spirituality practice as a "game with minutes," the goal of which was to keep God in mind for at least one second of every minute of each day. Clearly, such an approach to the pursuit would require some sort of self-assessment at each day's end.

But what form should such a self-assessment take? What criteria should be our focus? These are important questions to address.

To begin, I want to point out that Laubach's experiences with the "game" led him to do more in his writings than simply identify as many pursuit-related techniques as possible. He also focused on the kind of commitments necessary for Christ's followers to succeed at the game with minutes. This is why so many of Laubach's proposed strategies actually read as requirements. For example, according to Laubach, if we want to succeed at the game, we must prayerfully immerse ourselves in ministry to others rather than be preoccupied with our own needs. He writes, "So if anybody were to ask me how to find God I should say at once, hunt out the deepest need you can find and forget all about your own comfort while you try to meet that need. Talk to God about it, and—he will be there. You will know it."[23]

In other words, we experience God most profoundly when our focus is on what he is focused on: the plight of hurting people. One of the best ways to sense God speaking to us is to be continually posing to him this question: "Okay, Lord, what are you up to *in this person's life*, and how can I cooperate with you in it?" The fact that Laubach was a career missionary and brought a ministry mindset into the pursuit is apparent. His approach not only to ministry but to spirituality as well held that instead of simply asking Christ to bless us and what we are up to, we must sense where he is already at work around us, then make the quality decision to partner with him there!

Moreover, Laubach's missionary heart is also evidenced when, in another place, he states that success at the game with minutes requires that we also make a habit of actually talking about God to other people. He explains, "The week with its failures and successes has taught me one new lesson. It is this: 'I must talk about God, or I cannot keep Him in my mind. I must give Him away in order to have Him.' That is the law of the spirit world. What one gives one has, what one keeps to oneself one loses."[24] Put differently, another prerequisite for success in the pursuit, according to Laubach, is that we not keep our engagement in it a secret. The more we own Christ and confess our devotion to him before others, the greater will be our sense of his empowering presence in our lives.

Now, my contention is that if these two commitments are indeed prerequisites for success in our participation in the pursuit, it would only make sense for us to focus on them as we ponder nightly how we are doing at it. In other words, keeping the two commitments just presented in mind, I am proposing that we conclude each day by posing to ourselves these crucial questions:

- To what degree did the spirituality practices I engaged in today enable me to experience a vivid sense of Christ's real presence?
- To what degree did the experience of Christ's presence in my life today empower me to speak and act into the lives of others in a way that honored him?

23. Frank C. Laubach, *Man of Prayer: Selected Writings of a World Missionary* (Syracuse: Laubach Literacy International, 1990), 11.
24. Laubach, *Man of Prayer*, 31.

I often tell my students that, given the Golden Rule provided by Jesus, the question we should be asking ourselves each night when we put our head on the pillow is *not* "Was I careful today to avoid hurting anyone? Rather, the question I believe Jesus would have us ponder at each day's end is this: "How many people did I bless today in Christ's name?"

Now, it is inevitable that there will be evenings when this moment or two of soul-searching will serve to disturb rather than soothe one's conscience. Indeed, we will have times when we must admit to ourselves that we seem to be failing miserably at the game with minutes! When this is the case, we probably should, as Brother Lawrence instructs, forthrightly acknowledge this reality to God, resolving to do better going forward. Going further, we might also, as a repentant King David models for us, humbly appeal to God for a fresh experience of spiritual empowerment (see Ps. 51:10–12). Going further still, I recommend that we also revisit our previous discussion of what is involved in keeping in step with the Spirit. In other words, every so often we simply must ask ourselves questions such as these:

- Am I greeting and surrendering to the Spirit each day?
- Am I praying in the Spirit in a "continual" and "always" manner?
- Am I discerning the Spirit's promptings, obeying those promptings, and then trusting God with the results?

I am convinced that any day-ending exercise that leads us to prayerfully recommit to these behaviors is worthwhile. Why? Precisely because keeping in step with the Spirit really is crucial to a successful engagement in the hot pursuit that, in turn, enables an ongoing mentoring relationship with the risen Jesus. In other words, this is how we see our abiding in Christ go to the next level!

Easy Does It! Hang in There! Enjoy the Journey!

Before I conclude this chapter, I want to provide some additional words of encouragement. Even some of the spiritual-life experts cited in this chapter understood how daunting the hot pursuit of Christ's empowering presence will sometimes seem. Because of this difficulty, we need to be patient with ourselves and persist in the practice. A couple of quotations have personally inspired me to become adept at both. In his book *The Pursuit of God*, pastor A. W. Tozer blessed his readers with an acknowledgment that even though the pursuit will indeed be difficult at first, it becomes easier with practice:

"Believing, then, is directing the heart's attention to Jesus. It is lifting the mind to 'behold the Lamb of God,' and never ceasing that beholding for the rest of our lives. At first this may be difficult, but it becomes easier as we look steadily at His wondrous Person, quietly and without strain. Distractions may hinder, but once the heart is committed to Him, after each brief excursion away from Him the attention will return again and rest upon Him like a wandering bird coming back to its window."[25]

Likewise, in her book *Enjoying the Presence of God*, spiritual-life author Jan Johnson bids us recognize that the pursuit is a lifelong journey that must be eased into rather than rushed, and enjoyed rather than endured: "This experiment in keeping constant company with God cannot be rushed because God is doing the work in us and we cannot hurry God. We let go of the desire to perform and ease into this practice, knowing that intimacy is never instant. We are embarking on a lifelong journey of welcoming the invasion of our soul by the Holy Spirit so that moments with God are sprinkled throughout the day like manna in the desert."[26] No one is saying the pursuit is easy, but with God's help it can be engaged in successfully. We simply must be patient with ourselves and persevere in the process.

Going further, I will also offer that doing these things requires that we view the pursuit as the very heart of Christian spirituality. After all, how does one put a value on a Spirit-empowered, moment-by-moment mentoring relationship with the risen Jesus that makes it possible for us to embody in ourselves his wisdom, courage, and compassion, as well as his capacity to love God supremely and his neighbor as himself? Such a possibility strikes me as being, in a word, priceless!

In sum, it is my hope this second DIY discussion will get some "likes." As promised, I have done my best to make this tutorial inspirational as well as informational. Did I succeed? Were you inspired to either commence or continue in the hot pursuit? If so, I hope you will not only "like" this discussion but go on to "share" it with others.

Speaking of "sharing," the DIY discussion presented in the next chapter will focus on how we can make good on the third commitment at the core of a Pauline lifestyle spirituality: the cultivation of a missional faithfulness before God. What if it were possible to also take our sharing of the gospel to the next level? I am convinced that this is doable. Let's find out how.

---

25. A. W. Tozer, *The Pursuit of God* (Camp Hill, PA: Christian Publications, 1993), 84.
26. Johnson, *Enjoying the Presence of God*, 21.

TOPICS FOR REVIEW

1. What is your take on the Pursuit? Is it really a thing? If so, how important do you consider it to be to an "I-Thou" lifestyle spirituality?

2. How important to you is the stipulation that there is no one right way to engage in the Pursuit? If this is important to you, why?

3. What was your primary takeaway from this chapter's discussion of "Pursuing Christ in the Morning"?

4. What was your primary takeaway from this chapter's discussion of "Pursuing Christ throughout the Day"?

5. What was your primary takeaway from this chapter's discussion of "Pursuing Christ at Day's End"?

6. To what degree did you need this chapter's concluding admonition for readers to be patient and to persist at this point in the journey? How will you seek this sort of encouragement in the future?

8

COMPLETING THE CIRCUIT

Forging a Missional Spirituality

> The first thing that went through my mind was: "Make sure you touch all the bases!"
>
> —Joe Carter, Sports Collectors Digest

We are approaching the end of our spirituality-forming journey. In previous chapters, we discussed the how-tos of keeping in step with the Spirit and enjoying a moment-by-moment mentoring relationship with the risen Christ as a result. It is time now to complete the circuit by examining the spirituality moves necessary for us to honor the third commitment that is at the heart of a Pauline spirituality: to render to God the Father the missional faithfulness he desires and deserves.

This is an especially important chapter. Let me use an analogy to illustrate why. I recently came across an online sports article titled "Joe Carter Still Relishes in the Glory of His Game-Winning Home Run in the 1993 World Series." The lead-in reads as follows: "One of the biggest home runs in World Series history was hit by Joe Carter in 1993, winning the series for the Toronto Blue Jays."[1] I'm not exactly a Toronto Blue Jays fan, but I enjoy being happy with

---

1. Bert Lehman, "Joe Carter Still Relishes His Game-Winning Home Run in the 1993 World Series," *Sports Collectors Digest*, December 5, 2016, https://sportscollectorsdigest.com/news/joe-carter-world-series-home-run.

someone as they relive a moment when they felt really special. This is why I continued reading the interview with Blue Jays outfielder and first baseman Joe Carter that was conducted years after he slammed a game-ending home run that put him in the history books. Indeed, according to the article, "Not only did that round-tripper give the Jays its second consecutive World Series title, it also enabled Carter to join Bill Mazeroski as the only other player in Major League Baseball history to end a Fall Classic with walk-off homers."[2]

In the interview, Carter described the tension of the moment—the thoughts that were going through his mind right up to and after his bat connected with the ball. First, he prayed that the ball would stay fair. Then, when it did, he was momentarily stunned. "It was all kind of surreal as I headed down the first base line, he recalled. The first thing that went through my mind was: 'Make sure you touch all the bases.'"[3] Ironically, though Joe couldn't hear him at the time, the mic caught the game's announcer encouraging him to do just that. According to the article, "Blue Jays broadcaster Tom Cheek said during that memorable trot: 'Touch 'em all, Joe. You'll never hit a bigger home run in your life.'"[4]

What a great story! And, as it happens, it reminds us of a very important life lesson: the need to touch all the bases. In baseball, a cardinal rule is that a run isn't earned if a base runner fails to touch all three of the bases before arriving at home plate!

Not a sports fan? Maybe a science analogy will work better for you. For an electrical circuit to work, it must be completed (closed). There can't be any missing links (breaks, gaps, openings) in the wiring. Such a gap or opening will stop the flow of electrons from the power source to the device. Incomplete or open circuits don't work. *Only completed circuits get the job done!*

The point I'm making here is that, like missing one of the bases after hitting a home run, or leaving a gap or break in a circuit, not engaging in this third DIY discussion is simply not an option. We have not come close to approximating a Pauline, Spirit-empowered, Christ-emulating, and God the-Father-pleasing lifestyle spirituality if what we end up with fails to play out in an intentionally missional manner!

We know that Paul's own ministry methodology changed slightly from one ministry setting to another. For example, when Paul preached in the synagogue located in Pisidian Antioch (Acts 13:14–41), his message was filled with references to and actual quotations from the Hebrew Scriptures. But when

2. Lehman, "Joe Carter."
3. Lehman, "Joe Carter."
4. Lehman, "Joe Carter."

Paul presented the gospel on Mars Hill to the Areopagus (i.e., an Athenian tribunal, or court, that dealt with judicial and religious matters), he did not cite one Bible verse! While always faithful to the essence of the Jesus story, Paul's ministry message was contextually sensitive so as to be missionally impactful (see Acts 17:32–34).

That said, we also know that it was not simply Paul's ministry message that was contextually sensitive, but his manner as well—that is, the way he worshiped and lived out his faith before others. In other words, I am suggesting that the apostle has his *spirituality* as well as his ministry methodology in mind when he writes,

> To the Jews I became like a Jew, to win the Jews. To those under the law I became like one under the law (though I myself am not under the law), so as to win those under the law. To those not having the law I became like one not having the law (though I am not free from God's law but am under Christ's law), so as to win those not having the law. To the weak I became weak, to win the weak. I have become all things to all people so that by all possible means I might save some. (1 Cor. 9:20–22)

If what I am suggesting is true, then Paul's spirituality was contextually sensitive and, therefore, missional as well as devotional in nature.

Likewise, some support for the concept of a missional spirituality is provided by the apostle Peter. I have in mind the pastoral and missional exhortations presented in 1 Peter 2. Peter's readers are apparently new in the faith, having just recently "tasted and seen" for themselves how real and risen Jesus is. After encouraging these new converts to continue to grow in their salvation (1 Pet. 2:1–3), he immediately begins to hint at their ministry responsibility when he refers to them as a "spiritual house" and "holy priesthood" (1 Pet. 2:4–5).[5] Eventually, Peter clarifies the missional role his readers are to play. It begins with *proclamation*, giving witness to our personal experience of God as we worship and share our testimony with others: "But you are a chosen people, a royal priesthood, a holy nation, God's special possession, that you may declare the praises of him who called you out of darkness into his wonderful light" (1 Pet. 2:9; cf. Acts 26:15–18). But then Peter goes on to clarify that our priestly responsibilities also involve *demonstration*—the way we live day by day as Christ's followers. In the same passage, Peter says,

> Live such good lives among the pagans that, though they accuse you of doing wrong, they may see your good deeds and glorify God on the day he visits us.

5. See also Rev. 1:6; 5:10; 20:6; cf. Phil. 4:18; Heb. 13:15.

. . . For it is God's will that by doing good you should silence the ignorant talk of foolish people. (1 Pet. 2:12, 15)

When we consider these Petrine passages alongside similar ones located in the Pauline corpus (see Eph. 5:15–16; Col. 4:5–6; 1 Thess. 4:12; Titus 2:3–10; cf. 1 Tim. 5:14; 6:1), it becomes clear that both apostles were convinced that the way Christian disciples live into their faith (day in and day out) can and will possess a missional significance. This is an important observation. It leads me to suggest that if our *ultimate aim* is to please the God of the Bible, we simply must commit to the cultivation of a *missional spirituality*—a lifestyle spirituality that is intentionally and thoroughly missional in its orientation, performance, and impact.

How to do this is what this chapter is about. This third DIY discussion concerns some very important, circuit-completing stuff. In other words, and at the risk of mixing my metaphors, let's make sure that we touch all the bases! We do that by committing ourselves to the cultivation of a missional spirituality.

The Purpose of a Missional Spirituality

In a nutshell, a missional spirituality is a Christian lifestyle spirituality that is deliberate about the way it impacts not only the practitioner but also his or her family members, friends, neighbors, and coworkers who are not currently walking with Christ. More specifically, it is a spirituality practiced in a contextually sensitive manner so that those currently outside the faith might be encouraged by our example as Christ's followers to "taste and see" (Ps. 34:8) or "come and see" (John 1:46) for themselves who Jesus is and what he is about. Similarly, it is hoped that a relationship with someone practicing a missional spirituality will provide those who consider themselves post-Christian with some compelling reasons why they should take another look at Christ and his church.

The Particulars of a Missional Spirituality

I have found several personal attributes and communal associations to be especially relevant to a successful contextualization of the Jesus story for the increasingly post-Christian environment in which we Christians in the West now find ourselves in. An elementary goal of a missional spirituality is to intentionally cultivate these essential attributes and associations. Presented below is a simple list that not only provides an overview but also can be useful later on as a quick reference.

Essential Personal Attributes

- A *Christlike attitude:* showing care, gentleness, humility, and respect for those who currently do not share our faith in Christ (and may even be critical of it)
- A *Christlike listening skill:* a willingness to listen with empathy to the stories of others, thus earning the right to speak and act into their lives
- A *Christlike conversational skill:* a learned ability to dialogue with pre- and post-Christians about difficult biblical, theological, and philosophical issues, answering questions and clearing away misconceptions that are keeping them from even entertaining the idea that Christ could really be risen and Christianity true
- A *Christlike ability to identify with those outside the faith without going native:* a personal growth toward a spiritual and moral faithfulness that evidences in our lives the most important type of differentiation—the cardinal spiritual and ethical virtues identified in Micah 6:8 and embodied by Jesus himself

Essential Communal Associations

- An *invitational missional community* that is willing to allow good-hearted though imperfect people to belong before they believe
- An *incarnational missional community* whose gatherings to worship, pray, study, fellowship, and serve are theologically, pneumatologically, and christologically real

These, I suggest, are the primary characteristics of a missionally impactful way of being in the world. In the section below, I will briefly indicate how and why each of these is vital if we are to make a difference in our world for Christ.

The Process of a Missional Spirituality

A genuine, good-faith effort on our part to honor the first two core commitments at the heart of a Pauline lifestyle spirituality will allow the Holy Spirit and the risen Jesus to effect in us the same three dynamics that were so spectacularly evident in Jesus's God-the-Father-pleasing, incarnational ministry: identification-differentiation-transformation. Here is a brief sketch of how the primary characteristics listed above work together to do this.

A Gracious Rather Than Graceless Attitude toward Others

In my own work as a professor teaching undergraduate students, I've become acutely aware of just how very cynical members of the emerging generations can be toward organized religion in general and Christianity in particular. I would venture that this attitude of wariness and cynicism, while due in part to the impact of postmodern philosophy and culture, is also indicative of some deep disappointment with God, the church, and its members. In their book *Unchristian*, Barna researchers David Kinnaman and Gabe Lyons write,

> Our research shows that many of those outside of Christianity, especially younger adults, have little trust in the Christian faith, and esteem for the life-style of Christ followers is quickly fading among outsiders. They admit their emotional and intellectual barriers go up when they are around Christians, and they reject Jesus because they feel rejected by Christians.[6]

Later, they elaborate:

> Painful encounters with the faith also have a strong influence on what a person thinks of Christianity. In fact, we discovered that one-fifth of all outsiders, regardless of age, admitted they "have had a bad experience in a church or with a Christian that gave them a negative image of Jesus Christ." This represents nearly fifty million adult residents of this country—including about nine million young outsiders—who admit they have significant emotional or spiritual baggage from past experiences with so-called Christ followers. Church leaders are not unaware of this issue. Among pastors of Protestant churches, three-quarters said they often encounter people whose negative experiences create major barriers to their openness to Jesus.[7]

At the same time, however, I have discovered that our cultural peers are not opposed to ministry conversations as long as they involve a genuine dialogue rather than a rehearsed monologue, are not condescending or coercive, and do not give the impression that an ongoing friendship requires conversion. What our contemporaries cannot abide is an arrogant, judgmental, pugilistic,

6. David Kinnaman and Gabe Lyons, *Unchristian: What a New Generation Really Thinks about Christianity . . . and Why It Matters* (Grand Rapids: Baker Books, 2007), 11.
7. Kinnaman and Lyons, *Unchristian*, 31–32.

separatist, graceless (essentially pharisaical) religiosity.[8] All of this argues for an attitude of gentleness, humility, and respect for those who do not share our faith in Christ and may even be critical of it.

Empathic Listening

What's more, the current postmodern emphasis on truth being entirely subjective (rather than objective) means that if we are to succeed at enticing folks to take another look at Christ and his church, something more is needed than a rehearsal of the four spiritual laws or some other generic, scripted presentation (our care to utilize colloquial speech and culturally sensitive analogies notwithstanding). To reiterate, what is required is a gospel re-contextualization—a fresh retelling of the story of Jesus that, while maintaining a commitment to the four christological verities that are at the heart of the Christian faith, is profoundly shaped by an empathetic understanding of the non-Christian's deepest fears and aspirations. We must, in a Christlike manner, work hard at building the kind of humble, reciprocal relationships that convince our pre- and post-Christian peers that we genuinely care. Only this will provide them with the psychological air they need to be able to "breathe," to relax in our presence rather than maintain a wary, defensive posture. Not until they are convinced that their questions, disappointments, issues, and hurts have really been "heard" will they become open to a dialogue regarding the radical claims of Christ and an encounter with his transformative Spirit. In other words, we must possess a willingness to listen with empathy, thus earning the right to speak and act into the lives of others. We are never more like the incarnate Christ than when we seek first to understand the pain of the other before we attempt to minister to them.[9]

Conversations That Clear Away Misconceptions

Of course, simply listening empathically does not equate to opening a dialogue. We must also engage in conversations in which we gently encourage our cultural peers to consider the possibility that what they have experienced thus far in their lives was not necessarily the only or best way of understanding who Jesus is and what he is about. To put a finer point on it, I have found that

8. For more on how the phenomenon of Christian pharisaism feeds into the post-Christian dynamic, see Gary Tyra, *Defeating Pharisaism: Recovering Jesus' Disciple-Making Method* (Downers Grove, IL: IVP Books, 2009), 37–76.

9. For more on the skill known as empathic listening, see "Empathic Listening: Going beyond Active Listening," Mind Tools, accessed September 20, 2021, https://www.mindtools.com /CommSkll/EmpathicListening.htm.

dialogue can lead to a new openness to Jesus being who the New Testament says he is. This involves helping pre- and post-Christians recognize that the biblical, theological, and philosophical questions that have previously created so much doubt within them can be addressed in ways that rob these issues of their discipleship-defeating power. I am talking about such issues as the reliability of the biblical documents as a resource for understanding the self-revelation of God; why the Old Testament's "texts of terror" need not lead us to conclude that the God of Israel is a moral monster; why the claims to divinity found in the New Testament's portrayal of Jesus are game changers that simply cannot be ignored or explained away; why the notion that Jesus's death on the cross was necessary for the redemption of all creation makes perfect sense from a metaphysical point of view; why the case for Christ's resurrection, though not provable, really is compelling; why it is important to always keep in mind the difference between genuine Christianity (the teachings of Jesus himself) and *churchianity* (the sometimes egregiously imperfect manner in which his human followers have represented him to one another and to those outside the faith); why the biblical message regarding the telos of human history not only completes the biblical story in a stunningly coherent manner but also provides the human heart with what it most desperately needs—existential hope in the face of temporal suffering.

These and other issues like them can be responded to in faith-restoring and faith-imparting ways. But for this to happen, Christ's followers must take the steps necessary to develop the capacity to dialogue with pre- and post-Christians about difficult biblical, theological, and philosophical issues, clearing away misconceptions that are keeping some folks from even entertaining the idea that Christ could really be risen and Christianity be true.

Imagine someone in your world who has been wary of Christianity someday saying to you, "Well, no one has ever responded to my questions the way you have. I must admit that what we've talked about these past few days, weeks, months is resonating with me. In fact, our conversations have become increasingly compelling! So if I were to, as you put it, 'taste and see' for myself whether Jesus is real and risen, how would I do so?" Wouldn't hearing someone respond to you in this way be a powerful indication of the work of the Holy Spirit in their heart? Wouldn't it be worth all the time you have spent building an honest-to-goodness friendship with them and lovingly speaking into and acting in their life?[10]

10. Of course, we must also invest some time into improving our ability to answer difficult questions and clear away misconceptions regarding genuine Christianity, being careful to do so in a relationally sensitive manner. Two resources I can recommend with this goal in mind are Timothy Keller, *The Reason for God: Belief in an Age of Skepticism* (New York: Penguin

The Dramatic Difference Not Going Native Makes

And yet more is needed if our relational approach to Christian apologetics (defending, explaining, promoting the faith) is to prove fruitful. Those with whom we are in dialogue about spiritual matters must see something in us that seems just as compelling as our answers to their questions. I am talking here about the presence of the risen Christ in us.

While it is vital for us to identify with those we are trying to reach with the Christian gospel, we must take care not to *over-identify* to the point of going native. In missiological parlance, the phrase "going native" refers to occasions when missionaries end up adopting the moral values and ethical behaviors of the target culture even though some of these values and behaviors may conflict with biblical teaching.

Now, one might think that going native was something the apostle Paul would endorse, since his missional practice was to "become all things to all people" in order to "win as many as possible" (1 Cor. 9:22, 19). However, while Paul makes it clear that he felt the freedom in Christ to contextualize the way he lived out his faith (1 Cor. 9:20–21), this only applied to the ceremonial and ritual aspects of his faith, not the moral and ethical aspects. Thus, he provides these parenthetical clarifications: "though I myself am not under the law," and "I am not free from God's law but am under Christ's law" (1 Cor. 9:20–21).

This is where the differentiation dynamic that is also part of the incarnational ministry model comes in—the *differentiation* that, when accompanied by some sincere *identification*, results in actual *transformation*. It is important, therefore, to emphasize here how important it is for our spiritually disenchanted friends, family members, and coworkers to sense in us a genuine personal growth toward a spiritual and moral faithfulness before God. Jesus vociferously condemned the hypocrisy he spied in the lives of the religious leaders of his day.[11] Unfortunately, as was indicated above, the notion that contemporary Christian churches are rife with this and other anti-virtues inimical to fruitful Christian witness is virtually ubiquitous.[12] If we want to commend to our family members, friends, neighbors, and coworkers a real relationship with God that is genuinely transformational in its

---

Books, 2009); and Dan Kimball, *How (Not) to Read the Bible: Making Sense of the Anti-women, Anti-science, Pro-violence, Pro-slavery and Other Crazy-Sounding Parts of Scripture* (Grand Rapids: Zondervan, 2020).

11. See, e.g., Matt. 6:2, 5, 16; 7:5; 15:7–9; 23:13, 15, 23, 25, 33.

12. For more on this, see Tyra, *Defeating Pharisaism*, 62–68; Tyra, *A Missional Orthodoxy: Theology and Ministry in a Post-Christian Context* (Downers Grove, IL: IVP Academic, 2013), 38–40.

impact, some actual life change (for the good) needs to be observable in our own lives![13]

In particular, it is especially important that friends, family members, neighbors, and coworkers witness in us some evidence of the most important type of differentiation there is: the ever-increasing presence within us of the cardinal spiritual and ethical virtues identified in Micah 6:8 and embodied by Jesus himself. It is hard to overstate how vital to the younger generations are these three ethical virtues: to act justly, to love with mercy, to walk humbly and faithfully before God. A missional spirituality will be intentional about the prayerful cultivation of these virtues.[14]

A Missional Inclusivity

Also critical to a fruitful contextualization of the gospel in our increasingly postmodern, post-Christian ministry context is a missional community that is willing to allow people to belong before they believe. Historically, churches have insisted that inquirers make a decision for Christ *before* they are considered part of the community and *before* the process of spiritual, moral, and ministry formation commences. However, in an increasingly postmodern world, our apologetic must become increasingly relational and experiential. Many of our cultural peers will need to feel as well as think their way into the faith. Relationships with loving, caring, and humble yet thoughtful Christians are therefore critical. With this thought in mind, many missional communities are deliberately inviting both pre- and post-Christian acquaintances to "hang" with them *while* these acquaintances consider the claims of Christ either for the first time or anew, allowing these wary ones the opportunity to genuinely *experience* Christ as well as ponder him intellectually. This ministry move finds some biblical support in the call of Philip to the skeptical Nathanael: "Come and see" (John 1:46).

What is more, we should keep in mind that this emphasis on relationality was at the heart of St. Patrick's super-successful missional ministry in the early fifth century to the pagans who populated Ireland. The story is a remarkable one. Patrick (ca. 385–ca. 461) was only sixteen years old when he was kidnapped by a band of Celtic pirates, taken to Ireland, and sold into slavery. After about six years of captivity, Patrick escaped, made his way back

13. See Roger Helland and Leonard Hjalmarson, *Missional Spirituality: Embodying God's Love from the Inside Out* (Downers Grove, IL: IVP Books, 2011), 24–25.

14. For a more thorough discussion of the way these three virtues seem to be grounded in the character of God himself and of the role they play, therefore, in a moral faithfulness before him, see Gary Tyra, *Pursuing Moral Faithfulness: Ethics and Christian Discipleship* (Downers Grove, IL: IVP Academic, 2015), 167–79.

to England, trained for the ministry, and served for a couple of decades as a Roman Catholic parish priest. Eventually, however, Patrick formed what might be referred to today as a "missional team" made up of priests, seminarians, laymen, and laywomen and returned to Ireland with them around AD 432.[15]

I have written elsewhere at length about the contextual nature of St. Patrick's missional ministry and the spirituality that funded it.[16] Breaking with the traditional practice of Roman Catholic missionaries (which called for the *civilization* of people groups before their *Christianization*), the missional communities led by Patrick would invite pagan village members to pray, worship, study, and converse with them. What they discovered was how effective this was at having non-Christians *experience* their way into the Christian faith. In his book *The Celtic Way of Evangelism*, George Hunter explains that after a few days or weeks, it was not unusual for these seekers to find themselves "believing what these Christians believe." Once this occurred, they were invited to commit their lives to Christ and formally begin their discipleship training.[17] This "come and see" approach was not the only ingredient in Patrick's successful missional ministry, but it was certainly key. Here is the big takeaway: the identification-differentiation-transformation process of Christian ministry contextualization works in an optimal manner when we allow seekers to pray, worship, study, fellowship, and serve along with us as they consider the claims of Christ.

Taking Sacramental to the Next Level

And yet I must quickly include this critical caveat: this phenomenon of unbelievers experiencing as well as thinking their way into the faith only works if the missional community employing the "come and see" approach is one whose gatherings to worship, pray, study, fellowship, and serve are experienced as theologically, pneumatologically, and christologically real! This makes sense, doesn't it? For good-hearted but wary seekers to experience how real and risen Jesus is as they pray, worship, study, fellowship, and serve along with us presumes that Jesus really is there in our midst and that, through the manifesting, convicting, and convincing work of his Spirit (John 16:7–15), they may at some point come to the place where they exclaim, "Whoa! God is really among you!" (see 1 Cor. 14:24–25).

15. Tyra, *Pursuing Moral Faithfulness*, 2–3.
16. See Gary Tyra, "Welcome to Paul's World: The Contextual Nature of Missional Spirituality," in *Spirituality for the Sent: Casting a New Vision for the Missional Church*, ed. Nathan A. Finn and Keith S. Whitfield (Downers Grove, IL: IVP Academic, 2017), 123–44.
17. George G. Hunter III, *The Celtic Way of Evangelism: How Christianity Can Reach the West . . . Again* (Nashville: Abingdon, 2010), 42.

I want to suggest that a sacrament is best understood as an ecclesial rite or ritual that serves not only as a *sign* or *symbol* of a spiritual reality but also possesses the potential to actually enable participants to *experience* that reality. A broad definition such as this allows me to argue that it is not just water baptism and the Eucharist that can be considered sacraments; other ecclesial dynamics also can, when anointed by the Holy Spirit, enable us to *experience* the reality (presence and power) of the risen Jesus. Thus, I am convinced that any of the four cardinal components of Christian discipleship—worship, nurture, community, and mission—can be experienced in a sacramental, encounter-effecting manner.

I will also suggest that this paradigm—this broadened, theologically real understanding of the sacramental dynamic—is a game changer when it comes to just about everything related to Christian spirituality and ministry. My theology mentor in grad school, the late Ray Anderson, following Karl Barth and T. F. Torrance, described Jesus as the "primary sacrament," the primary point of connection between God and man.[18] In his book *The Soul of Ministry*, Anderson went on to speak of the church as the continuing sacramental presence of Jesus Christ: "The church as the body of Christ now lives between the cross and the return of Christ (*parousia*). The original sacramental relation of God to humanity through Jesus Christ is now represented through the enactment of the life of the church itself."[19] In other words, says Anderson, the local church, as a tangible expression or "body" of the resurrected and ascended Christ, is called to function as a point of connection (sacrament) between hurting people and Jesus Christ, who in turn functions as the primary point of connection (sacrament) between them and God. The local church can and should be a place where hurting people can find and touch the hem of Jesus's garment, so to speak, in order to experience the grace of God through him. This is good news: there are places where people can go to meet with and be encountered by the resurrected and ascended Jesus!

This is what I mean when I suggest the need for the readers of my book to take sacramental to the next level. As church members, every time we attend a worship-, teaching-, fellowship-, or mission-oriented event, we can and should do so with an openness to the possibility that we may, like the prophet Isaiah, experience a genuine, real, life-story-changing encounter with God (Isa. 6:1–8). It also means that church leaders—those of us who plan and preside over such events—should be very careful to do so in a prayerfully

18. Ray Anderson, *The Soul of Ministry: Forming Leaders for God's People* (Louisville: Westminster John Knox, 1997), 167–69.

19. Anderson, *Soul of Ministry*, 169–70. See also David J. Bosch, *Transforming Mission: Paradigm Shifts in Theology of Mission* (Maryknoll, NY: Orbis Books, 2011), 383–85.

expectant manner. Every ecclesial event is potentially holy ground—a sacred space where, for this or that person, the phenomenon of a burning bush might occur (see Exod. 3:1–6).

If this sacramental dynamic can be at work in the life of the local church as a whole, it can and must also earmark the worshiping, praying, studying, encouraging, sharing, and serving of its missional teams. It is only then that the missionally inclusive "come and see" so as to "taste and see" approach to ministry will prove fruitful. We simply must take sacramental to the next level if we want to be successful at emulating the identification-differentiation-transformation dynamic of Jesus's incarnational ministry.

But nothing that is "next level" can occur unless we take seriously the three core commitments that were discussed in part 2 of this book: (1) keeping in step with the Spirit, (2) pursuing Christ's empowering presence, and (3) cultivating a God-the-Father-pleasing (missionally faithful) lifestyle. It is only when all three of these core commitments are being honored, at the same time, that one's lifestyle spirituality begins to play out as a fruitful missional spirituality as well. We simply must be careful to complete the circuit, touching *all* the bases in the process!

At this point some readers, especially those familiar with Dallas Willard's seminal work *The Spirit of the Disciplines*, might be wondering how all the other spiritual disciplines traditionally associated with Christian spiritual formation fit into this proposal for a lifestyle, missional spirituality. Some might also be curious about the role spirituality practices of a more recent vintage might play in a Pauline "I-Thou" lifestyle spirituality. I will endeavor to address these important, potentially controversial topics in the final chapter of this book.

TOPICS FOR REVIEW

1. Is the notion of a *missional* spirituality new to you, or were you already familiar with the idea? How would you explain to someone what is distinctive about this type of Christian spirituality?

2. Did the lists of essential personal attributes and essential communal associations presented in this chapter ring true for you? Why or why not? What emendations would you make?

3. How would you explain to someone the ministry importance of a gracious rather than graceless attitude toward others and the practice of empathic listening?

4. How would you explain to someone the ministry importance of being able to engage in conversations that clear away misconceptions and *to not* go native?

5. How would you explain to someone the ministry importance of a missional inclusivity and taking sacramental to the next level?

6. Reflect on how you might respond to this chapter. What is your biggest personal takeaway? Is the Holy Spirit prompting you in any manner?

9

ALL THE SPIRITUAL DISCIPLINES

Not Just Any Engagement Will Do!

In fact, spiritual practices can become bondages of performance that miss the purpose of practicing the presence of God, if undertaken "according to the flesh" rather than "by the Spirit" (Gal. 5:16–17; 6:8). In Jesus' day, the teachers of the law and the Pharisees were prime examples of the former (Matt. 23:13–36). When motivated by a pure heart (Matt. 5:8) to commune with God, however, spiritual practices become doorways for the Spirit to work deeply in the human heart, drawing us further into worship by way of a reciprocal love relationship.

—Diane J. Chandler, *Christian Spiritual Formation*

So far, the primary focus of this work has been on the need to keep in step with Christ's Spirit, to engage in the pursuit of Christ's empowering presence, and to thereby cultivate a God-the-Father-pleasing, missionally faithful lifestyle. Some of the customs or spiritual practices by which the Holy Spirit enables a fruitful engagement in "the pursuit" were discussed in chapter 7. As we near the end of our journey together, I can imagine some readers wondering what role the classic spiritual practices—such as fasting, giving, solitude, silence, service, secrecy, and submission—play in the trinitarian "I-Thou" lifestyle spirituality we seem to see the apostle Paul promoting.

To be clear, I am committed to the belief that there is not only room for *all* the classic disciplines of the Spirit in a Pauline spirituality but a necessity for them as well. And yet, for any of these disciplines to enable a *lifestyle* that is Spirit-empowered, Christ-emulating, and God-the-Father-pleasing, it must be practiced in a certain manner. Not just any kind of engagement will do.

Thus, the aim of this final discussion is to be frank about what must happen for all the spiritual disciplines we engage in to have the effect in us that our relational, holy, missional God desires. Along the way, I will also indicate how my understanding of the *enabling* role of the spiritual disciplines compares with the understanding put forward by my former mentor, the late Dallas Willard.

As an advance organizer, here is an overview of what will be discussed in this final chapter. In order for the spiritual disciplines to impact us the way Jesus and Paul anticipated, they need to be understood in a functional manner and then practiced in a way that is theologically informed, theologically real, pursuit prioritizing, pneumatologically real, and mission minded. Let's have a look now at each of these dynamics.

A *Functional* Understanding of the Disciplines

There are numerous books that treat the topic of spiritual disciplines currently on offer. While I am sure all of them possess value, I am going to suggest that the best ones will be careful to encourage a *functional* understanding of the disciplines. In other words, in addition to surveying the disciplines and explaining what they entail, these books will also provide readers with (1) a clear awareness of why these practices were promoted in the first place by Jesus, his apostles, or those recognized as Christian spiritual masters and (2) a criterion for how to assess the degree to which one's engagement in them is having the effect that Jesus, his apostles, or the spiritual masters had in mind.

This need for a careful, thoughtful, functional understanding of the disciplines is indicated by Jesus in his Sermon on the Mount (Matt. 5–7). In the middle of this discipleship teaching, Jesus presents a biting critique of the hypocritical way *some* religious leaders of his day were engaging in some otherwise very useful spiritual disciplines—giving, prayer, and fasting (see Matt. 6:1–18).[1] This suggests the critical need for a nuanced understanding of the "what," "why," and "how" of one's engagement in spiritual disciplines. Otherwise, we run the risk of approaching the disciplines as ends in themselves

---

1. On the basis of passages such as Matt. 22:15–18; 23:13, 15, 23, 25, 27–29; Mark 7:5–8; 12:13–15; Luke 12:1, most biblical scholars agree that the hypocrites referred to in Matt. 6 were some members of the party of the Pharisees. For more on the notion that Jesus is using the Pharisees in his Sermon on the Mount as an anti-model as he engages in the spiritual, moral, and ministry formation of his disciples, see part 2 of Gary Tyra, *Defeating Pharisaism: Recovering Jesus' Disciple-Making Method* (Downers Grove, IL: IVP Books, 2009), 79–189.

rather than as means to the end that Jesus, Paul, and the spiritual masters originally had in mind. This could mean that we actually end up cultivating a spirituality that not only fails to play out in a God-pleasing, missional manner but actually succeeds at doing just the opposite: pushing people away from Christ and his church and greatly displeasing God in the process!

A *Theologically Informed* Engagement in the Disciplines

Looking more closely at Jesus's critique of the spirituality of "the hypocrites" in Matthew 6:1–18, we find him finding fault with both the *motive* behind their practice of giving, prayer, and fasting and the *manner* in which they did these things. As we will soon see, these two aspects of one's spirituality are integrally related.

With respect to their *motive*, Jesus essentially accuses the hypocrites of possessing something other than the "theocentric starting point" and "theo-sensitive ultimate concern" discussed in chapter 2 of this book. To review, a spirituality that fails to be theocentric in its starting point, one that begins with an anthropocentric orientation instead (i.e., the self's "petty feelings and needs, ideas and capacities"[2]), tends to become narcissistic and utilitarian (i.e., self-serving rather than God-pleasing) in essence and effect. It is hard not to have this warning come to mind when we "hear" Jesus assert in a rather matter-of-fact manner that the motive of the "hypocrites" when engaging in their spiritual practices was not to please and commune with their God but was, instead, to be "honored" (Matt. 6:2), "seen" (v. 5), and highly regarded by their peers (v. 16).

Not surprisingly, this theologically impoverished motive for engaging in the disciplines produced a theologically bankrupt manner of doing so. This explains (1) why Jesus kept referring to these bad actors as "hypocrites" and (2) his repeated warnings that their "reward" was dreadfully temporal and not at all transformational (Matt. 6:2, 5, 16). Moreover, judging by what Jesus had to say to and about these "hypocrites" in chapter 23 of Matthew's Gospel, he considered the effect of their spirituality to be anything but missionally helpful (Matt. 23:13–15)!

A *Theologically Real* Engagement in the Disciplines

Looking again at Matthew 6, Jesus obviously has a theologically real "I-Thou" (rather than "I-It") approach to prayer in mind when he instructs his disciples

2. Evelyn Underhill, *The School of Charity: Meditations on the Christian Creed* (Wilton, CT: Morehouse, 1991), 6.

with these words: "But when you pray, go into your room, close the door and pray to your Father, who is unseen. Then your Father, who sees what is done in secret, will reward you. And when you pray, do not keep on babbling like pagans, for they think they will be heard because of their many words. Do not be like them, for your Father knows what you need before you ask him" (vv. 6–8). According to British theologian Michael Green, Jesus breaks some new ground when he instructs his disciples to address God as "Father" as they pray. Says Green of Jesus's sidebar discussion of prayer in the sermon, "It begins with the word of intimacy, *Father*. In the Aramaic Jesus spoke, that would be 'Abba,' Jesus' own characteristic address to God. Nobody had ever addressed God like that. The word was used by little children of their daddy. And Jesus, who alone had that intimacy or relationship with God as his dear daddy, gives his disciples the right to come in on the same level of intimacy, and call God Abba. Amazing!"[3]

This is an important observation. It is one thing to pray, worship, study, fellowship, celebrate, or serve with just the idea of God in mind; it is another to engage in these practices fully reckoning with God's real, loving, holy, empowering presence. It was because Jesus modeled for us an "I-Thou" rather than "I-It" approach to spiritual formation that the apostle Paul was all about this type of spirituality as well.

With the notion of a missional spirituality in mind, we simply must recognize that the goal is not simply to invite curious pre- and post-Christians to "hang" with us as we worship, pray, study, fellowship, celebrate, and serve the poor but for those seekers, because of our theologically real approach to these spirituality practices, to genuinely sense the real, awesome, yet gracious presence of God among us as we do so! This is why we must never allow ourselves to forget how important a *theologically real* engagement in the spiritual disciplines is to a missional spirituality. When it comes to the spiritual life, expectation tends to impact experience, as evidenced by those biblical passages that link promises of the *experience* of God with encouragements to proactively call to him (Jer. 33:3), wait upon him (Isa. 40:31), or draw near to him (James 4:8) in an *expectant* manner.

A *Pursuit-Prioritizing* and *Pneumatologically Real* Engagement in the Disciplines

I hope it is apparent by now that my main mentor when it comes to Christian spirituality (this side of Jesus himself) is the apostle Paul. A close second to

---

3. Michael Green, *The Message of Matthew* (Downers Grove, IL: InterVarsity, 1988), 100.

him, however, is the late Dallas Willard, through his doctoral seminar, writings, and some email exchanges. At the risk of oversimplifying Willard's take on the spiritual disciplines, I will simply indicate here that both Willard and I insist that Jesus himself should be at the focal point of the Christian's spiritual formation, and that an engagement in the spiritual disciplines makes it possible for us to experience the reality of Christ in our lives.[4] Anyone familiar with Willard's writings is aware of the importance he placed on how the spiritual disciplines—by training the body as well as the mind, will (heart and spirit), social dimension, and soul—enable Christ's followers to react "on the spot" to all types of life situations as Jesus would react if he were us.[5] For instance, near the beginning of *The Spirit of the Disciplines*, Willard provides his readers with a summary statement that emphasizes the importance of the spiritual disciplines for the process of Christian spiritual formation:

> This book is a plea for the Christian community to place the disciplines for the spiritual life at the heart of the gospel. When we call men and women to life in Christ Jesus, we are offering them the greatest opportunity of their lives—the opportunity of a vivid companionship with him, in which they will learn to be like him and live as he lived. This is that "transforming friendship" explained by Leslie Weatherhead. We *meet* and *dwell* with Jesus and his Father in the disciplines for the spiritual life.[6]

In another early passage of the same work, Willard explains,

> The chapters that follow are written to aid you in understanding the absolute necessity of the spiritual disciplines for our faith, and the revolutionary results of practicing these disciplines intelligently and enthusiastically through a full, grace-filled, Christlike life.[7]

Clearly, Willard's approach to Christian spiritual formation placed the disciplines front and center as the key to spiritual formation in Christ. However, what these quotations also make apparent is the *enabling* role the disciplines play. According to Willard, they contribute to or facilitate a "vivid companionship" and "transforming friendship" with Christ Jesus. We know already, from discussions in previous chapters, that Willard would in later writings

---

4. Dallas Willard, *The Spirit of the Disciplines: Understanding How God Changes Lives* (New York: HarperOne, 1988), xii, 96.

5. Willard, *Spirit of the Disciplines*, 5, 7, 9. For an extended, very thorough discussion of Willard's holistic take on spiritual transformation, see Dallas Willard, *Renovation of the Heart: Putting on the Character of Christ* (Colorado Springs: NavPress, 2002), 95–216.

6. Willard, *Spirit of the Disciplines*, xi (emphasis original).

7. Willard, *Spirit of the Disciplines*, xii.

also encourage a hot pursuit of Jesus Christ.[8] While he does not use the phrase "hot pursuit" in *The Spirit of the Disciplines*, he does emphasize, more than once, the enabling connection that exists between the spiritual disciplines and the experience of Christ's empowering presence. Well into the book, we find these two passages:

> A discipline for the spiritual life is, when the dust of history is blown away, nothing but an activity undertaken to bring us into more effective cooperation with Christ and his Kingdom.[9]

> When through spiritual disciplines I become able heartily to bless those who curse me, pray without ceasing, to be at peace when not given credit for good deeds I've done, or to master the evil that comes my way, it is because my disciplinary activities have inwardly poised me for more and more interaction with the powers of the loving God and his Kingdom. Such is the potential we tap into when we use the disciplines.[10]

Moreover, Willard sounds a similar note in his book *The Great Omission*. Only, in this case, he seems to explicitly indicate that the result of the hot pursuit is something akin to what I have been referring to as an ongoing, mentoring relationship with the risen Jesus:

> The movements of the Spirit of Christ in the embodied personality are often identifiable, tangible events. Frequently they come in the form of individualized "words" from Christ to his apprentices who are involved in Kingdom living. He is our living teacher, and we are not asleep while we walk with him. Spiritual formation in Christ is not simply an unconscious process in which *results* may be observed while the One who works in us remains hidden. We actually experience his workings. We *look* for them, expect them, give thanks for them. We are consciously engaged with him in the details of our existence and our spiritual transformation.[11]

Finally, in one of his most recent books, *Knowing Christ Today*, Willard speaks of the possibility of living one's life with a "Christ focus," one aspect of which involves "the practice of Christ's constant presence."[12] He refers also

---

8. Willard, *Renovation of the Heart*, 42.
9. Willard, *Spirit of the Disciplines*, 156.
10. Willard, *Spirit of the Disciplines*, 157.
11. Dallas Willard, *The Great Omission: Reclaiming Jesus's Essential Teachings on Discipleship* (San Francisco: HarperSanFrancisco, 2006), 75.
12. Dallas Willard, *Knowing Christ Today: Why We Can Trust Spiritual Knowledge* (New York: HarperOne, 2009), 156.

in this book to our need to open ourselves to the "Presence,"[13] thus achieving something he refers to as the "with God" life.[14]

So, in sum, I believe that a thoughtful pondering of all these quotations, when considered alongside the arguments presented in previous chapters of this book, will suggest that both Willard and I agree that the spiritual disciplines are important not only because of the way they directly impact our bodies, minds, wills, social dimensions, and souls but because they enable the cultivation of a mentoring relationship with Jesus, who then equips us to live "on the spot" the way he would were he in our shoes. In other words, we do not participate in the spiritual disciplines as ends in themselves. We participate in them because they are key to experiencing Christ's empowering presence in our lives. This is what I mean when I refer to the need to engage in the disciplines in a "pursuit-prioritizing" manner. When we engage in any spiritual discipline, we should have the pursuit in mind.

That said, I have also argued in this work that it is only through a pneumatologically real engagement in the disciplines that we experience the empowering presence of Christ and that such an engagement requires us to continually surrender ourselves to the leadership of the Spirit and pray in the Spirit, thus becoming increasingly sensitive and responsive to the Spirit's devotional and lifestyle promptings. In other words, we must seek to keep in step with the Spirit (Gal. 5:25) because there seems to be a dialectical relationship between the Spirit and Christ. It is through the Spirit that we experience Christ's real presence, but it is also through the Spirit that the risen Jesus communicates with us, providing the spiritual direction and empowerment we need to experience spiritual transformation.

The question I have occasionally asked myself since Willard's passing is this: How would he have felt about this emphasis I have come to place on Paul's call to keep in step with the Spirit—that is, my contention that we must practice the spiritual disciplines in a pneumatologically real, pneumatologically expectant manner for them to succeed at what Jesus intended for them to do in our lives? I wouldn't dare to simply presume that Willard would have affirmed this emphasis on the need to keep in step with the Spirit, but I have some reasons to believe he might have.

While it is true that Willard does not discuss Galatians 5:25 in *The Spirit of the Disciplines*, he does do so in *The Great Omission*: "As Paul points out, living in the Spirit allows us to 'walk in' the Spirit (Gal. 5:25). This all-powerful, creative personality, the promised 'strengthener,' the Paraclete of

13. Willard, *Knowing Christ Today*, 159.
14. Willard, *Knowing Christ Today*, 161.

John 14, gently awaits our invitation to him to act upon us, with us, and for us."[15] Then, in that same work, Willard seems to provide some implicit support for the thesis I have presented in this book when he goes on to explain, "What brings about our transformation into Christ-likeness is our direct, personal interaction with Christ through the Spirit. The Spirit makes Christ present to us and draws us toward his likeness. It is as we thus behold the 'glory of the Lord' that we are constantly 'transformed into the same image from one degree of glory to another; for this comes from the Lord, the Spirit' (2 Cor. 3:18)."[16]

While this is not an explicit endorsement of the necessity of a pneumatologically real approach to the disciplines, it does affirm my contention that it is the Holy Spirit who enables us to experience Christ's power and presence and that it is through the Spirit that Christ provides us, his apprentices, with the direction and empowerment that leads to our spiritual transformation. Supporting this conclusion are several passages in Willard's book *Hearing God*, which cite, with evident approval, some observations provided by several other theologians and churchmen that seem to reflect a realist rather than nonrealist understanding of the Holy Spirit.[17] Here is but one example, a quotation from a lecture once delivered by C. H. Spurgeon:

> Even so we have felt the Spirit of God operating upon our hearts, we have known and perceived the power which he wields over human spirits, and we know him by frequent, conscious, personal contact. By the sensitiveness of our spirit we are as much made conscious of the presence of the Spirit of God as we are made cognizant of the existence of souls, or as we are certified of the existence of matter by its action upon our senses. We have been raised from the dull sphere of mere mind and matter into the heavenly radiance of the spirit-world; and now, as spiritual men [and women], we discern spiritual things, we feel the forces which are paramount in the spirit-realm, and we know that there is a Holy Ghost, for we feel him operating upon our spirits.[18]

All this is to say that, while both Willard and I heartily affirm Paul's call for us to "exercise [ourselves] unto godliness" (1 Tim. 4:7 KJV),[19] we also both seem to agree on the need to reckon with the apostle Paul's call to keep in step

15. Willard, *Great Omission*, 27. There is also a reference to Gal. 5:25 in Dallas Willard, *Hearing God: Developing a Conversational Relationship with God* (Downers Grove, IL: InterVarsity, 1999), 150.

16. Willard, *Great Omission*, 28.

17. Willard, *Hearing God*, 151, 166, 199.

18. C. H. Spurgeon, *Spurgeon's Lectures to His Students*, ed. David Otis Fuller (Grand Rapids: Zondervan, 1945), 172, cited in Willard, *Hearing God*, 151.

19. See Willard, *Spirit of the Disciplines*, xii.

with the Spirit. We must never forget that, ultimately, it is a Spirit-enabled, Spirit-prompted engagement in the disciplines that makes them effective at enabling us to experience that mentoring relationship with Christ that, in turn, provides us with the direction and empowerment necessary for the cultivation of a God-pleasing lifestyle spirituality.

A *Mission-Minded* Engagement in the Disciplines

Furthermore, given the missional nature of God, a theologically informed, theo-sensitive approach to the spiritual disciplines mandates that we engage in *all* our spirituality practices with the goal of cultivating a *missional spirituality* in view. This concept provides us with help on two important fronts: such a commitment not only serves to ensure that our spirituality practices function in our lives in ways that are genuinely missionally impactful but also opens the door to just about *any* activity functioning as a spirituality practice if the motive behind it is to be missionally faithful before God. With that latter thought in mind, let's identify several categories of spirituality practices we have not focused on yet.

A *Missional Spirituality and* Christian Liturgy

In recent years, more and more evangelicals, even those who identify as Pentecostal or Charismatic, have indicated a deep appreciation for the way "ritual and liturgy" have enabled them to experience the presence of Christ during worship gatherings. Indeed, an increasing number of my students are testifying that they are now more likely to sense the presence of the risen Jesus in a High Church rather than a Low Church (i.e., evangelical or Pentevangelical) worship gathering. While I must admit to possessing a theological concern whenever I hear someone assert that liturgical worship is not simply *a* way to experience the Spirit of Christ but *the* way, it would appear that, depending on how it is engaged in, liturgical worship should be viewed as a very valuable spirituality practice that possesses both formational and missional value precisely because the Holy Spirit is indeed using it to effect sacramental encounters with the risen Jesus in people's lives.

In his book *Spirit and Sacrament*, Andrew Wilson seems to be describing a healthy, balanced, pneumatologically real version of liturgical worship:

> Imagine a service that includes healing testimonies and prayers of confession, psalms, hymns and spiritual songs, baptism in water and baptism in the Spirit, creeds that move the soul and rhythms that move the body. Imagine young men

seeing visions, old men dreaming dreams, sons and daughters prophesying, and all of them coming to the same Table and then going on their way rejoicing. Can you see it? That's what it means to be Eucharismatic.[20]

I do see it. Indeed, I want to encourage everyone reading this book to become adept at (or at least open to) really *experiencing* Christ in worship regardless of the ecclesial setting in which that worship is occurring. God forbid that those of us who consider ourselves fully devoted Christ followers would allow ourselves to come to the place where we can encounter Christ only when worshiping in a particular ecclesial environment. To cultivate this devotional dexterity, however, will require that we approach the practice of worship (whether liturgical or not) in the same ways we approach any spiritual discipline: in a functional, theologically informed, theologically real, pneumatologically real, pursuit-prioritizing, and mission-minded manner. And we must do this not because we are prioritizing mission over worship but because the God we are worshiping is a missional God who cares deeply about the lost and is eager to have his people render to him a spiritual, moral, and *missional* faithfulness.

A Missional Spirituality and Christian Praxis

Can an engagement in political action be considered a spirituality practice—in this case, an activity that not only evidences one's connection to Christ but strengthens it as well? The short answer is "yes," but it comes with some important caveats.

In the preceding chapter, we took notice of the fact that there is such a thing as "sinful praxis," an application of one's theological beliefs to a social problem that ends up doing more harm than good. One thinks of the assassination of abortion providers as an example.[21] It is with this thought in mind that I want to suggest that, though the Bible clearly calls Christians to advocate for justice, and even though a democratic form of government makes it possible for many contemporary Christ followers to do this through political means, there is a right and wrong way to go about this. Given our overarching call as Christ's followers to fulfill the Great Commission, the goal for our involvement in the political process should be—in addition to seeing justice done for hurting, powerless, voiceless people—the cultivation of a

20. Andrew Wilson, *Spirit and Sacrament: An Invitation to Eucharismatic Worship* (Grand Rapids: Zondervan, 2018), 15–16.
21. Cheryl Bridges Johns and Vardaman W. White, "The Ethics of Being: Character, Community, Praxis," in *Elements of a Christian Worldview*, ed. Michael D. Palmer (Springfield, MO: Logion, 1998), 304.

social environment that enables more and more lost people to come to faith in Christ (see 1 Tim. 2:3–4). Therefore, however involved we become in the political process, whatever informed action we feel God calling us to engage in, we must always conduct ourselves in an honest but loving and Christlike manner! No matter how strongly we may feel about a political or cultural issue, no matter how much righteous indignation we may feel compelled to exhibit, we must first and foremost act as fully devoted followers of Jesus Christ who are committed to emulating his spiritual, moral, and missional faithfulness before the Father. This is a missional faithfulness that is informed by the Great Commission (Matt. 28:19) as well as the Great Commandments (Matt. 22:36–40). Thus, if our political engagement ends up pushing people away from faith in Christ rather than making them hungry and thirsty for him, we need to take pause. How can an engagement in Christian praxis function as a legitimate spirituality practice if it works against rather than toward God's ultimate concerns?

Our engagement in political action only functions as a spirituality practice when we do so prayerfully, always keeping the entirety of God's character and mission in mind. We can and should engage in Christian praxis as a spirituality practice. But, like all the spiritual disciplines, it must be performed in a pursuit-prioritizing, mission-minded manner. The good news is that doing this will make a profound difference in the way Christians participate in the political process. We can also hope that it will have a Christ-honoring, God-pleasing effect on the way we engage in political discourse as well!

A Missional Spirituality and Just About Every Other Activity

The concept of a missional spirituality has implications not only for our engagement in the political process but for other activities as well. A serious engagement in the pursuit can mean that just about every aspect of one's lifestyle can be missionally impactful!

For example, a mission-minded participation in various nonecclesial communities (clubs, boards, service-oriented associations, etc.) can put us in proximity to the very people in our cultural context to whom Christ is calling us to minister. I know from personal experience that such involvement in one's community can be taxing at times. Yet we do so prayerfully in the hope that the identification-differentiation-transformation process of incarnational ministry will play out.

Moreover, a mission-minded imbibing of pop culture (music, literature, theater, and various forms of visual media) can be engaged in with the same identification-differentiation-transformation dynamic in mind. While we should be careful *not* to "go native" (see Prov. 4:20–27), our prayerful participation in the culture in which we are embedded can serve to help us *understand* the people we are called to identify with—that is, to understand the discourse that shapes their values, the stories that define their hopes, and the shared experiences that engender the fears and anxieties that keep them up at night. Such an understanding can be used by the Spirit of mission to inspire us toward ministry speech and actions that serve to contextualize the Jesus story in a way that is not only comprehensible but compelling as well! In addition, the deeper comprehension of the social imaginary that a mission-minded, prayerful participation in pop culture provides can enable Christ's followers to better and more proactively address the questions and clear away the misconceptions that have thus far kept our cultural peers from tasting and seeing for themselves just how real and risen Jesus is.

The bottom line is that we need to broaden our sense of what may be thought of as a spirituality practice and how such practices are to be performed. The notion of a missional spirituality blows the doors off our traditional way of thinking about spiritual disciplines: how many there are, what they are supposed to do, how to measure the degree to which our engagement in them is being effective. To review, I am arguing here for a functional understanding of the spiritual disciplines and an engagement in them that is theologically informed, theologically real, pneumatologically real, pursuit prioritizing, and mission minded. This type of engagement is necessary whether the spirituality practice has been known for ages (prayer, fasting, giving, solitude, service, silence, submission, etc.) or is of more recent vintage (unplugging, detachment, sobriety, slowing, waiting, hospitality, justice, community involvement, cultural research, etc.).

Over the years, many books have been produced that function as surveys and how-to manuals.[22] What this discussion has sought to contribute to the conversation regarding spiritual disciplines is an indication of how important it is, given God's missional nature, for all of them to be approached in a way that is missionally sensitive. This really is a game changer. It explains why the spirituality to which the apostle Paul keeps calling his readers to is not just Christian but fully trinitarian and "I-Thou" in nature—a spirituality that is designed to produce within Christ's followers a *lifestyle* that is spiritually, morally, and missionally faithful.

---

22. For a comprehensive compendium of possible spiritual disciplines, see Adele Ahlberg Calhoun, *Spiritual Disciplines Handbook: Practices That Transform Us*, rev. ed. (Downers Grove, IL: IVP Books, 2015).

The question we must grapple with is this: Will we take Paul's call to a lifestyle spirituality seriously? In the brief conclusion that follows, I will provide a final reason why we should.

TOPICS FOR REVIEW

1. According to this chapter, what two things does a functional understanding of the spiritual disciplines provide us with? How important do you think these things are?

2. According to Matthew 6:1–18, in what sense was the hypocrites' motive for engaging in spiritual disciplines "theologically impoverished" and their manner "theologically bankrupt"?

3. How would you explain to someone what this chapter has to say about what a theologically real engagement in the disciplines involves and how it is important for missional ministry?

4. Do you agree or disagree with the assertion that "when we engage in any spiritual discipline, we should have the 'the pursuit' in mind"? Why?

5. How convinced are you that Dallas Willard would affirm the emphasis this book places on the importance of our keeping in step with the Spirit to the cultivation of a Pauline "I-Thou" lifestyle spirituality?

6. How would you explain to someone the argument that the concept of a missional spirituality "opens the door to just about *any* activity functioning as a spirituality practice if the motive behind it is to be missionally faithful before God"? Do you tend to agree or disagree with this notion? Are there any qualifications?

CONCLUSION

And the peace of God, which transcends all understanding, will guard your hearts and your minds in Christ Jesus.

—Philippians 4:7

A major theme of this work has been that a God-the-Father-pleasing spirituality will necessarily be missional in the way it plays out. But surely another important earmark of a biblically informed spirituality is the way it enables Christ's followers to deal with the seasons of *adversity* they experience in this life and the *anxiety* these distressing seasons produce. As it happens, I have reason to believe that the spirituality the apostle Paul commends in his writings is just what the doctor ordered. Accordingly, this brief conclusion to the book will be somewhat personal in nature.

In more than one of my previously published works, I have referred to a "dark night of the soul" experience I had nearly four decades ago. I will not rehearse that story in its entirety here but will simply indicate that for an eighteen-month period in the mid-1980s, I wrestled with a serious anxiety disorder that I am convinced possessed a diabolical component. Both of my parents had succumbed to cancer while still relatively young. My dad died at the age of forty-eight of liver cancer (when I was sixteen years old); my mom passed away just a few years later from breast cancer. When I was in my late twenties, I experienced a physical ailment that defied easy treatment. Tests were administered to determine whether I had developed cancer of the kidney. Though the results proved negative, my doctor at the time remarked in a rather cavalier manner that, given my family history, I was likely to eventually experience a cancer diagnosis of my own.

This comment produced in me an irrational but nevertheless debilitating cancer phobia. In other words, I became convinced that it was my destiny to, like both of my parents, die young. I also feared that, like them, I would never see my children graduate from high school, go to college, get married, start a career, have kids, and so forth.

Irrational or not, the suffering produced by this battle with what seemed to be a spirit of fear was real. It affected me mentally, emotionally, physically, and professionally. It is hard to provide pastoral care for hurting, dying people when you are dealing with a persistent fear of your own imminent demise.

My experience-based definition of a "dark night of the soul" identifies it as an indeterminate amount of time—a season—during which a child of God feels compelled by adverse circumstances and a concomitant inability to sense any divine succor to wonder whether God is there—and if he is, the degree to which he cares. Objectively, my suffering did not compare to that experienced by Job. Then again, his story is in the Bible for a reason. Because the experience of suffering is subjective, it is possible for all of us at times to think we know how he felt: profoundly bewildered, anxious, and therefore desperate for a personal encounter with God.

And eventually, like Job's, my dark-night experience came to an abrupt end. Indeed, it was because of the dramatic, theologically real, life-and-ministry-shaping way I eventually experienced what I consider to be a "deliverance" from this dreadful extended season of spiritual desolation that I have alluded to this story before.[1] Though I did not intend to refer to my dark-night experience in this work, some recent developments have caused me to change my mind.

The publishing project I worked on just before this one focused on what the authors of the New Testament had to say about the significant relationship between Christian discipleship and spiritual warfare. While writing that book, I developed a form of cancer. Granted, it was a nonlethal version of skin cancer (basal cell carcinoma), but since it appeared just before the onset of the COVID-19 pandemic and did not initially alarm my primary care physician, it took nearly two years for it to be formally diagnosed. As a result, it had time to flourish.

1. See Gary Tyra, *The Dark Side of Discipleship: Why and How the New Testament Encourages Christians to Deal with the Devil* (Eugene, OR: Cascade Books, 2020), 11–14, 199–205; Tyra, "God with Us . . . Really!," *Influence Magazine*, November–December 2020, 28–36.

The eventual diagnosis occurred just after I began working on this current book. Thus, for just about the entire time I have been writing this introduction to Christian spirituality, I have also been dealing with something I have dreaded for most of my adult life: a cancer diagnosis. For sure, it was not the worst kind of cancer, but it was cancer still! Early on in the story of Job we hear him lament: "What I feared has come upon me; what I dreaded has happened to me" (Job 3:25). Once again, I felt I could relate.

Having come to terms with the reality that the cancer diagnosis I had dreaded for four decades had finally occurred, I was eager to have the affected area on the right temple of my forehead surgically treated. The problem was that, because of how long it took for the cancer to be diagnosed, it had had the opportunity to develop in a way that rendered the surgery only partially successful. The final postsurgical pathology report suggests that some deeply embedded "nests" of cancer cells may remain. For a variety of reasons, my plastic surgeon recommends that we monitor the situation, hoping for the best.

Now, for sure, given the type of cancer I am dealing with, this is not the end of the world. I get that. But the irony is significant, is it not? As someone who once wrestled for a year and a half with a seriously debilitating cancer phobia, I now find myself having to live for an indefinite period of time with the possible presence of a malignancy in my body. Lethal or not, because of my previous dark-night experience, my current situation is earmarked by multiple ambiguities that have given rise to several nagging questions, the chief of which is this: Will my cancer phobia reappear and my battle with a spirit of fear resume?

I am happy to report that no resurgence of my previous dark-night experience has occurred. On the contrary, this experience has evidenced the ability of the Christian spirituality I have promoted in this book to pass the anxiety-abating test. My wife, Patti, suggested the other day that it is like I have been given my own "thorn in the flesh"—something Satan has sent with the intent to torment me but that God has allowed not only to "prove" (or provide evidence of) my resolve to render to him a spiritual, moral, and missional faithfulness (cf. 1 Pet. 1:3–9) but also to effect in me a greater missional fruitfulness (see 2 Cor. 12:1–10).

At the beginning of our journey together, I suggested that learning to keep in step with the Spirit—and thereby experiencing a moment-by-moment mentoring relationship with the risen Christ—will function in our lives not only as a *missional* spirituality but as a *mental health* spirituality (Rom. 8:15; 2 Tim. 1:7), a *warfare* spirituality (Eph. 6:10–20), a *holiness* spirituality (Heb. 12:14), a *faithfulness* spirituality (Matt. 25:21, 23), and ultimately an eschatological *readiness* spirituality (Matt. 22:44). This was a bold assertion. I have more reason than ever to consider it true. As someone who genuinely desires to hear Jesus someday refer to me as a "good and faithful servant," I can attest that, despite some serious testing, my faith in Christ has not flagged and my experience of his empowering presence is real and ongoing—as is my commitment to, like him, stay on mission no matter what. All of this is due in no small part to the lifestyle spirituality we have been exploring in this book.

So let's stay the course, shall we? Now that we have begun the race, let's finish it together. And, while we're at it, let's invite our friends, family members, neighbors, coworkers, and so forth to take this nuance-requiring and nuance-affording journey into the "rabbit hole" with us. It won't always be easy, but—as I tell my students—"If you think the Christian life is boring, you're not doing it right!" Indeed, the fact that the Bible nowhere promises us a life in this age that's completely free of adversity and the anxiety-producing ambiguities that result from it is ultimately a good thing. It "speaks" to us of the need for a Pauline, fully trinitarian "I-Thou" *lifestyle* spirituality.

Coram Deo!

RECOMMENDED RESOURCES

Brother Lawrence. *The Practice of the Presence of God with Spiritual Maxims*. Grand Rapids: Baker, 1967.

Chandler, Diane J. *Christian Spiritual Formation: An Integrated Approach to Personal and Relational Wholeness*. Downers Grove, IL: IVP Academic, 2014.

Downey, Michael. *Understanding Christian Spirituality*. Mahwah, NJ: Paulist Press, 1997.

Finn, Nathan A., and Keith S. Whitfield, eds. *Spirituality for the Sent: Casting a New Vision for the Missional Church*. Downers Grove, IL: IVP Academic, 2017.

Foster, Richard. *Celebration of Discipline: The Path to Spiritual Growth*. New York, HarperCollins, 1998.

———. *Prayer: Finding the Heart's True Home*. San Francisco: HarperSanFrancisco, 1992.

Johnson, Jan. *Enjoying the Presence of God: Discovering Intimacy with God in the Daily Rhythms of Life*. Colorado Springs: NavPress, 1996.

Lane, George. *Christian Spirituality: An Historical Sketch*. Chicago: Loyola, 1984.

Ortberg, John. *The Life You've Always Wanted: Spiritual Disciplines for Ordinary People*. Grand Rapids: Zondervan, 1997.

Tozer, A. W. *The Pursuit of God*. Camp Hill, PA: Christian Publications, 1993.

Tyra, Gary. *Christ's Empowering Presence: The Pursuit of God through the Ages*. Downers Grove, IL: IVP Books, 2011.

———. *The Dark Side of Discipleship: Why and How the New Testament Encourages Christians to Deal with the Devil*. Eugene, OR: Cascade Books, 2020.

———. *Defeating Pharisaism: Recovering Jesus' Disciple-Making Method*. Downers Grove, IL: IVP Books, 2009.

———. *Getting Real: Pneumatological Realism and the Spiritual, Moral, and Ministry Formation of Contemporary Christians*. Eugene, OR: Cascade Books, 2018.

———. *The Holy Spirit in Mission: Prophetic Speech and Action in Christian Witness*. Downers Grove, IL: IVP Academic, 2011.

———. *Pursuing Moral Faithfulness: Ethics and Christian Discipleship*. Downers Grove, IL: IVP Academic, 2015.

Willard, Dallas. *The Divine Conspiracy: Rediscovering Our Hidden Life in God*. San Francisco: Harper, 1998.

———. *The Great Omission: Reclaiming Jesus's Essential Teachings on Discipleship*. San Francisco: HarperSanFrancisco, 2006.

———. *Hearing God: Developing a Conversational Relationship with God*. Downers Grove, IL: InterVarsity, 1999.

———. *Knowing Christ Today: Why We Can Trust Spiritual Knowledge*. New York: HarperOne, 2009.

———. *Renovation of the Heart: Putting on the Character of Christ*. Colorado Springs, NavPress, 2002.

———. *The Spirit of the Disciplines: Understanding How God Changes Lives*. New York: HarperOne, 1988.

SCRIPTURE INDEX

SUBJECT INDEX